SEMINAR STUDIES IN HISTORY

The Collapse of the Soviet Union, 1985–1991

DAVID R. MARPLES

PEARSON
Longman

Harlow, England • London • New York • Boston • San Francisco • Toronto
Sydney • Tokyo • Singapore • Hong Kong • Seoul • Taipei • New Delhi
Cape Town • Madrid • Mexico City • Amsterdam • Munich • Paris • Milan

PEARSON EDUCATION LIMITED

Edinburgh Gate
Harlow CM20 2JE
United Kingdom
Tel: +44 (0)1279 623623
Fax: +44 (0)1279 431059
Website: www.pearsoned.co.uk

First edition published in Great Britain in 2004

© Pearson Education Limited 2004

The right of David R. Marples to be identified as author
of this work has been asserted by him in accordance
with the Copyright, Designs and Patents Act 1988.

ISBN-10: 0-582-50599-2
ISBN-13: 978-0-582-50599-5

British Library Cataloguing in Publication Data
A CIP catalogue record for this book can be obtained from the British Library

Library of Congress Cataloging in Publication Data
Marples, David R.
    The collapse of the Soviet Union : 1985-1991 / David R. Marples.
        p. cm. — (Seminar studies in history)
    Includes bibliographical references and index.
    ISBN 0-582-50599-2
        1. Soviet Union—Politics and government—1985–1991. 2. Soviet Union—Economic
    conditions—1985–1991. I. Title. II. Series.

    DK288.M383 2004
    947.085'4—dc22

                                                                2004044404

10 9 8 7 6 5 4 3 2

Set by 35 in 10/12.5pt Sabon
Printed by Malaysia

The Publisher's policy is to use paper manufactured from sustainable forests.

For Aya Fujiwara

CONTENTS

INTRODUCTION TO THE SERIES

Such is the pace of historical enquiry in the modern world that there is an ever-widening gap between the specialist article or monograph, incorporating the results of current research, and general surveys, which inevitably become out of date. *Seminar Studies in History* is designed to bridge this gap. The series was founded by Patrick Richardson in 1966 and his aim was to cover major themes in British, European and world history. Between 1980 and 1996 Roger Lockyer continued his work, before handing the editorship over to Clive Emsley and Gordon Martel. Clive Emsley is Professor of History at the Open University, while Gordon Martel is Professor of International History at the University of Northern British Columbia, Canada, and Senior Research Fellow at De Montfort University.

All the books are written by experts in their field who are not only familiar with the latest research but have often contributed to it. They are frequently revised, in order to take account of new information and interpretations. They provide a selection of documents to illustrate major themes and provoke discussion, and also a guide to further reading. The aim of *Seminar Studies in History* is to clarify complex issues without over-simplifying them, and to stimulate readers into deepening their knowledge and understanding of major themes and topics.

ACKNOWLEDGEMENTS

We are grateful to the following for permission to reproduce copyright material:

Academic International Press for an extract adapted from *USSR Documents Annual 1991, Volume 2: Disintegration of the USSR*; Andrew Nurnberg Associates for an extract adapted from *Against the Grain* by Boris Yeltsin; Basic Books Ltd. for extracts adapted from *Ten Years That Shook the World: The Gorbachev Era as witnessed by His Chief of Staff* by Valery Boldin, translated by Evelyn Rossiterre; Ed Victor Limited for a letter adapted from *Voices of Glasnost Letters from the Soviet People to Ogonyok Magazine 1987–1990*; HarperCollins Publishers for an extract adapted from *Perestroika: New Thinking for Our Country and the World* by Mikhail Gorbachev; HarperCollins Publishers and G. Merritt Corporation for an extract adapted from *The Man Who Changed the World: The Lives of Mikhail S. Gorbachev* by Gail Sheehy; The Pennsylvania State University Press for an extract adapted from *My Six Years with Gorbachev* by Anatoly Chernyaev © 1995 The Pennsylvania State University Press, translated and edited by Robert English and Elizabeth Tucker; Princeton University Press for an extract from *The Rise of Russia and the Fall of the Soviet Empire* by John B. Dunlop © 1993 Princeton University Press, 1995 paperback edition and Transworld Publishers and Doubleday, divisions of The Random House Group Limited and The Random House Group Inc. for an extract adapted from *Mikhail Gorbachev: Memoirs* by Mikhail Gorbachev published by Doubleday © 1995 Mikhail Gorbachev, English translation © Wolf Jobst Siedler Verlag GmbH, Berlin.

Map 1 redrawn from map European Russia from http://www.lonelyplanet.com, © Lonely Planet Publications Ltd. 2004, reprinted by permission of Lonely Planet Publications Ltd.; Map 3 redrawn from map Europe, The Baltic States from http://www.worldatlas.com, reprinted by permission of Graphic Maps; Map 4 redrawn from map Moscow from http://www.lonelyplanet.com, © Lonely Planet Publications Ltd. 2004, reprinted by permission of Lonely Planet Publications Ltd.

In some instances we have been unable to trace the owners of copyright material, and we would appreciate any information that would enable us to do so.

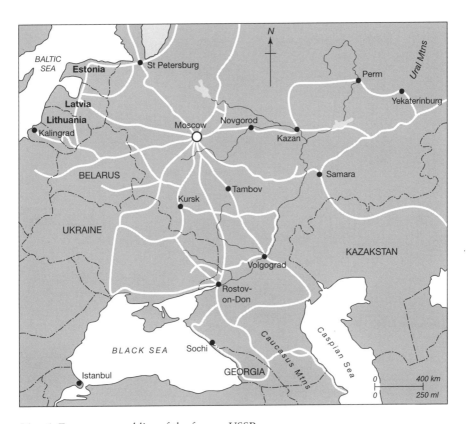

Map 1 European republics of the former USSR

Source: Redrawn from map 'European Russia' from http://www.lonelyplanet.com, © Lonely Planet Publications Ltd. 2004. Reprinted by permission of Lonely Planet Publications Ltd.

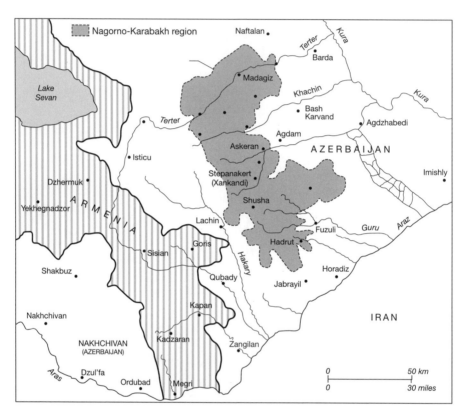

Map 2 Nagorno-Karabakh
Source: Redrawn from http://www.osce.org.

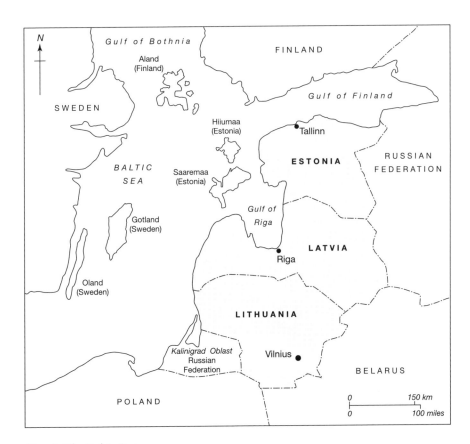

Map 3 The Baltic States
Source: Redrawn from map 'Europe, The Baltic States' from http://www.worldatlas.com.
Reprinted by permission of Graphic Maps.

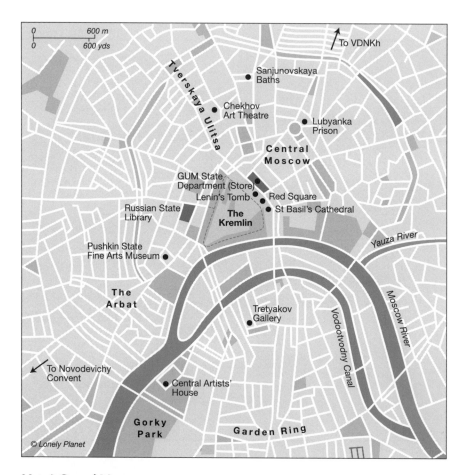

Map 4 Central Moscow

Source: Redrawn from map 'Moscow' from http://www.lonelyplanet.com, © Lonely Planet
Publications Ltd. 2004. Reprinted by permission of Lonely Planet Publications Ltd.

CHRONOLOGY

1985
10 March	Death of Konstantin Chernenko.
11 March	Gorbachev becomes the General Secretary of the Central Committee of the CPSU.
26 April	Warsaw Pact renewed for another twenty years.
2 July	Eduard Shevardnadze appointed Minister of Foreign Affairs.
November	First summit meeting between Gorbachev and Ronald Reagan in Geneva.
December	Boris Yeltsin becomes Communist Party leader for Moscow.

1986
February/March	Gorbachev denounces Brezhnev era as 'the Epoch of Stagnation' at the 27th Congress of the CPSU.
26 April	Fourth nuclear reactor unit explodes at Chernobyl power station north of Kyiv.
12 May	*Gospryomka* (State Inspection of Production) created to monitor quality of production.
July	Gorbachev announces removal of six Soviet divisions from Afghanistan by end of year.
October	Gorbachev and Reagan discuss nuclear arms reduction and end of testing at Reykjavic, Iceland.
December	Andrey Sakharov allowed to return from exile; his wife Yelena Bonner freed from prison; riots break out in Kazakh capital of Alma-Ata.

1987
August	Demonstrations in Estonia, Latvia and Lithuania.
2 November	Gorbachev creates commission to rehabilitate Stalin's victims.
November	Yeltsin dismissed as Moscow party leader.
December	Gorbachev visits Washington for first time and agrees to elimination of medium-range nuclear missiles.

1988

January	Law about the State Enterprise reforms industrial enterprises and reduces state subsidies.
February	Demonstrations begin in Armenia to incorporate Nagorno-Karabakh into Armenia.
May	The Soviet Union agrees to remove all troops from Afghanistan by February 1989.
May/June	Gorbachev and Reagan summit meeting in Moscow.
1 October	Gorbachev elected chair of Supreme Soviet.
November	First major reform demonstration held in Kyiv, Ukraine.
6 December	Gorbachev, addressing United Nations, declares intention to reduce Soviet armed forces by 500,000 over next two years.
December	Supreme Soviet approves creation of Congress of People's Deputies.
	Basic Criminal Code revised to reduce prison sentences, the number of offences that could result in death penalty and ending policy of deporting dissidents.

1989

January	USSR declares direct rule over Nagorno-Karabakh in order to end conflict between Azerbaijan and Armenia.
9 April	Soviet troops attack supporters of Georgian independence, killing twenty marchers.
May	Baltic reform movements meet in Tallinn to promote economic and political sovereignty.
8 June	Ryzhkov appointed chairman of USSR Council of Ministers.
10 July	Coal miners of Kuzbass coalfield go on strike.
30 July	Radical deputies create the Interregional Group with goal of moving USSR from totalitarianism to democracy.
September	CPSU Central Committee Plenum proposes reform of political and economic terms of USSR federation.
November	New governments replace communist regimes in Bulgaria, Czechoslovakia and Hungary; Berlin Wall falls.
1 December	Pope John Paul II receives Gorbachev in Vatican and arranges for restoration of diplomatic relations between Roman Catholic Church and the USSR.

1990

January	*Time* magazine declares Gorbachev 'Man of the Decade'. Nakhichevan Autonomous Republic declares secession from both Azerbaijan and USSR. People of Tiraspol Raion vote in favour of self-government and establishment of a Dnestr Autonomous Republic.
19 January	Soviet security forces sent into Baku, where they clash with Azerbaijan People's Front.
20 January	Democratic Platform of Communist Reformers formed in Moscow.
5–7 February	Central Committee Plenum of CPSU resolves to create presidential system in USSR.
7 February	CPSU formally relinquishes monopoly on power.
17 February	Armenia declares illegal the decision of USSR to make Nagorno-Karabakh part of Azerbaijan.
25 February	Belarusian Popular Front holds demonstration attended by 100,000 in Minsk.
27 February	Supreme Soviet approves creation of a Soviet presidency.
11 March	Lithuanian Supreme Soviet issues declaration of independence from USSR.
12 March	Unofficial parliament convened in Estonia, demanding immediate departure of Soviet troops.
15 March	Moscow Congress rejects Lithuanian declaration of independence.
March	Elections in Russia, Ukraine and Belarus demonstrate popular support for radical reformers. Presidential Council established in Russian Federation. Ukrainian Supreme Soviet announces Chernobyl plant to be phased out over next five years.
April	Soviet government admits responsibility for deaths of 15,000 Polish officers in Katyn forest massacre of 1940.
29 May	Yeltsin wins election for chairmanship of Supreme Soviet of the RSFSR.
May/June	Gorbachev and George Bush agree to reduce strategic weapons at Washington summit meeting.
June	Hungary announces intention to leave Warsaw Pact before end of 1991.
July	Donbas miners strike, demanding material improvements and dismantling of party control over mines.

31 July	Gorbachev and George Bush sign START Treaty in Moscow.
September	500 Days program economic reforms outlined in public.

1991

7 January	Soviet tanks and paratroopers enter Lithuania.
14 January	Valentin Pavlov replaces Ryzhkov as prime minister following the latter's heart attack.
January	Pavlov announces monetary reforms that include freezing of savings accounts until currency reforms instituted.
19 February	Yeltsin calls for resignation of Gorbachev.
22 February	400,000 people attend demonstration in Moscow in support of 'Democracy and Glasnost'.
February	Members of Warsaw Pact announce that it will cease existence by end of March.
10 March	Yeltsin, calling for Gorbachev's resignation, inspires demonstration of 500,000 in Moscow.
17 March	Referendum on a renewed federation held in USSR; 99 per cent of Georgians voting in referendum support independence.
28 March	100,000 people march in Moscow, supporting Yeltsin and defying Supreme Soviet ban on political demonstrations. RCPD votes 532–286 to defy ban on demonstrations.
12 April	USSR suspends rail and sea shipments to Georgia.
23 April	The 1+9 agreement is signed between Gorbachev and leaders of the nine republics. ·
26 April	50 million people stage one-hour strike protesting rising prices and falling quality of life.
4 May	Donbas miners end coal strike.
12 June	Yeltsin elected Russian president.
1 July	New Democratic Movement initiated by well-known political figures.
12 July	USSR Supreme Soviet approves draft Union Treaty.
20 July	Yeltsin bans activities of political parties and public organizations in entities belonging to the state.
18–21 August	Putsch in Moscow attempts overthrow of Gorbachev.
24 August	RSFSR recognizes independence of Latvia and Estonia. Ukrainian parliament declares independence.
25 August	Belarus declares independence and suspends Communist Party.
27 August	Moldavia declares independence.

29 August	USSR Supreme Soviet bans activities of CPSU in all regions of USSR.
1 September	Gorbachev announces that he and leaders of ten republics agree to sign treaty on a Union of Sovereign States.
21 September	99 per cent of voters in referendum in Armenia support secession from USSR.
1 December	90 per cent of voters in referendum in Ukraine support secession from USSR; Leonid Kravchuk elected first president of independent Ukraine.
8 December	Meeting of presidents Yeltsin and Kravchuk (Russia and Ukraine) and Belarusian parliamentary leader Shushkevich agrees to form Commonwealth of Independent States (CIS).
10 December	Parliaments in Russia, Belarus and Ukraine approve formation of CIS.
26 December	USSR Supreme Soviet votes to dissolve itself.
27 December	Yeltsin and colleagues seize Gorbachev's office in Kremlin.
31 December	Soviet flag on Kremlin replaced by Russian tri-coloured flag.

PREFACE

Like any scholar who works on the USSR and post-Soviet republics, I find the events of the recent past very difficult to assess because I feel part of them. I have attended dozens of lectures and talks on the fall of the Soviet Union and indeed delivered not a few as well. I can recall the euphoria among Western analysts with the advent of Mikhail Gorbachev in March 1985 and the possibilities for change that his elevation seemed to augur. The next six years were so tumultuous that to confine them within the pages of a small book seems inappropriate. During that period there was a remarkable outpouring of analyses in the West and of revelations within the Soviet Union. Over the past twelve years, however, that period seems to have been confined to the more distant past than the Stalin years (events of which are still commemorated in most republics) or even the revolutions of 1917. Visiting former Soviet regions one can only be struck by the rapidity of change and the thoroughness with which the physical symbols of the Soviet era have been removed. It may be time therefore to revisit them and offer a new assessment. It is not an easy task. As with any such venture, this manuscript is bound to contain controversial statements. The two main actors, Gorbachev and Yeltsin, are still alive; both maintain supporters and critics. Both have written several books defending their actions of 1985–91 (and afterward in Yeltsin's case) and neither, frankly, has received an altogether critical press.

In the interim of twelve years, many of the participants in the events of 1985–91 have written memoirs – those translated into English have been included in the bibliography. Collections of documents have been made available on the Internet. Yet the debates continue: over Gorbachev and his relative success or failure; the roots of the August 1991 putsch; the role of the national republics in the fall of the USSR; the relative significance of the economic crisis, and the role of the main adversary, the United States in the Cold War and the downfall of the Communist regimes of Eastern Europe. I should confess to a certain bias, in that I have long felt that the national question was of key significance, and conversely that the arms build-up and Cold War conflict were overrated as factors in the dissolution of the Soviet state. In writing this book I also came to the conclusion that the role of personalities was of much greater importance than had initially appeared to be the case. Personal friendships and animosities often played a critical role, as did misconceptions of political alliances and intrigue. In my view there was nothing inevitable about the events of 1991 and I would not pretend to have discovered any kind of definitive truth about why things happened as they did.

This book was written with the aid of a grant from the Support for the Advancement of Scholarship, Faculty of Arts at the University of Alberta, which permitted research trips to Moscow and to the archives of the Open Society at the Central European University in Budapest (RFE/RL Archives). These latter proved invaluable and I owe a debt to the various writers of RFE/RL, sometimes for citations that are too brief to be acknowledged here: Alexander Rahr, Elizabeth Teague, John Tedstrom, Keith Bush, Vera Tolz, Roman Solchanyk, Saulius Girnius, Dzintra Bungs and others monitored events in the Soviet Union and its constituent republics assiduously for many years. In the late 1990s in Minsk, I interviewed Stanislau Shushkevich, the former leader of Belarus about the events of Belavezha, and I have used some excerpts of that interview in my interpretation of the events of early December 1991.

I would like to thank Anna Yastrzhembska, who provided advice, ideas, and proofread the manuscript in its initial form; and Ilya Khineiko, one of my PhD students in the Department of History and Classics at the University of Alberta, who was my research assistant during the latter stages of preparation. Thanks are due also to the series editor, Dr Gordon Martel, for his keen attention to the manuscript, and to Casey Mein and Melanie Carter at Longman for their prompt responses and advice. I also thank my wife Lan, and my two sons Carlton and Keelan, for their constant support.

David R. Marples
Edmonton, Canada
October 2003

ACRONYMS

BPF	Belarusian Popular Front
CC	Central Committee
CIS	Commonwealth of Independent States
CNS	Committee of National Salvation (Lithuania)
CPSU	Communist Party of the Soviet Union
GDR	German Democratic Republic (East Germany)
GRU	State Military Intelligence
IAEA	International Atomic Energy Agency
IRG	Interregional Group (parliamentary deputies)
KGB	Committee of State Security
NATO	North Atlantic Treaty Organization
NEP	New Economic Policy
NKVD	People's Commissariat of Internal Affairs
OMON	Special police troops
RBMK	Graphite-moderated nuclear reactor
RCPD	Russian Congress of People's Deputies
RSFSR	Russian Soviet Federated Socialist Republic
SDI	Strategic Defence Initiative (Star Wars)
START	Strategic Arms Limitation Treaty

INTRODUCTION

The collapse of the Soviet Union was largely unpredicted and today there are various interpretations of the event. Similarly, the rule and legacy of Mikhail Sergeevich Gorbachev are much debated, both in Russia and the outside world. Gorbachev came to power at a time when the Cold War seemed to have been reignited. In 1983, the Soviet Union shot down Korean Airlines Flight 007 and then denied responsibility. The Soviet leaders were also incensed when Ronald Reagan termed their country an 'evil empire.' For decades, the Soviet media had hidden from its citizens economic statistics, and venerated the ageing group of leaders in power. It seemed to be a country living within a shell, cut off from the outside world, yet potentially very dangerous as a nuclear power that had attained by the late 1970s theoretical parity with the United States after a lengthy arms race. The years 1985–91 thus constitute something very different: a time of unparalleled change and ultimately the collapse of the Soviet system. The figure of Gorbachev is tied irrevocably to these events. Initially, Western observers regarded him with skepticism, then wonder, and finally delight, so that in the United States and other countries he had become practically a cult figure by 1990, the recipient of a Nobel Peace Prize and a man unlike any other Soviet leader for his love of the camera and public appearances.

Historians and political scientists thus faced two interrelated questions. First, how far apart were the perceptions of Gorbachev and the reality? And second, what were the main causes of the collapse of the Soviet Union? The latter question needs to take into account a variety of factors and interpretations: the ending of the Cold War; an economic crisis and virtual collapse; the rise of the national republics, which were making more and more demands on the centre, and in some cases lapsing into ethnic conflicts that predated Soviet power; and political in-fighting within the leadership. The events of 1991, though cataclysmic, are also puzzling. How could the world's largest remaining empire fall so suddenly? How could the new republics essentially maintain the same ruling personnel as in the Soviet period? What did this signify? Was it a revolution or merely a change of name and the replacement of communist states with nationalist ones without really altering the existing structure?

Dealing with the first question, the problem may derive from Western misconceptions about the new leader. Here some background comments are necessary. The Soviet Union, by and large, was a totalitarian state. True, it experienced some periods of thaw or liberalism, most notably during the later years of Lenin's leadership and the early years of Khrushchev's. But the defining period was that of Stalin (1928–53), and his appalling legacy of slaughter, deportation, internment, and purges. During the 1930s and 1940s it became difficult for Western observers to delineate an accurate picture of life and events in the USSR. With the onset of the Cold War in the late 1940s, it became almost impossible. The Soviet authorities presented a single version of events and official images. The United States reacted in similar fashion – or so it seems now – overreacting to the intrusion of real and alleged Communists into American society. The very nature of the Cold War belied interpretation: was it a war for freedom against tyranny, or was it a defensive war of communism against capitalist expansion? Both the main protagonists were ideological states, and the United States took over Britain's mantle as the main power of the capitalist world.

Western writings on the Soviet Union during the Cold War can be divided, simply, into liberal and conservative. The liberal school considered Stalin a monster, but admired Lenin, and believed that the Soviet Union had achieved some benefits for its population. The conservatives believed that a quest for world Communism was a fight to the death that would result in the total defeat of one side or the other. Ultimately, the conservatives probably expressed their case more successfully, largely because of the collapse of the Communist regimes of Eastern Europe in 1989 and the Soviet Union in 1991. Peaceful coexistence, the great watchword of Soviet foreign policy, was no longer necessary. The West had won. This perspective continues to permeate many works about the Gorbachev and post-Gorbachev periods – in my opinion, falsely. However, this is to advance too quickly. The key issue was not how people saw the USSR, but the way in which they gleaned their information. How does one analyze a state that is secretive by nature, has muzzled its media, and much of which is off-limits to foreigners, including government officials and reporters? Certainly some information was available from refugees, or underground literature (*samizdat*), and during the war the Germans captured an entire archive in Smolensk that revealed some of the inner workings of the Soviet Union, and these materials came into the hands of the Americans at the end of the war.

In terms of the leadership, however, the prevailing pseudo-science was termed Kremlinology, or 'Kremlin-watching.' It required detailed analyses of all official announcements and speeches; reading between the lines; observing the way the leaders were listed in official publications; or seeing who had pride of place at a major parade or public function. It was, clearly, made up mostly of guesswork. It led to the division of the Soviet hierarchy into 'hawks' and 'doves' (much as the US leadership had been categorized during the Vietnam

War), or 'hard liners' and 'liberals.' It was a science of speculation and fore-casting. These comments are not meant to denigrate those who took up this kind of occupation. Indeed it was possible to make some deductions from these analyses, but it was also likely to result in some significant misconceptions and misplaced hopes. This book has suggested that the first misconceptions pertained to Gorbachev himself, i.e. that he was a 'liberal' bent on 'reforms,' and curtailing the tyrannies of Communism in the face of the old Brezhnev supporters in the Politburo. Gorbachev, it is postulated, was neither to the 'right' nor 'left' of the Soviet political spectrum. He was a provincial leader who had risen rapidly through making important contacts and remaining essentially loyal during what was subsequently termed 'the time of stagnation' under Brezhnev. In one sense he was revolutionary: he adhered to the principles laid down for the Bolshevik Party by V.I. Lenin.

The image of Gorbachev, especially in works published during the early years of his leadership, thus tends to be misleading. Too much was expected of him. His relative approachability and openness suggested a new style of Soviet leader, though any figure under the age of 60 and able to walk unaided would have made a similar impression. Not only was the image of Gorbachev misleading, but the Western media tended to focus on the individual rather than the ruling group. By the late 1980s headlines like 'Man of the Century' continued to follow Gorbachev's name like an epithet. By that same time, the Soviet public had already become quite cynical. The man of the people did not get along with the people. He was ill at ease with workers; he was patently uncomfortable whenever anyone opposed his point of view in the Congress of Deputies, notwithstanding the fact that Gorbachev had done more than any-one to establish that body and empower the legislature in order to overcome his opponents in the Communist Party. Nonetheless, he retained his links with the latter organization and wielded enormous power within it. In 1991 he was manifestly unwilling to relinquish his position of General Secretary even when his closest allies willed him to do so. Gorbachev, then, was a man of his time, a committed Communist and follower of Lenin, who tried to reform a system through what was termed 'restructuring' (not revolution) and honesty and self-criticism in reporting.

In this mission – and very few Western analysts make such a comment outright even today – he failed; honorably perhaps, but catastrophically. No one in March 1985 could have predicted what the country might look like in 1991: strikes among the workforce; demonstrations in major cities; fighting in the Caucasus; near uprisings in the Baltic States; and an empire destroyed by the loss of Eastern Europe, the satellite states established under Soviet occupa-tion in the aftermath of the Second World War. At the same time, a dramatic fall in the living standards of the population only exacerbated matters. In these circumstances the sight of Gorbachev and his well-dressed wife Raisa at foreign summits served to infuriate the Soviet public, which now regarded him as one of the most disastrous leaders in living memory. Even Brezhnev had maintained near full employment, civil peace, and the solidity of the Warsaw Pact, albeit with dangerous sideshows such as the invasion of Afghanistan. Yet at the very moment that Soviet citizens were growing disillusioned with Gorbachev, through his unilateral military cuts, the Soviet leader was cementing his image in the Western world. Here was a leader who put into practice Soviet rhetoric about peace initiatives; one who did not wait for the United States to reciprocate. Small wonder that some Kremlin watchers saw no danger to Gorbachev's authority in 1990 and even late 1991! In this way, and from the perspective of 12 years, it is evident that Western writers often presented a false image of Gorbachev, overestimating his abilities, and also his impact on Soviet society.

The second major question under review is: why did the Soviet Union collapse? The problem continues to elicit discussion. The simplistic view is that the West won the Cold War, which ended the Warsaw Pact and ultimately led to the dissolution of the USSR. Gorbachev, in some interpretations, abetted the process by dismantling the Communist Party, which he had come to see as an obstacle to further progress. An integral facet of this perspective is that the arms race took on new dimensions in an era of high technology. Simply put: the Communists could not keep up with the West. The SDI research program forced the Soviet side to try to match Western escalation, thereby leading the country to virtual bankruptcy. Gorbachev had the wisdom to end this contest by giving up, making concession after concession to the West and turning on the party that had nurtured him. Like all theories about the Soviet period, it may contain an element of truth without revealing the whole picture. Throughout post-Second World War history, the Soviet side had been behind and then made a supreme effort to catch up, often without attaining the sort of quality of weaponry that would have made them a truly formidable adversary. But there is no clear indication that the Soviet Union fell because the Cold War ended. Indeed the end of foreign challenges might also have led to internal stability, ostensibly the main goal of Gorbachev's 'peace initiative.'

This leads naturally to the second theory: that the Soviet Union collapsed economically from within. This theory is more plausible than the Cold War explanation, but prompts an immediate question: how then did countries such as Russia and Ukraine, which emerged from the former Soviet state, manage to survive an even greater drop in living standards in the period 1992–98, leading in Russia's case to an almost fatal economic collapse? At what point does economic decline constitute a danger to the political order? Analysts do not dispute the existence of an economic crisis. But during revolutions, there is a tight link between the crisis and the group advocating a state takeover. What happened in 1991 was rather different: if there was truly an economic crisis, it was one between the republics and the centre; when republics, and particularly Russia, were failing to contribute to the state budget so that state coffers were empty. Yet this occurred at a relatively late stage, and behind the scenes. The economic argument needs to be examined more thoroughly and receives treatment below, but by itself it does not seem to be a convincing explanation for the demise of the Soviet empire, particularly one that had undergone a similar experience in the late 1970s with the declining revenues from oil and gas.

Historians have begun to pay significant attention to the Soviet republics and the rise of nationalism. Indeed in the early 21st century, the topic seems to be reaching a peak. Few serious analysts would attempt to construct a theory for the dissolution of the Soviet Union that does not include the national question. Some observers, such as Taras Kuzio of the University of Toronto, have long argued that the Western academic world was incurably Russo-centric and tended to ignore events in the non-Russian republics. Added to that is the fact that Moscow and Leningrad were undoubtedly the main centres for the Western media. Many republics lacked a foreign correspondent, and newspapers would have their Moscow man (or woman) make occasional trips to the periphery of the empire, only to return with instant observations and deductions. This is not to suggest that the non-Russian republics were totally neglected – in fact there was a growing interest in Ukraine, while the Baltic States had never been accepted as an integral part of the USSR – but like the focus on Gorbachev, the concentration on the Moscow centre to the detriment of the republics did not always allow for a broad perspective on events in the Soviet Union as a whole. Who, other than Azeri or Armenian specialists, for example, could have predicted the depth of feeling over the fate of Nagorno-Karabakh? Or that Kazakhs would protest en-masse in the streets of Alma-Ata in December 1986 with the appointment of a Russian as the new party leader?

Western analysts were not the only ones to neglect the national question. Gorbachev, it seems, did not have a national policy, despite the fact that he grew up in the Caucasus among dozens of different national groups. Given the rise of the national republics to sovereignty, and then the mass 'flight' to independence in the summer of 1991, it is evident that national issues must have been at the forefront of the collapse of a federal centre like Moscow. That the response to events in Moscow was so rapid adds weight to that statement. But then another question arises: would the national problem alone explain the dissolution of Gorbachev's government? And what was the relationship between growing national sentiment in the various republics and the disaffection with the centre of the Russian Federation? How did Russia relate to the national question? Attention here needs to be centred on the events of 1991: from the March referendum to the failed Putsch in August, and the consequent independent path of Russia under its new president, Boris Yeltsin. The latter, incidentally, has elicited the same sort of extremes of opinion as Gorbachev. The West (especially new US president George Bush) at first seemed reluctant to embrace Yeltsin, but later came to regard him as the best hope for preserving 'democracy' in Russia. The Russian president aided his own case by penning three volumes of memoirs, a feat matched only by Gorbachev's publication of a single volume that equalled in size all three of those of his rival. Whereas Gorbachev was distant from the Soviet public, Yeltsin was a populist, very much at home with workers or peasants.

In the area of high-level politics, a controversy developed between what might loosely be called the Gorbachev and Yeltsin schools. Thus, one group of scholars maintains that Gorbachev was practically thrown out of office by Yeltsin in a virtual coup in the latter part of 1991. Yeltsin took over the reins of power while Gorbachev was under house arrest at his villa in Foros. The opposing group has come close to accusing Gorbachev of outright collaboration with the leaders of the Putsch – he, after all, had appointed all the leaders of the so-called Emergency Committee. This second school perceives Yeltsin rather than Gorbachev as the bearer of democratic values; the man who almost single-handedly defied the plotters and at every stage of his rise to power subjected himself to elections and judgment by his peers and public. Gorbachev, in contrast, remained within the comfort of the party circle, unelected by the people, and clung to power long after his popularity had waned. Often overlooked during these analyses is the depth of the bitterness of this rivalry – though it is obvious enough from Yeltsin's memoirs – and how far Yeltsin would be prepared to go to take power. Analysts also have to measure the extent of the correlation between the actions of Yeltsin and those of the Russian Federation *per se*. Russia was also the centre of the sort of hard-line Communists who carried out the coup, and even in the presidential election of 1991, Yeltsin received less than 60 per cent of the vote.

The issues are thus complex and it seems unlikely that there will be a consensus on why the Soviet Union fell, at least in the near future. The events are also too recent for any unity of opinion. Many of the players are still alive (Gorbachev, Yeltsin, Kravchuk, Shevardnadze, Kryuchkov, and others), though relatively few are in positions of prominence today. At the time of writing, there is a minor but fractious border dispute taking place between Ukraine and Russia. The disintegration of the empire may have been relatively peaceful but it has produced many problems that still require resolution. However, what is clear is that no party in any republic is advocating a return of the Soviet Union. The events of 1985–91 proved to be the decisive death knell of the Bolshevik regime. Gorbachev may have been unlucky or he may have taken on too much, or he may have been a leader who was simply not up to the task of reforming a Communist system that was essentially defunct in many respects. This volume, while outlining the various areas of significance and the possible factors behind the collapse, will offer an assessment concerning the plausibility of each theory. Ultimately, it is posited, the empire fell because of a particular combination of factors and circumstances rather than any one specific cause.

PART ONE BACKGROUND

CHAPTER ONE

GORBACHEV COMES TO POWER

POLITICAL OVERVIEW

The Gorbachev era began on 11 March 1985, following the deaths in rapid succession of the three previous General Secretaries of the CC CPSU, Leonid Brezhnev (November 1982), Yury Andropov (March 1984), and Konstantin Chernenko (March 1985). Though Andropov, a former KGB chief, had begun his period in office with a campaign against corruption and absenteeism in the workplace, his tenure had been too short to herald any major changes. Chernenko's time at the top provided the farce toward the end of a long drama: a virtual clerk of Brezhnev with few ideas and lacking in intellect, taking over the reins of the country. Like Andropov, he was too ill to rule for long. The new secretary, Mikhail Sergeevich Gorbachev, aged 54, was evidently the unanimous choice of the ruling Politburo's members following his nomination by the veteran foreign affairs minister, Andrey Gromyko. A possible contest for the leadership with Moscow party boss Viktor Grishin failed to materialize. A robust, balding, stocky man with a prominent birthmark, Gorbachev was endowed with remarkable energy. He had risen through the Soviet system, but was now in a position to determine its direction.

Gorbachev's background was not untypical for the late Brezhnev period. He was born on 2 March 1931 in the village of Privolnoye, Krasnogvardeisk district of the Stavropol oblast in the Caucasus. His parents were peasants and his maternal grandfather had been one of the early collective farmers during the initial phase of collectivization. His paternal grandfather, on the other hand, had declined to join a kolkhoz and was arrested in 1934. In 1937, his maternal grandfather had also been arrested during the purges and accused of being a member of a 'Trotskyite' association. Though both grandfathers were able to recover their careers and lives, Gorbachev was well aware of the restraints placed upon farmers during the Stalin period. In 1949, on the other hand, his father received the Order of Lenin when the annual harvest plan in Privolnoye was overfulfilled. The Stavropol area was under German occupation for about five months during the Wehrmacht's summer offensive of

1942, but the Red Army had removed the invaders by January 1943. One can thus describe Gorbachev's early life as eventful. In 1950, three years before Stalin's death, he had entered the prestigious law faculty at Moscow State University and become a candidate member of the Communist Party. Two years later, he was accepted as a full-time member of the party.

His subsequent career as an adult was a combination of graft, patience, and good fortune. In September 1953, he married Raisa Titorenko, an expert on Marxism-Leninism who was to become his close partner throughout his life. In 1955, he graduated from Moscow State University and began to pursue a party career in his home region of Stavropol, rising through the Komsomol and district organizations until he was appointed the First Secretary of Stavropol city committee of the party in September 1966. He also added to his qualifications by taking agronomy courses at the Stavropol Agricultural Institute. By April 1970 he was head of the Stavropol regional party committee, an important local boss and on good terms with KGB leader, Yury Andropov, who came to the area for periods of relaxation. At the 24th Party Congress in 1971, Gorbachev became a full member of the Central Committee of the party. Seven years later, as he recounts in his memoirs, he met Brezhnev and Chernenko at the spa of Mineralnye Vody. By this time Gorbachev had a reputation as a hard-working regional leader with a promising party career. Because of his reputation as an agricultural expert he could expect to be singled out for future work in Brezhnev's ambitious Food Program, elaborated in the late 1970s and scheduled to last from 1980 to 1990. Though ill fated, the Food Program continued to be trumpeted in the official media as a device to end the USSR's increasing reliance on grain imports, first begun in the later years of Khrushchev's administration. In October 1980 Brezhnev appointed Gorbachev a full member of the ruling Politburo.

It was perhaps not the most suitable time to be rising to the top of the hierarchy. Less than a year earlier, Soviet troops had crossed the border into Afghanistan and installed a puppet ruler – Babrak Karmal – in Kabul. Several harvest failures in a row directly threatened Gorbachev's career. The Politburo comprised mainly elderly figures that resented anything that would affect their comfortable lifestyles and privileges. Brezhnev himself was barely coherent in his speeches, relying on cue cards and prompting, and had been in poor health since a heart attack in the mid-1970s. His vanity had risen to the point at which he lived for praise and the presentation of new medals glorifying his contributions to all walks of life. Since the Khrushchev period, the Soviet system had been notable for security of high party and government positions. Politburo and Central Committee members were no longer replaced with regularity and generally ended their days in office. By the late 1970s and early 1980s, there was a succession of funerals. Several local leaders who had attempted reforms, or who had spoken out against the corruption and nepotism endemic in Moscow had been removed or had died in staged 'accidents.' However, when Brezhnev died on 10 November 1982, following his appearance at the Revolution Day parade three days earlier in bitterly cold weather, his successor was Andropov, a man who could be expected to promote Gorbachev's career, while embarking on reforms against corruption and lack of discipline in the workplace. The 'opposition' in the Politburo gathered around Konstantin Chernenko, Brezhnev's faithful clerk who wished for no more than a continuation of the system unchanging.

Ill health prevented Andropov from accomplishing much. Moreover, when he was succeeded by Chernenko, Gorbachev's ambitions potentially may have been limited. Yet by this time (February 1984) he had made himself indispensable, principally in the area of agriculture but also in other fields such as foreign affairs. In September 1984, he went to Bulgaria for the 40th anniversary of the liberation of Sofia from German occupation. He also visited Canada and Britain in 1984–85, and made a notable impression on the British Prime Minister Margaret Thatcher. Because of Chernenko's ill-health, Gorbachev took on the role of 2nd Secretary and frequently ran Politburo meetings in the leader's absence. Perhaps there were some rivals for the succession, but again the main threat to Gorbachev's rise continued to be harvest failures. Agriculture was the stumbling block of the Soviet economy, and Gorbachev, as others before him, failed to come up with any viable solutions. There is no evidence that Gorbachev was ever outspoken or disloyal to the members of the Brezhnev clique. That same clique had no reason to suspect that his elevation would herald any major changes. On paper at least, the country had remained a superpower and under Brezhnev it had come close to numerical military parity with the United States. Gorbachev was a typical product of the Brezhnev system, while aware of its faults and failings.

Thus there was little initial indication that a new era had begun or that Gorbachev was likely to implement fundamental changes. He had been a protégé of Andropov. Effectively, Gorbachev had been running the country during the administration of the gravely ill Chernenko, who suffered from emphysema, among other ailments. Gorbachev had responsibility for agriculture, an area that was unlikely to win him any public acclaim. He was given to ritualistic long-winded speeches, a characteristic that did not alter when he came to power. At meetings he exerted almost complete control, often allowing those in attendance only perfunctory remarks. On paper, his authority was substantial, and he did not shy away from making personnel changes. Though from a modest peasant background, Gorbachev as noted was well educated, and had taken up acting as one of his hobbies. In general, he had few close friends and liked to take responsibility himself for decisions and initiatives.

In the political sphere, personality changes were at once introduced. Over the first year of the Gorbachev leadership, 70 per cent of the ministers were changed, along with 50 per cent of the leadership cadres in the Soviet republics. By the end of 1986, after nine months in office, 40 per cent of all first secretaries had lost their positions, and the Central Committee membership suffered an even more drastic replacement of 60 per cent of its members. Within the Politburo itself, two obvious rivals for the leadership had been the Leningrad party chief, Grigory Romanov, as well as his Moscow counterpart, Grishin, noted above. Neither was to remain in the highest office for long. On 1 July 1985, Romanov was removed. Grishin survived for a further six months before being relieved of his duties and sent into retirement. In the same month, the Minister of Internal Affairs, Vitaly Fedorchuk also lost his post.

Several other leaders might have been considered candidates for early dismissal, taking into account their role as long-time and faithful followers of Brezhnev. However, they retained their posts for some time. Most notable was the Ukrainian party leader, Volodymyr Shcherbytsky, often referred to as a 'hard-line' leader (a term used to denote strict adherence to the official line and a lack of tolerance for dissidence), who remained in office until he was retired with full honours in the fall of 1989. Perhaps Shcherbytsky was retained because he had proved capable of keeping things quiet in Ukraine, a potential trouble spot for a period in the 1960s and early 1970s when it had seen a strong dissident movement and an undercurrent of nationalist sentiment under previous party leader Petro Shelest.

More significant as an indicator of the sort of leadership that Gorbachev would offer were the replacements brought into the ruling circle. On 23 April, at a Plenum of the party's central committee, Viktor Chebrikov became the chairman of the KGB, and two key figures originally advanced by Andropov also came to prominence. Yegor Ligachev was appointed a Central Committee secretary for ideology and cadre policies (perhaps at the time the key position after that of General Secretary) and Nikolay Ryzhkov was given similar responsibility over the economy. Both these men were to remain in the leadership for the next few years. On 27 September, Ryzhkov replaced Nikolay Tikhonov as the Chairman of the Council of Ministers (Prime Minister).

More startling was the elevation of the former party leader of the republic of Georgia, Eduard Shevardnadze, as the Minister of Foreign Affairs on 2 July 1985 following his promotion to full member of the Politburo a day earlier. He replaced Gromyko, who took on the role of ceremonial president of the USSR, the position of chairman of the then relatively powerless Supreme Soviet. Shevardnadze was not only a relative unknown in Moscow, but also his command of Russian was less than fluent. Nevertheless, the choice proved to be an inspired one, and Shevardnadze was to remain one of the more determined supporters of détente with the United States, a key element in Gorbachev's strategy. Of equal importance was the virtual removal from a position of influence of Gromyko, whose impact on foreign relations for the previous four decades could charitably be regarded as negative. Moreover, under previous Soviet leaders, Gromyko had been given a virtual free hand in formulating Soviet initiatives and responses to the Americans and their allies. Remarkably, Gromyko seems to have supported Gorbachev unequivocally, though his views (as espoused in his memoirs) remained unchanging and bitterly opposed to any rapprochement with the United States.

Also in July, Aleksandr Yakovlev, a former member of the nomenklatura who had been sent into relative exile under Brezhnev as Soviet ambassador to Canada for a lengthy ten-year term, received the position of head of the propaganda section of the Central Committee. Yakovlev has been termed 'the father of Glasnost,' though such an epithet seems exaggerated. Yakovlev was not really a leader figure, but worked well within the more tolerant environs created by the new period of Perestroika. He was nonetheless a close associate of Gorbachev who is identified with the policy of more frank reporting and accountability of the leadership to the Soviet public. Lastly, the July Plenum elected as Central Committee secretaries L.N. Zaikov and Boris N. Yeltsin. The latter, a native of Ekaterynoslav in Siberia and the same age as Gorbachev, enjoyed a spectacular rise when in December 1985, he replaced Grishin as the party leader in the city of Moscow. He was elevated at the same time to a Candidate Member of the ruling Politburo.

Was it evident from the first that the new Soviet leader was replacing former Brezhnev 'cronies' with figures more dedicated to reforming Soviet society and reducing the corruption so endemic during the Brezhnev years? One can say that such a statement is partially true. The change from the previous era may have been superficial, but was clear from certain events. For one thing, the new leader was less distant than his predecessors. He seemed to scorn the typically obsequious adulation that had customarily followed holders of the office. His photograph was not constantly in *Pravda* or *Izvestiya*, and he appeared to be a populist leader who was happy to talk to the public, especially to workers, about the problems that they faced. In March 1986, for example, Gorbachev travelled to Kuibyshev (Samara) to visit a Volga car factory where he criticized local bosses for their unwillingness to allow their workers to talk openly about their situation. That these events were carefully staged was not initially evident.

Gorbachev was outspoken about the problems facing Soviet society, believing firmly that the country could not continue under recent political and economic policies. It was necessary for a break with the past, for the accelera-tion of the economy, and an end to parochialism, nepotism, corruption, and a ruling elite that appeared to be distanced from the general population other than on national holidays and ceremonies during which they decorated them-selves with medals to assuage their vanity. Brezhnev was perhaps the supreme example of this phenomenon, and though it was Brezhnev who had elevated Gorbachev to the Politburo, his protégé from Stavropol in southern Russia quickly tried to erase the memory of his benefactor once he achieved the highest post.

It was not uncommon for Soviet leaders to dissociate themselves from those who had preceded them. A General Secretary wielded enormous power and had scope to introduce direction within the general confines of 'Marxism-Leninism,' itself a nebulous concept. Gorbachev was no exception, though there is little evidence of any far-sighted strategy and where he wished to take the country. The first real opportunity to make a break with the immediate past came at the 27th Congress of the Communist Party (CPSU), which was held from 25 February to 6 March 1986. At this Congress, Gorbachev gave a speech that was the length of a small book and around four hours in delivery. He dismissed the entire Brezhnev era as 'the Epoch of Stagnation,' and demanded fundamental changes in the economy along with the 'democratization' of Soviet society. The comments were sensible. They allowed Gorbachev essentially to begin anew, but without a radical departure from current policies, other than the appearance and vitality of the new leader. Indeed, the contrast in personalities was the most marked change of Gorbachev's first year in office.

One observer of the Congress was the French political scientist and journalist Michel Tatu. He noted that the election at the end of the Congress saw the return of a surprising number of typical Brezhnev personnel, despite the avowed reforms (Tatu). These included Nikolay Tikhonov, the retired prime minister and Nikolay Baibakov, the chairman of the State Planning Commission (Gosplan), a man that even Khrushchev had attempted to remove. The implication here was that the Congress was hardly a forward-looking body and that the changes were cosmetic. One could argue also that even the new faces contained many people who were far from committed reformers.

Insofar as Gorbachev had a vision of the future, it was of a country that had returned to the principles put forward by Lenin in the spring of 1921, a society that ran more efficiently, and an economy in which labor productivity re-attained the sort of growth levels reached in the 1970s. These reforms were to be encapsulated under the general name of 'Perestroika,' a term that included not only economic, but also social and political restructuring. But like other leaders before him, the essential task initially was to consolidate his authority in the ruling structures. The possibility of radical change within the system manifested itself at an early stage. By late January 1987, for example, Gorbachev was advocating that elections to local Soviets should take place through a secret ballot and that there should be more than one, officially sanctioned candidate. The CPSU Plenum at which he made these remarks also tinkered with the idea of holding an all-Union party conference. However, in the elections to local Soviets that followed in June 1987, some 96 per cent of districts had only one name on the ballot paper.

Nevertheless, the new leadership slowly undermined the former Brezhnev structure, in which it had been a rare event to make personnel changes at the top. Gorbachev received an opportunity to make changes to the sensitive military leadership, when a young German, Matthias Rust, managed to land a small plane in Moscow's Red Square, to the acute embarrassment of the Soviet authorities. Though Rust was given a light sentence (four years, of which he served a little more than one), Marshal S. Sokolov was dismissed as Minister of Defence, as was Marshal A. Koldunov, commander of the Soviet armed forces. Sokolov's successor was D. Yazov, who proved to be a controversial choice, and turned against Gorbachev during the serious political crisis of August 1991.

The summer 1987 Plenum of the Central Committee saw the advancement of several committed supporters of Perestroika to the ruling Politburo. They included the new Belarusian party leader, Nikolay Slyunkov, and A. Yakovlev. Yazov was appointed a Candidate Member of the body. A few months later, Gorbachev declared his intention to remove all those who did not support his new policy line. However, in November of this year, Boris Yeltsin, who had begun a thorough program of rooting out corruption in the city of Moscow, was removed from his position suddenly, and replaced by Lev Zaikov. According to the former US ambassador to the Soviet Union, Jack Matlock (Matlock, p. 119), this decision was Gorbachev's first major political mistake, and the reason behind it was envy of a man who was attracting more attention than Gorbachev himself. The attack on Yeltsin by the Politburo members was brutal and unrestrained, and it left lasting scars. Perhaps most galling to Yeltsin was the fact that he had been removed from a hospital bed (following a stroke) at Gorbachev's demand, to face a haranguing from the members of the Central Committee. Two months later, Yeltsin lost his candidate membership of the Politburo, his political career apparently over.

Perhaps the key event during these early years of the new administration was the 19th Party Conference in Moscow, ostensibly an occasion for debate rather than the implementation of radical changes. Some 5,000 delegates took part, in a raucous atmosphere during which it became a struggle to attain the podium in order to make speeches. On several occasions, delegates disagreed sharply with the Soviet leader on various policies, and it was also evident that there were wide divisions within the CPSU. The focus was the reform of the existing system and the continuing struggle with the Soviet bureaucracy, changes to the legal structure, and the twin policies of Glasnost and Perestroika.

The major innovation was the concept of a new law on the election of people's deputies. The Gorbachev leadership decided to elect a new Congress of People's Deputies, effectively a lower house of parliament, made up of 2,250 delegates. The Congress, in turn, was to elect a Supreme Soviet from its ranks, led by a chairman. The elections were to be multi-candidate, allowing for a substantial minority of non-party people to take part. These changes received the approval of the Supreme Soviet on 1 December 1988. The intention of this change, which required amendments to the Soviet Constitution (1977), was to empower the Soviet while reducing that of the party structure.

On paper, it did not yet indicate the elimination of the authority of the Communist Party, but it did signify that the Supreme Soviet was to be more than the 'rubber stamp' authority of the past. Above all, it seemed to outsiders that Gorbachev was seeking an instrument through which to introduce his disputed reforms.

Of the initial Gorbachev team, Ligachev was the most outspoken critic of the sort of changes envisaged by the Soviet leader. He became the target of those who wished to make more rapid reforms. Political analysts applied the term 'conservative' or 'rightist' to those political figures that were opposed to change, ambiguous adjectives when used to refer to committed Communists. More accurate might be the phrase: supporters of the status quo. At the September Plenum of the Central Committee, Ligachev was moved from ideology to agriculture. His replacement was Vadim Medvedev. Several other members of the Brezhnev 'old guard' were ousted, including Vladimir Dolgikh, a key figure in Soviet industry, and Gromyko lost his posts as chairman of the Supreme Soviet and as a Politburo member. At an extraordinary Supreme Soviet session on 1 October Gorbachev was elected Gromyko's successor as chair, with an avowed policy of 'accelerating reform.' At the same time, Vladimir Kryuchkov took over from Chebrikov as the chairman of the KGB.

Thus by the end of 1988, and after almost four years in power, a Gorbachev team had been established. It still could not be considered a team of democrats or committed reformers. Rather, it was a mixed group, with Gorbachev often adopting a central position between two wings, a not untypical maneuver in a party that traditionally relied on unanimity. An essential difference from past policy was the openness of debate. Yet the style of presentation – the General Secretary offering lengthy speeches in defence of his methods – was not something unusual for the Soviet public. What was different, and it proved for many a heady experience, was the possibility of offering criticism, in public, against official policy, whether this be on the economy, society, or the continuing Soviet war in Afghanistan (described below). Gorbachev did not like public criticism and he often grew impatient at some of the speeches being offered. But he did not prevent his opponents from speaking. That this was possible was a result of Glasnost, an integral part of the general policy of Perestroika.

GLASNOST

The policy of Glasnost or frankness saw the development of overt public opinion in the Soviet Union. Over the years of Soviet rule, certain topics had been taboo. The most obvious examples – aside from nuclear weapons and military-security matters – were the economy, societal problems such as corruption and crime, and self-criticism among the ruling elite. It was not a question of lack of analysis, but rather the way that analysis was formulated in the official media and in party and government decrees and publications. Since the 1960s, outspoken activists, termed dissidents by the regime, had noted the gap between the theoretical basis of Soviet power and the way that it was exercised. In the case of the Gorbachev administration, it is sometimes hard in retrospect to distinguish symbolic changes in media accounts and examples of the desire to see more honest reporting both of the past and present. As a lawyer, Gorbachev was interested in protecting the rights and legal interests of Soviet citizens. At the same time, the policy of Glasnost again required the replacement of several party members in the media and the development of a free press. Lastly, Glasnost, in Gorbachev's view, required a reanalysis of the past, and particularly the period of Stalin's rule (1928–53). The Soviet authorities introduced Glasnost but after an experimental period they soon failed to control it as writers, cultural figures, and media personalities began to test its limits, often to the chagrin of the party leadership.

Two events at the very start of the Gorbachev administration signalled the future path. In May 1985, Gorbachev visited Leningrad and to the surprise of his audience he spoke without notes; an unedited version of his speech later appeared on central television. In September, he agreed to an interview with *Time* magazine, with questions submitted in advance by American journalists. When the interview took place, Gorbachev elaborated on his answers, and a frank account appeared in *Pravda*. The following month, Gorbachev provided a live broadcast interview with three French journalists. At the least, such occasions illustrated that the new General Secretary had a thorough grasp of the Soviet situation and was prepared to discuss his problems with the Western as well as the Soviet media. Among the questions invariably raised when the Western media had an opportunity to interrogate the Soviet leadership were those pertaining to detained dissidents. While Gorbachev and his colleagues did not acknowledge at first that these figures had been imprisoned or exiled unfairly, they were nonetheless prepared to take steps to change this situation.

The first such case was that of the Jewish 'refusenik,' Anatoly Shcharansky, who was exchanged for an East European secret agent on 11 February 1986 in Berlin. Though several spies changed hands at this time, Shcharansky was treated separately and flown first to Germany and subsequently to Tel Aviv. The noted scientist Andrey Sakharov up to that time had been in exile in Gorky (Nizhniy Novgorod), along with his wife, the poet Yelena Bonner. In mid-December, Gorbachev phoned Sakharov and informed him that he was free to return to Moscow, a move that he may later have regretted given the popular support that Sakharov was to achieve from his outspoken comments, particularly against the continuing Soviet presence in Afghanistan. Bonner, who had been serving a five-year sentence of exile in Gorky, was also freed on the orders of the Supreme Soviet Presidium on 19 December. Sakharov made a triumphant return to Moscow on 23 December.

The leadership was anxious to get suitable editors in place in key newspapers and journals through which they conveyed Soviet policies to the public. Among them were the party newspaper, *Pravda*, and the political monthly, *Kommunist*. The editor of *Pravda*, V. Afanasyev, was the subject of many complaints from readers, while at *Kommunist*, R. Kosolapov was almost immune to the influx of new ideas. In both cases the replacement editor was Ivan T. Frolov, a man two years older than Gorbachev, a university professor and chairman of the Council on Philosophical and Social Problems of Science and Technology at the Soviet Academy of Sciences. *Pravda* evolved from a dull party mouthpiece to one that could keep pace with the rapid changes in other press organs. The changes in reporting did not begin immediately, but by early 1987, several newspapers began to adopt more radical stances, particularly *Ogonyok*, *Argumenty i fakty*, and *Moskovskie Novosti*, a newspaper that had earlier been intended for foreign audiences. Editors such as Vitaly Korotych (*Ogonyok*) and Yegor Yakovlev (*Moskovskie Novosti*) were valued highly by the government, which protected them from persecution.

In general, the changes in the media were mixed. True, for the first time journalists were given license to express views that would not have been permitted hitherto. However, there were limits, though not always clearly defined. Further, there was a natural tendency to adopt a dogmatic tone and a subjective point of view. Often, reports were written in the form of a polemic. This was characteristic of the first officially sanctioned media campaign: the denigration of Stalin and his rule. Here, the media followed the instructions of the Soviet leadership. The policy continued that of Khrushchev's campaigns of 1956 and 1961 but took them a stage further, to the point of rehabilitating the main victims of Stalin's purges and revealing what were described as 'blank spots' in history. The evident intention was to point out to readers that Lenin's vision of Soviet society remained intact, despite the deviations that had occurred under Stalin. Democratic centralism must again replace an administrative-command system; the abuses that occurred under Stalin, with trials and executions of thousands of innocent people, were not to be repeated.

This process began on 2 November 1987, when Gorbachev announced the creation of a commission to rehabilitate Stalin's victims, and by February 1988, dozens of party personnel condemned as a result of the third Moscow show trial were declared to have been innocent, including Nikolay Bukharin and Aleksey Rykov, the leaders of the so-called Right Opposition, and Marshal Mikhail Tukhachevsky, the most prominent victim of the purge of the military. It was only a matter of time before the most senior figures were reinvestigated, and on 13 June 1988, the USSR Supreme Court rehabilitated Grigory Zinoviev, Lev Kamenev, Georgy Pyatakov, and Karl Radek, the main figures from the two earlier show trials of 1936. A week later, Bukharin and Rykov were readmitted posthumously to the CPSU, a dubious honour.

The exception to the unravelling of the complex 1930s was the position of L.D. Trotsky, though his case and that of the former chief of the secret police, Lavrenty Beria were also under examination.

After the visit of Polish president, Wojtiech Jaruzelski, to Moscow in April 1990, the Soviet government for the first time admitted its responsibility for the deaths of some 15,000 Polish officers in 1940, about one-third of them at the Katyn Forest near Smolensk. In the Slavic republics, it became quite common to uncover mass graves of NKVD victims, executed in the period 1937–41. These included one at Bykivnya near Kyiv, and another at Kurapaty in a northern suburb of Minsk. In contrast, the current regime was anxious to demonstrate that such days were long gone. A new draft of the Basic Criminal Code, published in December 1988, reduced prison sentences, cut drastically the number of offences that could result in the death penalty, and ended the policy of deportation. More and more dissidents were released, and Sakharov had become something of a cult figure. He had been re-elected to the Soviet Academy of Sciences in October 1988, and when he died in mid-December 1989, his Moscow funeral was a truly national event, with tens of thousands in attendance. The dissidents of the past had, albeit for a short time, become the heroes of the present.

Gorbachev later reflected on the enormous psychological shock brought about by the exposure of past crimes and atrocities. They led ultimately to a re-evaluation of Lenin and Marx, in addition to Stalin and Brezhnev and what Gorbachev saw as the depiction of the October Revolution in an entirely negative light. Such an acute historical inquiry, expressed through the media for the most part, was undoubtedly damaging. It led even party members to question the legitimacy of Soviet rule, as well as a revival of monarchism and Russian nationalism (demonstrated in part by the Pamyat society). The atmosphere of the Stalin years was recreated by the publication of Anatoly Rybakov's novel, *Children of the Arbat*. In 1989, *Novyi Mir* began to publish Solzhenitsyn's early 1970s treatise about the Gulag camps, *Gulag Archipelago*, for which he had been deported from the Soviet Union in 1974, with a print run of some 1.5 million copies of the journal. The icons of Soviet rule thus came crashing down, and along with political and economic events, this development had a profound impact on the way Soviet citizens perceived the Gorbachev regime. It did not amount yet to a full betrayal of what was seen as the glorious past, but it raised profound fears among party stalwarts that Gorbachev and his followers, particularly Aleksandr Yakovlev, seemed only too willing to 'bite the hand that fed them.' For some members of the public also, the process of revisiting the past had gone too far (*Voices of Glasnost*, pp. 269–71).

De-Stalinization also raised questions about Soviet ideology. Since the Khrushchev period, the ideological aspects of the Soviet Union had been in decline, confined to ritualistic programs and statements about the success of

Soviet plans and the ideas of Lenin. The ageing leadership under Brezhnev and his successors could hardly inspire the Soviet population, let alone a prospective Communist world. What was there about the USSR to encourage nations to join the Communist camp? There could be few economic gains. Capitalism had not disappeared; indeed even the Soviet leadership could only acknowledge its surprising longevity. When Gorbachev hoped to revive the Soviet system, what did he have in mind, other than a reversion to a nebulous Leninism, which signified that the Lenin of the NEP period was the true Lenin, rather than Lenin of the Civil War and War Communism? That Gorbachev was a Leninist is not in doubt, at least for the most part of his leadership. But how relevant was Lenin, now dead for more than 66 years, to Perestroika? The danger of de-Stalinization was that it undermined some of the basic conceptions on which the Soviet state had survived for so long, but did not offer any adequate replacement formulae.

The first public reaction to the directions of Glasnost was an article in *Sovetskaya Rossiya* (13 March 1988) by a Leningrad chemistry teacher, Nina Andreeva, which sharply attacked the policies of Perestroika in a lengthy and authoritative essay that seemed to many to signal a change of direction. Andreeva felt that Gorbachev's policies constituted a betrayal of the Soviet past, and was treating with scorn a venerable era, with particular targets being Stalin and Russian national pride. Though Andreeva claimed that she was not a Stalinist, she felt that it was impossible to deny the positive impact of Stalin on Soviet society. Ligachev was the obvious supporter and perhaps even initiator of such an article, and many observers believed that he might even have written it (it appeared at a time also when Gorbachev was absent from Moscow.). Ligachev denied any such authorship. However, Andreeva herself remained quite vocal for the remainder of the Soviet Union's existence. Three weeks later, Gorbachev replied in *Pravda* condemning the sentiments expressed in the rival newspaper. The events at least indicated that there was a serious debate among the Soviet leadership, in itself, not an unhealthy development. However, Gorbachev and the supporters of Perestroika came under increasing pressure to impose limits on Glasnost in the media and gradually they did so. By 1990, the period of license was effectively over, at least as far as the central media was concerned and restrictions on the media were very much in place. But by that time, the political situation had changed irrevocably.

SOCIAL, ENVIRONMENTAL AND NUCLEAR POWER ISSUES

How far Gorbachev was genuinely concerned about the environment prior to the Chernobyl disaster is debatable. Certainly scientists had been given license to criticize some of the more foolish plans of previous periods, such as the one to divert Siberian rivers to irrigate the dry lands of Central Asia. In the Sibarral Project, planners intended to divert waters from two rivers – the north-flowing Onega and Pechora – into the Volga, which flows into the Caspian Sea. It was the most ambitious of several irrigation projects that had got under way in the Brezhnev period. There were several others, including the Danube-Dnipro and North Crimean canals. In general, Soviet economic development could be described as supportive of grandiose projects, announced in a blaze of media publicity. Nuclear power development was an attempt to cut some corners, to supply with electricity both the large populations and industries of the European part of the Soviet Union, in addition to economic partners in Eastern Europe, which lacked natural energy resources.

The Chernobyl disaster, from the perspective of the Soviet government, was not merely a national tragedy, but it was also a result of shocking inattention to safety procedures, a chance event that could only have occurred through an unlikely combination of circumstances: an experiment on safety equipment conducted on a holiday weekend by inexperienced operators, with automatic shutdown systems dismantled. It was a combination of human error and equipment failure (a reactor that became unstable if operated at low power). The impact of the accident, however, was enormous and far-reaching, both from the perspective of official reporting, the health and environmental consequences, and the resentment against centralized planning that it aroused in the most affected republics, Belarus and Ukraine. After Chernobyl, the country could never be quite the same again, and ultimately the disaster served to lessen the distance between the Soviet Union and the outside world since, as was often stated, 'Radiation knows no boundaries.'

The accident, an explosion that blew the roof off the fourth reactor unit at the Chernobyl power station, 137 kilometers north of Kyiv, occurred in the early hours of 26 April 1986. Reports were spasmodic and unclear, and were not even issued at all until some 40 hours had expired. That they appeared eventually was due to the discovery of a substantial rise in atmospheric radiation coming from the Soviet Union by the authorities at a nuclear power plant in Sweden. The Soviet media began to issue information only when the Swedes had detected the location of the radiation. The population learned that there had been an accident, two people had died, and that a government commission had been appointed to deal with the situation (its first chairman was Boris Shcherbina). Initially, an area of 10 kilometres in radius around the reactor, including the main town of Pripyat, three kilometres to the north of the power station, had been evacuated. Ligachev and Ryzhkov flew to Kyiv and arrived at Chernobyl on 2 May. Thereafter the zone of evacuation was expanded to 30 kilometres. Under Ryzhkov's guidance the Politburo set up its own Operations Group to monitor the effects of the accident.

Matters were made worse by a transparent attempt by the health author-ities to play down the impact of the disaster, particularly (though not solely) at the Union level. Health information was classified, and offers of foreign assistance were turned down unless it came from people (like US industrialist

Armand Hammer) who were long-established friends of the Soviet Union. The Politburo debated the safety of Soviet nuclear power stations in July, with Gorbachev and others raising the question of how such flawed technology could have been put into place in a nuclear plant. When a Soviet delegation went to Vienna to report on the causes of the accident to the International Atomic Energy Agency (IAEA), it placed the blame squarely on human error rather than the make-up of the graphite-moderated (RBMK) reactor. In the summer of 1987, the chief officials at Chernobyl were put on trial and given sentences of 2–10 years of hard labor. The longest sentence was administered to plant director, Viktor Bryukhanov, who had not been present during the events. In the West meanwhile, according to Gorbachev in his television address of 14 May, 'mounds of lies' had been assembled about the accident in the media. It became quite common for Soviet newspapers to compile lists of accidents at Western power stations while virtually ignoring what was happening at Chernobyl.

Subsequently, the tone of Soviet articles began to change, and the struggle to deal with the effects of Chernobyl was compared to that against the German occupants in the Second World War. This time, the articles stressed, the enemy could not been seen, and the risks were therefore even greater. This approach at least allowed journalists to uncover some of the more harrowing events, such as the removal of graphite chunks from the roof of the destroyed reactor unit. Gorbachev was undoubtedly quite ignorant of the scale of the accident at first. In what seemed like callousness at the time, he used Chernobyl to justify his new avowed policy of removing all nuclear weapons from the earth by the year 2000. Chernobyl, he explained, provided an example of what a nuclear attack might be like. While this was at least partly true, it appeared to designate the event as a part of official propaganda. And while the death toll continued to mount, and observers could name individual colleagues who had died after working on the decontamination campaign, the official death toll never rose above 31, of which 28 deaths were attributed to radiation sickness.

Though the attention to the effects of Chernobyl ceased to be a matter of international concern by 1987–88, it continued to be a national issue for the Soviet authorities. Further the development and progress of Glasnost in the media was to have a direct impact on the Soviet population. The media continued to investigate certain aspects in spite of official obstacles and denials that anything was amiss. The key issue was the extent of the radioactive fallout. If it had remained within the 30-kilometer zone, Soviet reports that the accident had been contained could be justified. However, significant hotspots were uncovered miles from the reactor site. Finally in the spring of 1989 new maps of radiation fallout appeared in the major Moscow newspapers. They revealed that about 20 per cent of the territory of the Belarusian SSR was contaminated as were areas of Ukraine well to the south of Kyiv, and west as far as the Polish border. In Russia, large areas of Bryansk and Smolensk oblasts, as well as parts of Tula and Leningrad areas were now within the affected zones. New evacuations were hastily organized. The general attitude among the population was one of panic and disbelief. How could official reports ever be believed again? Ultimately, the Moscow authorities suffered a drop in credibility after the spring of 1989. The published maps directly fostered new environmental movements and renewed attention to the question of the development of nuclear power stations in general.

Chernobyl turned public attention to the state of the Soviet environment, and particularly the way in which the country had been subjected to heavy industrial development without regard for the ecological effects. At first the main issue, unsurprisingly but unjustifiably, was nuclear power. The first protests against nuclear power started at the republican level, especially in Lithuania (which had a giant RBMK-1500 plant at Ignalina, close to the border with Latvia and Belarus), and spread into Ukraine, Armenia, and other republics. The scale of the development of nuclear power, given the way in which Chernobyl had happened, gave cause for concern. Activists and investigative journalists discovered that Moscow-based planners had rarely visited the areas in which plants were to be built. As a result, there were proposed nuclear plants in seismic zones (Crimea, Armenia), and nuclear power and heating stations were planned within the vicinity of major cities (such as Kharkiv, Minsk, and Kyiv). Campaigns against the continued development of nuclear power caused the postponement or cessation of a significant portion of future reactor units.

The outcry of protests that resulted from Chernobyl had a significant impact on Soviet industrial development. No longer could the planners ignore the public reaction to their decisions. Moreover, the focus soon switched to other spheres of industry: chemical and ferrous metallurgy factories, and encroachments on the natural environment of Siberia and Central Asia. On 30 September 1988, a decree was issued to improve the ecological situation of the Aral Sea, the erosion of which was cited as one of the country's biggest ecological catastrophes. By March 1990, the Ukrainian Supreme Soviet announced that the Chernobyl plant would be gradually phased out over the next five years (though this did not happen until December 2000) and that there would be a moratorium on any new reactor construction. The outcry that resulted from Chernobyl thus spurred an environmental concern that had an impact on virtually every aspect of economic (and ultimately political) life. Planners could no longer simply construct a new industrial complex without consultation with the local population. They had to respond to protests and public concerns. Some newspapers, such as *Sotsialistychna Industriya* and *Rabochaya Gazeta* were filled with articles protesting industrial projects that were causing damage to the environment. The nuclear power program in the USSR was brought to a virtual halt.

   The period of Glasnost saw some changes in other areas of Soviet life. Reporting of subsequent accidents gradually became more timely and accurate. Gorbachev seemed to be a leader beset by unforeseen disasters. Only four months after Chernobyl, a passenger liner, the *Admiral Nakhimov* collided with a freighter called *Petr Vasev* on the Black Sea with the loss of over 300 lives. The accident received prompt coverage in the media, including reports about drunkenness among the crew of the liner under its new captain. In December 1988, an earthquake in Armenia was not only reported in detail, but also the Soviet authorities welcomed external assistance. Gorbachev himself decided to cut short a visit to the United States to visit the accident scene. Formerly, the Soviet Union had never released figures on the number of accident victims, or highlighted social problems, such as AIDS (initially blamed on the United States) and the decline in living standards. Though progress was gradual, by the early 1990s, the Soviet population had been made aware of the high rates of infant mortality, the decreasing birth rate, and the spread of HIV across the country. The reports issued under Glasnost refocused attention to the state of the Soviet economy. The self-praise and complacency of the past began to dissipate.

PART TWO

THE YEARS OF PERESTROIKA

CHAPTER TWO

PERESTROIKA IN ACTION

THE ECONOMY, 1985–90

Acceleration and anti-alcohol campaigns

Perhaps in no other sector has the Soviet leadership under Gorbachev been criticized so severely as the economy. The reason perhaps is that he was dealing with an area about which he knew little, but in which he became deeply enmeshed. In short, he seemed unwilling to delegate major decisions to experts. According to an American economist, 'Gorbachev did not understand the basic economic principles of the reforms he sought to introduce' (Tedstrom, 1991, p. 12). The period of Perestroika is replete with attempts to improve the performance of the Soviet economy, of frank assessments of hitherto concealed problems, and ultimately of the frustration felt by many economists at the limited reforms that were actually implemented. Arguably, Gorbachev considered the economy as the most critical factor for his administration, sacrificing any foreign policy ambitions in order that he might give it undivided attention. Perestroika, first and foremost, signified economic restructuring. For our purposes, the failure of economic reform demonstrates the limitations of the Gorbachev leadership, but one still needs to assess to what degree the economic crisis that was evident by 1991 was a key factor in the collapse of the Soviet Union.

The first notable attempt at reform was the campaign against drunkenness and alcoholism that was launched in May 1985. The USSR Institute of Sociology maintained that the yearly losses to the economy from alcohol amounted to around R80 billion. Gorbachev noted the link between alcoholism and poor work discipline, low life expectancy, along with its perennial drag on the Soviet economy. However, the key architect of this reform was Ligachev. Before long, Gorbachev was complaining that the campaign had been introduced with too much zeal and enthusiasm, effectively ruining a good initiative. Instead, the campaign lowered the popularity of the new leader, who became known derisively as 'Comrade Orange Juice.' The goal was to lower the production of vodka by 10 per cent over five years, but this amount was already attained by 1986. Similar to the anti-corruption drive of the Andropov leadership, the campaign was extended to the workplace, and even to public transport, where police would sometimes conduct breath tests on passengers. In the cities, the number of outlets selling liquor dwindled, causing long queues. Vineyards closed down, and the general public began to purchase items to make samogon. Sugar disappeared from stores. Having initiated the program, Gorbachev had little time to monitor its progress, and it was perhaps fortunate for him that he could blame Ligachev once the reform went awry.

At the same time, Gorbachev began to focus on scientific and technical issues, and the poor work discipline that had been manifest in the workplace since the Brezhnev years. The latter took the form of a personal critique as the new Soviet leader visited factories in Dnipropetrovsk (Brezhnev's home town, and a key industrial base in Ukraine) and the oil and gas regions of Western Siberia, such as Tyumen and Surgut. The first measures applied were extensions of those tried under Andropov, namely to expand an economic experiment to raise the control of enterprises and make them more responsible for production targets. Surpluses achieved at these factories could be reinvested at the same place. By July 1985, the system was extended to all enterprises in the sectors of light industry, food, machine building, and meat and dairy products, with a starting date of 1 January 1986, to be extended to the whole of industry one year later. Paradoxically, the regime worsened the bureaucratic structure of Soviet industry with the formation of the State Committee for the Agro-Industrial Complex, in November 1985, which was created to amalgamate the various agricultural ministries under the leadership of the First Deputy Chairman of the Soviet government.

In 1986, further changes occurred in the area of planning and control. The development of light industry was to be more oriented to demand of wholesale markets, and industrial ministries were permitted to trade through their own firms. More radically, a new system to monitor quality of production was introduced at a trial 1,500 factories, evidently causing uproar and resulting in mass protests. On 12 May, a decree on the fundamental improvement of the quality of production saw the introduction of a new organization, the *Gospryomka* (State Inspection of Production), to monitor quality control. The new system remained only for two more years, however, falling victim, like so many of the Gorbachev reforms, to the reluctance of the workforce to deal with major changes. More dabbling with the state economic system followed: 20 ministries received the right to export their products directly to the world market, while another 70 factories and associations were allowed to form partnerships with similar enterprises in the socialist bloc of countries.

In February 1986, the regime launched a new system of consumer cooperatives. One year later, it was extended to the production of consumer goods, general foods, and services. Sharp wage differentials were introduced in January 1987, linking salary to the results of labor. The cost of military spending was announced in the spring of 1987 to be up to 40 per cent of the state budget, which was more than twice the amount reported formerly by the Soviet authorities. Another major concern to Gorbachev was the cost of labor in agriculture, which was ten times more than in developed countries, and more than twice the amount for industry. The party and government noted that whereas in the past such excessive costs had been counterbalanced by the high prices at which the Soviet Union could sell its oil and gas assets in the 1960s and 1970s, this was no longer the case in the late 1980s.

But how was the situation to be improved? The authorities constantly announced what were described as 'radical' economic reforms with the goal of maximizing the potential of the existing system rather than dismantling it. A Central Committee Plenum of June 1987 was devoted to economic reform, and issued some ten decrees on the redistribution of authority from the central organs to the periphery, the development of wholesale markets to offset slowly the centralized system of supply, and the proposed revival of banking activities. Just four days after the Plenum, the authorities issued the Law about the State Enterprise (effective from 1 January 1988), which foresaw the election of factory managers, and a system of financing in enterprises. It also anticipated the reduction of state subsidies, signifying that in the future there would be the possibility of enterprises going bankrupt. The goal of the reform was to allow the state enterprise to become more independent from the government ministries. By December 1987, there were already reports that in the production sphere extensive layoffs would soon become inevitable, possibly resulting in some 16 million unemployed.

The coal miners' strike

By 1988, discontent had spread among the Soviet workforce. According to a survey published in *Argumenty i fakty* (No. 6, 1990), and comparing worker contentment with a similar survey of 1976, the newspaper reported that dissatisfaction of workers with their conditions had risen by 1.5 times among males, and had doubled among females. Most respondents maintained that labor productivity required material stimuli. According to official figures, the economy was not performing badly in this period. In 1989, the Soviet GNP had risen (compared to the previous year) by 3 per cent, national income had increased by 2.4 per cent, industrial output by 1.7 per cent, and labor productivity was up 2.5 per cent. The budget deficit also had fallen from $120 billion to $92 billion. The figures were nonetheless lower than the state plan, and these results were registered in the midst of a fierce debate about taking deeper steps in economic reform. The rate of crime meanwhile had risen some 32 per cent, and the country witnessed the first serious unrest for many years – the first that was ever reported in the media – when the coal miners of the Kuzbass coalfield started a strike on 10 July 1989.

The strike began as a result of working conditions at the coalmines, including shortages of soap. It soon spread from Kuzbass to the Donbas mines on the Ukrainian-Russian border, Pechora and Karaganda, as the number of strikers rose to around 180,000. Before long, particularly in the Donbas, the economic demands turned to political ones, with the miners forming an unofficial trade union to put forth their demands, made up of the various strike committees and based at the town of Gorlovka (Horlivka) in Ukraine. Ostensibly the target of the protests was the Soviet government (rather than the party leadership) and its chairman, Nikolay Ryzhkov. Gorbachev declared himself to be in sympathy with the miners' demands and promised to rectify them by improving both salaries and working conditions. Such promises proved far more difficult to put in place than to enunciate. In July 1990, the Donbas miners staged a repeat strike to demand material improvements and the dismantling of party control over the mines. The miners formed an unofficial trade union and began to evict mine party leaders from their offices.

These events proved to be a serious threat to the Gorbachev administration, and raised questions about whether essential industries should be permitted the right to strike. Workers from the steel industry sent letters of complaint to various newspapers (doubtless under management pressure) to complain that their own industries could not survive for long without supplies of coking coal. A law of 9 October 1989 declared the basic right of workers to strike, though it banned strikes in major economic areas, and its wording was vague. The miners' strike also indicated political activism in areas that had previously been quite passive, thus demonstrating that a discontented workforce might under certain conditions play a role alongside anti-Soviet political forces. For the Gorbachev regime, the strike belied the official figures on economic performance. One dilemma was that incomes were rising much faster than productivity and a cautious reform program introduced in December 1989 was only worsening the situation. In an interview in the London *Times* of 21 March 1990, Nikolay Petrakov, deputy director of the Mathematics-Economics Institute and a corresponding member of the Soviet Academy of Sciences, pointed out that the government had lost control over the question of people's incomes. In the first two months of 1990, wages had risen by 14–15 per cent, but productivity growth was hardly above zero. And there was a growing backlog of incomplete, over-budget projects.

Economic reform programs

By March 1990, some of Gorbachev's economic advisors released the results of discussions held by a working group on economic reform that was headed by Dr Leonid Abalkin, deputy prime minister. They proposed the more rapid introduction of a market system during the coming years, through price reform, anti-monopoly legislation, the creation of a central bank, and a law on foreign investment. Prices were to rise for several commodities and products, including energy supplies and electric power, and iron and steel, and the practice of state procurement was to be abandoned. On 11 March, through a government decree, the USSR Council of Ministers formed a Commission chaired by Mikhail Gorbachev to prepare a new reform package within a month, with the help of a group of economists led by Abalkin. There was some fear over the immediate results of a crash reform program. Abalkin remarked that there would be a sudden, sharp rise in the prices of consumer goods by 150–200 per cent, but subsequently prices would stabilize, and basic goods necessary for family subsistence would not be subjected to the increase (Rutland, 1990, p. 5).

On 24 May, Prime Minister Ryzhkov presented the new plan to the USSR Supreme Soviet (reported the following day in the newspaper *Izvestiya*), offering what was termed a phrased transition to a market economy. The goal was to cut down on state subsidies, which would result in much higher prices for many consumer products. Bread prices were expected to triple, while prices for many non-consumer goods would rise by 30–50 per cent. To a swell of protest from the assembled, Ryzhkov voiced his belief that in the short term, the Soviet public could expect high inflation rates, unemployment, and a drop in output. The Supreme Soviet urged Ryzhkov, a naturally cautious political leader, to re-examine or redraft the program.

In mid-July 1990, the 28th Party Congress noted the deteriorating economic situation in the country with a dramatic drop in living standards. It referred to a 'crisis phenomenon' with the collapse of the consumer market. The mass of the population, speakers asserted, had lost its faith in Perestroika. But how had this situation occurred? What had happened since the release of generally positive (albeit sluggish) figures on economic performance in earlier years? Writing in *Pravda* on 24 July, Yegor Gaidar maintained that the roots of the crisis lay as far back as 1985, with a budget shortfall of some R10 billion annually as a result of the abortive anti-alcohol campaign. Incomplete construction projects, he noted, had added a further R38 billion, and between 1985 and 1987, after all expenses had been taken off the budget, external trade had fallen by an estimated $21 billion per year because of the fall in world oil prices. By 1988–89, a sudden increase in average wages far surpassed the rise in national income, and by the end of 1989, and for the first time, the absolute volume of production in the country had begun to decline. Henceforth there would not be stagnation, but recession. The Gorbachev regime thus, in Gaidar's view, bore some but by no means all of the responsibility for an emerging and pressing economic predicament.

At the same time, Gorbachev's plans for economic reform now faced another problem: the concomitant drawing up of a reform program by the government of the Russian Federation, under the leadership of the Chairman of the Presidium of the Russian Supreme Soviet, Boris Yeltsin. The transformation of Russia into a sovereign state is dealt with below. Suffice it to say here that Yeltsin and his team rushed ahead of their Union counterparts, partly through the general beliefs of the economists involved, but partly to undermine the Union program and raise their own authority vis-à-vis Gorbachev and the USSR Supreme Soviet. The combination of politics and economic reform proved to be a lethal concoction that ultimately would play a key part in the demise of the Union state. On 16 August 1990, Yeltsin held a meeting with the Russian working group to come up with a program to transfer the Russian Federation to a market economy. The group included more radical economists, such as S. Shatalin, a member of the presidential council, N. Petrakov, and the Deputy Chairman of the Russian Council of Ministers, G. Yavlinsky. Its program, in which Abalkin also took part, was to be known as 'The 500 Days,' the amount of time it anticipated it would take to transfer Russia to a market economy.

Almost at once, steps were taken to try to coordinate the Union and Russian programs, as a Union plan was inconceivable without the support and cooperation of Russia. The Soviet side established a new team of experts under Academician Abel Aganbegyan, effectively signifying the creation of three working groups on economic reform: that of Ryzhkov, which was chaired by Abalkin; that of Shatalin (the 500 Days program, now operating for both the Union and Russian governments led by Gorbachev and Yeltsin respectively), and the Aganbegyan team that was under the jurisdiction of the USSR Council of Ministers and had a mandate to review all possible alternatives for the move to a market economy. It was left to the Shatalin team to outline its more fundamental ideas, and the other two groups then tried to moderate its plans to make the scheme more palatable, both to themselves and the population at large.

The 500 Days program was outlined by Yavlinsky in the newspaper *Sovetskaya Rossiya* on 20 September 1990. Beginning on 1 October, the first 100 days were to see a series of extraordinary measures, including the imposition of strict fiscal regulation and monetarism, along with the devolution of fundamental economic authority from the centre (Moscow) to the republics. After the first 100 days, the period of 100–250 days anticipated the freeing of prices and acute financial limitations, with the aim of creating the preconditions for the switch to a complete market economy. In this period, the consumer market was to be functioning fully, and the first stage of a land reform was to be complete by the spring of 1991. In the third period, 250–400 days, the market was to stabilize, and anti-monopoly policies were to be implemented. By its end, the country was to have ended state control over prices in up to 80 per cent of production and services, and a convertible rouble would be introduced. The period from 400 to 500 days was to be the 'take-off' period for the new program, with the removal of state control, the introduction of privatization, de-monopolization, and market economics. Over a six-month period, the budget deficit was to be reduced to zero through the public sales of land and housing, with state assets sold off over the subsequent year. The responsibility for taxes and foreign investment would devolve to the Union republics.

The 500 Days program was not only more radical than the Union authorities wanted, but it also implied a dramatic loss of authority to the republics for the Soviet regime. Yet Gorbachev was put under pressure to respond to the initiatives of the Russian government. On 3 September, Yeltsin made the program public and announced that the Russian parliament would vote on it on 11 September, the day after the USSR Supreme Soviet was to begin its session. This brought about the likelihood that the Russian government would be one step ahead of Gorbachev. From the outset, it was evident that there could not realistically be two economic programs in place. Yeltsin raised the tension also by demanding that Soviet Prime Minister Ryzhkov should resign. In turn, Ryzhkov apparently lost the confidence of Gorbachev, who surprisingly supported the 500 Days program when the USSR Supreme Soviet began its session. Ryzhkov had relied on Gorbachev's backing to introduce proposals that would have modified the radical plan. He described Shatalin's proposals as 'dangerous' and 'irresponsible.' Aganbegyan also remarked on 11 September that the plans of Shatalin and Ryzhkov were incompatible. Meanwhile, on this same day, the Russian Supreme Soviet supported the new program by 213 votes to 2, with 6 abstentions.

Ryzhkov's approach, outlined on 9 September in *Pravda*, seems in retrospect to have been eminently sensible, if lacking in adventure. He advocated the retention by the central government of some control over the economy, and that factories should deliver some of their taxes to the central budget. The central government in Moscow, in his view, should also continue to operate crucial industries, such as energy, heavy industry, and telecommunications. The diversity of approaches may have caused some problems, but ultimately it was the ambivalence of the Gorbachev government, and the Soviet president himself, that led to the undoing of the 500 Days program. Though ostensibly he supported the plans offered by Shatalin and Yavlinsky, Gorbachev could not bring himself to implement them. A key question is why he offered support for the program in the first place, given the reduction of his powers that it implied. Though he was under great pressure not to be outdone by the moves of Yeltsin and the Russian government, his actions at this time lacked logic or purpose. At the least, he showed no faith in his own Prime Minister, and ultimately he lost control over economic decision-making by refusing to put either plan into operation.

Initially, however, Gorbachev tried to take responsibility for economic reform. On 27 September he requested special executive authority to implement measures, following the failure of the USSR Supreme Soviet to agree on direction. A committee of scholars and officials under the chairmanship of

Gorbachev was given the task of coming up with a compromise plan that would be based on Shatalin's ideas, but with modifications elaborated by Leonid Abalkin, and with a deadline of 15 October for completion. The result, a combination of the two programs, appeared in *Izvestiya* on 27 October as 'The basic directions for the stabilization of the economy and transition to a market economy.' Predictably, the authors of the 500 Days program were unimpressed. Shatalin, Yavlinsky, and others published a letter in *Komsomolskaya Pravda* on 4 November, in which they declared that the Program could not now be fulfilled because the government had refused to introduce it.

Could it have worked? Western economists had strong doubts. The late American economist Ed Hewett, for example (cited in *Izvestiya*, 22 September 1990), commented that the transfer of all power to the republics would lead to constant debates between the republics. Philip Hanson, a British economist based at the University of Birmingham, also noted that the sharing out among the republics of the existing USSR debt and reserves would create problems and that without a centre, it would be very difficult to reach a consensus (Hanson, 1990). It seems fair to say that the 500 Days program would have led to the collapse of the centre almost upon its implementation. It may have worked at the republican level – indeed it was applied in part by Gaidar for the independent Russian Federation in early 1992. What happened subsequently was a similar process of division between republics and centre, but one that was slower and more painful, as the republics gradually took away economic power from the centre, and Gorbachev tried to introduce workable plans amid a disturbing economic climate.

Stagnation

In 1985, though the country may have reached a point of stagnation, there was no discernible crisis. Only by late 1990 and 1991 can one state that economic issues had become a priority. The evidence was plain. In January 1991, the Soviet government reported that industrial production had declined by 1 per cent in 1990. Output of oil had fallen by 6 per cent, and by 10 per cent in December 1990. In Ukraine, the Donetsk Coal Enterprise reported that output was 400,000 tons below the annual target, 15 out of the 21 enterprises having failed to meet the planned totals. GNP in 1990 dropped by 2 per cent and national income fell by 4 per cent. In March 1991, the Independent Miners' Union held a one-day warning strike across the Soviet Union, demanding that wages be doubled. Periodic stoppages then occurred over the next few days at coalmines in Ukraine, Kazakhstan, and the Arctic regions. By 19 March, 300,000 coal miners were on strike in the larger coalfields of the Donbas and the Kuzbass, and also in Vorkuta. Meanwhile, national income and industrial output continued to fall, along with what one newspaper described as 'increasing destabilization of the consumer market.' On 10 April,

Valentin Pavlov, who had replaced Ryzhkov as Prime Minister on 14 January after the latter had a heart attack on 25 December 1990, announced that Soviet GNP had fallen 10 per cent in the first three months of 1991.

Pavlov's first steps as Prime Minister were disastrous. On 19 January 1991, he announced a platform of monetarism that included a currency reform and freezing savings accounts until it was in place. By 22 January 50 and 100 rouble bills were no longer to be legal tender, and had to be exchanged for new bills. A decree of the USSR Cabinet of Ministers on this same date established a maximum limit for the exchange of old rouble notes: R200 for pensioners and R1000 for workers. The reform was intended to cut out speculators, counterfeit money and unearned income, but it came suddenly, and many banks were unprepared for the public reaction, which was one of great concern and anxiety, as large crowds descended on banks trying to exchange old bills. No account was taken of the reluctance of some parts of the population to save money at home rather than at banks, as had long been the tradition. Thus part of the population suffered badly as a result of the currency reform. Further, only about 5 per cent of money in circulation was confiscated.

On 4 March, Gorbachev appeared on the television program *Vremya*, and informed viewers of the sudden fall in industrial output and the supply of food in January and February. He laid the blame primarily on industrial unrest, which had resulted in shortages of coking coal and scrap metal for the steel industry. As a result steel exports had fallen sharply. Two weeks later, Gorbachev issued a decree on new retail state prices for goods, and a rise in the price of transport and communications. Income derived from these measures was to be used to compensate the population and to cover wage increases for workers in the spheres of health, education, social security, and culture. Current prices would be maintained for vodka, gas, and coal. In this same month, in the London *Financial Times* (27 March), Oleg Ozherelev, one of Gorbachev's financial advisors, attributed the collapse of the economy to a too rapid switch to a market system, declaring that it was essential to maintain a centralized system to maintain supplies between different state enterprises. In his view, managers of state companies simply lacked the experience for a sudden change to a market system.

By the spring of 1991 it was becoming difficult to separate economic reform from political decentralization. Already several republics were refusing to participate in Union endeavors (see below). More important those that did take part were anxious mainly to ensure greater power and control at the local level. Several republics began to withhold revenue from the central budget, giving credibility to declarations of state sovereignty that had been issued in the previous summer. The main 'culprits' were the three Baltic States, Ukraine, Georgia, Moldavia, and Russia. By early April, the Soviet Union began to experience a severe and unprecedented budget deficit, which reached over R30 billion in the first quarter of the year, compared to a planned deficit of only R26.7 billion for the entire year. Anxiously, the main financial leaders in the Union (Vladimir Orlov, the Minister of Finance, Viktor Gerashchenko, Chairman of the State Bank, and Viktor Kucherenko, Chairman of the USSR Supreme Soviet Budget and Planning Committee) sent a letter to Gorbachev, stating that the economy was on the verge of a catastrophe and that if the current deficit continued, it would not be possible to cover investment and spending on the military in the second quarter of 1991.

Was there a viable solution? The financial leaders advocated strengthening the hold of the central power over the economy, banks, and the republics. They did not say, however, how the Gorbachev government was supposed to carry out such a policy in the face of republican opposition. Moreover, Russia, represented by First Deputy Chairman of the parliament, Ruslan Khasbulatov, made it plain that it would oppose any attempts to centralize the economy. Gorbachev, however, entrusted Pavlov to come up with yet another program, and the consequence of the latter's approach to economic problems served to exacerbate the situation. Its introduction coincided with further bad news on economic performance, for the first quarter of 1991: GNP had fallen by 8 per cent, industrial output by 5 per cent, labor productivity by 9 per cent; national income by 10 per cent, agricultural output by 13 per cent, and production of livestock by 12 per cent. Foreign trade turnover had plummeted by 33 per cent; exports were down by 18.4 per cent, and imports by 45 per cent. Pavlov declared that economic collapse was imminent if his program were not adopted.

The Pavlov program

Strikes continued across the country, led by the coal miners but involving a broad portion of the Soviet workforce. The two major coalfields, Kuzbass and Donbas, were reported working at 50 per cent of capacity. On 9 March, Aleksandr Golikov, chairman of the Coordinating Council of Strike Committees, declared in Moscow the demand for a national index that would raise the wages of workers of all industries to meet the rising costs in living standards. It was reported that car factories were striking in support of the miners, and railway workers were threatening to halt all transport in Vorkuta if the lack of coal supplies continued. On 2 April the Soviet government introduced an increase of retail prices. Workers received an extra R60 in their monthly wages, but this amount did not compensate for the price rises. On 26 April, about 50 million people staged a one-hour strike in protest at the rising prices and falling quality of life, at the behest of the Independent Federation of Trade Unions of the Russian Federation. Thus a rising tide of worker unrest occurred that could not be ignored. Vladimir Shcherbakov, a Soviet deputy prime minister, met with republican leaders in this same month to reach agreement on the new economic reform program proposed by Gorbachev and

Pavlov. Eleven republics joined the discussion, as the Baltic States and Georgia refused to cooperate further in any Union plans.

Pavlov's program satisfied few people. As outlined to the USSR Supreme Soviet on 22 April, it anticipated limited privatization, and more controls over salaries, prices, and supply and output. There was to be a one-year ban on strikes and protests during working hours. The USSR Central Bank was to keep under control spending by republican governments. Emergency measures were to be put in place for the distribution of essential food products. It complemented proposals by Gorbachev two weeks earlier that advocated the reduction of defence spending and the conversion of military plants for the production of consumer products, along with a decrease in monopolies. In both cases, the two leaders stressed that the republics must sign the new Union Treaty, otherwise they would face much higher costs for energy and raw materials. Republican or local laws that were in contradiction of those at the all-Union level were to be suspended. Energy-inefficient factories were to be closed, and some 5 million hectares of arable land were to be set aside for private farming.

Pavlov's plan essentially tried to restore the balance of control in favour of the centre. It was the fifth attempt at a major reform program in the Gorbachev period. It was limited in scope by its creator's own aversion to a market economy, and it coincided with a period of intense labor unrest and popular discontent. A Western economist, Keith Bush, described it as 'perhaps fatally flawed' and '350 pages of dense prose,' and pointed out that in the spring of 1991, the Soviet economy was undergoing a process of disintegration (Bush, 1991, p. 5). Supporters of Shatalin's earlier program naturally deplored it, and it reflected the unwillingness of the USSR Supreme Soviet to take radical measures to deal with the economic crisis. There was to be no shock therapy for the Soviet Union. The question, however, was whether any program would work. The Supreme Soviet allowed the USSR Council of Ministers until 20 May to refine the new plan, in discussions with the republics. Already, Kazakh president Nursultan Nazarbayev had criticized Pavlov's plan for not taking into account the needs of the republics. Though it foresaw the eventual establishment of a market economy, there was no precise timetable.

Meanwhile the political games continued. With the issue of the draft Pavlov Plan, Gorbachev signed a statement on stabilization measures with representatives of nine Union republics (Russia, Ukraine, Kazakhstan, Azerbaijan, Moldavia, and the Central Asians). Boris Yeltsin then announced that Gorbachev's signature on the document signified his recognition of the republics as sovereign states. He gave further weight to this statement by taking it upon himself to bring an end to the festering miners' strike, meeting the miners' leaders in Novokuznetsk and offering a draft document of a settlement. He assured miners a week later that if he should win the Russian presidential election (scheduled for June), then he would de-politicize Russian state enterprises, i.e., curb the authority of the Communist Party within them. On 1 May, Yeltsin signed a resolution that saw the transfer of control over the Kuzbass coalmines from the Soviet Union to the Russian Federation. This dramatic move, which perhaps fatally undermined Gorbachev's authority, was undertaken with the backing of the Kuzbass Strike Committee and regional leaders. The Donbas miners ended their strike on 4 May, and also made it clear that they would support more regional power for the government in Kyiv. Gorbachev was prepared to go so far along this route, negotiating a share of revenue from republican enterprises for the central government. He was determined, however, not to permit the continuation of strikes in key industries, which brought him into direct conflict with the Independent Trade Union of The Russian Federation.

By the late spring and early summer of 1991, Pavlov was able to declare that the economic situation was 'stabilizing.' All the same the economic indicators remained grim, with the six-monthly figures revealing a fall in GNP of 10 per cent, a 12 per cent decline in national income, and 6.2 per cent drop in industrial output. Gorbachev was beginning to plead with Western governments to come to the aid of the Soviet Union arguing that the price was a small one to pay for the preservation of the new democracy. How far was the economic crisis responsible for the ultimate collapse of the Union state? Clearly it cannot be ruled out as a significant factor. However, the crisis itself was made worse by the political situation and the growing rift between Gorbachev's government and that of Russia. As noted below, this rift would be widened appreciably once Yeltsin was elected president of the Russian Federation. Though the Shatalin Plan offered one answer to the growing dilemma, it was essentially a recipe for disintegration in itself, as it would have brought an end to Union control over the economy.

Above all, the divergence between Union control and Russian control has to be placed alongside the quest for privatization and a rapid transition to a market economy. The Gorbachev regime lacked resolution and proved unable to settle on a viable economic program, swayed by the opposition of the USSR Supreme Soviet on the one hand, while being understandably reluctant to concede economic power to the republics on the other. The outbreak of strikes, beginning with that of the coalminers in 1989, made the picture far worse, as other related industries were affected, exports fell, and the overall impact of the strikes, added to the continuing decline of world oil prices, contributed to the worst economic year for the country since the war against Germany. Ultimately, the economic crisis of 1991 was a symptom rather than the cause of the country's disintegration. Later in 1991, when Russia was refusing to make its contribution to the Union budget, the situation for the central government was untenable. But this refusal was a political, not an economic decision.

FOREIGN POLICY

Ideology and propaganda

Soviet foreign policy under Gorbachev saw the reduction of tensions in and ultimately the end of the Cold War. As a result, it is easy to examine it retrospectively and to perceive an end product that simply was not on the negotiating table in 1985. By that date, in the United States, the administration of President Ronald Reagan was entering its second term. The first had been characterized by a new phase of hostility between the Super Powers, with the president's allusion to the Soviet Union as an 'evil empire,' and the proposed development of a defensive shield that might protect the United States from a nuclear attack, known as the Strategic Defence Initiative (SDI) or Star Wars. Since 1991, there have been numerous discussions about an American victory in the Cold War, and how the substantial build-up of arms, in addition to SDI, forced the Soviet Union to engage in a race that it could not win; to wit, it brought about the end of a conflict that dated from the end of the Second World War. Any analysis of the fall of the Soviet Union has to deal with this line of thought.

But it also has to encompass another factor: the emergence of Gorbachev as peace-maker, the man who initiated the series of leadership summits that eased tensions, often making unilateral reductions of troops and weapons systems, and exhibiting a personality, at once dynamic and friendly, and able to cultivate a warm relationship with Reagan, and later a workable friendship with the more cautious George Bush (senior), who at first appeared reluctant to adopt the policies and initiatives of his predecessor (as well as the personnel). There is no doubt that Gorbachev can take some credit for bringing about an end to the lengthy arms race. *Time* magazine, in a fit of hyperbole, declared him the Man of the Decade in 1990, referring to him as 'the Copernicus, Darwin, and Freud of Communism all rolled into one' and giving him the credit for ending the Cold War. What is harder to discern is a premeditated policy to ease tensions or to conduct negotiations of any form other than to be able to concentrate on the domestic economy and domestic politics. There is also little evidence that the arms race *per se* brought about the end of the Soviet Union. No doubt it was a contributing factor, as it had been in the fluctuating tensions of the previous four decades. As a main cause of the downfall of the Soviet empire, or Communism, however, the evidence is lacking.

Gorbachev can be described as an ideological leader, a believer in Leninism and the Soviet path to Communism. In 1985, there are several indicators that as a leader, his foreign policy outlook did not constitute a radical departure from the past. On 26 April 1985, for example, the Soviet Union and its partners renewed the Warsaw Pact for a further twenty years. Later in the same month, Nicaraguan president Daniel Ortega visited Moscow, and Gorbachev enthusiastically endorsed the Sandinista revolution. Speaking to the Soviet armed forces on the 40th anniversary of the end of the Second World War, Gorbachev also praised Stalin. His first summit with Reagan, in Geneva, in November 1985, was inconclusive. Shortly afterward, Vasily Petrov, the First Deputy Minister of Defence, reiterated a familiar Soviet demand for a total ban of the military build-up in space. At the end of the year, the US and Soviet leaders sent greetings to each other's countries. Gorbachev noted that although the Geneva summit had been useful, there was still a considerable rift between the two. Reagan, gaining an unusual audience in the Soviet public, staunchly defended SDI.

At this time, Gorbachev's main platform was largely propagandistic. It consisted of his program to eliminate all nuclear weapons from the earth by the year 2000, an idea that, given the lack of response from Washington, could be consigned to the realms of fantasy. On 15 January 1986, a detailed list of Soviet proposals appeared in the government newspaper, *Izvestiya* and later they were broadcast on Soviet television. There were to be three stages. In the first stage, over the coming five to eight years, the Soviet Union and the United States would reduce by half all the missiles that could reach each other's territory. In the second stage, and by 1990, other states would be invited to join the disarmament program, tactical nuclear weapons were to be eliminated, and there was to be a ban on all nuclear tests. The third stage, the complete removal of nuclear weapons, was to be under way by 1995 and completed by 1999. The Americans responded politely but without commitment.

A second theme used by Gorbachev was that of a common European home. This policy appeared to be a ploy to drive a wedge between the United States and its European allies. It was not new. Moreover, Gorbachev did not adhere to it for long since his focus was primarily on the US–Soviet relationship. The main obstacles to further progress were the intransigence of the Reagan administration on SDI, the continuing Soviet military presence in Afghanistan, and the question of monitoring any agreement on a test ban. Gorbachev was willing to make concessions in certain areas, but initially it was not always clear to what extent he did so for a propaganda triumph and how far the Soviet side was prepared to go in reality. On 18 January 1986, for example, Soviet officials held a news conference to announce that the Soviet Union would remove its medium range missiles from Europe, providing that NATO did the same. In the past, this demand had been linked to the elimination of the nuclear forces in Britain and France.

Arms control

The main distinction between Gorbachev and Soviet administrations of the past was the new leader's approachability and apparent flexibility. This clearly was not an old-style bureaucrat fumbling through cue cards and refusing to move an inch from the set list of demands (the styles reminiscent of Brezhnev and the long-time foreign minister Andrey Gromyko respectively). The Americans, for their part, were initially suspicious, and for some time conservative analysts wondered whether Gorbachev might be seeking to gain the upper hand in superpower politics through his apparent openness, i.e., to hoodwink the American negotiators. Initially, therefore, there were no breakthroughs between the two sides. In March 1986, Reagan made an offer to the Soviet side for a sharing of US nuclear test monitoring technology. The official Soviet response was angry: the Americans were evading the issue of a test ban. On 28 March, for example, the US held a test in Nevada. On 29 March, speaking on Soviet television, Gorbachev called on the American president to meet him as soon as feasible in Europe to discuss a test ban, noting that although the Soviet moratorium on such tests was about to expire, his country would not carry out further tests if the Americans agreed to do the same. The US declined the offer, maintaining that a summit merely to discuss a test ban was inexpedient.

Gorbachev continued to emphasize both arms and nuclear testing in his relationship with the Americans. After April, he began to use the Chernobyl issue to support his campaigns both for a test ban on weapons and for a common European home. Both sides discussed their mutual programs at the next summit in Reykjavic, Iceland on 11–12 October 1986. No breakthrough in relations occurred at the summit, despite high expectations, and it was perceived at the time, especially by the Americans, as a failure. On the other hand, the two leaders evidently had begun to establish a rapport. In other areas in 1986, the Soviet Union seemed to resort to a more traditional pattern of foreign policy, including the arrest of an American journalist, Nicholas Daniloff, of *US News & World Report* for alleged espionage. Though Daniloff was eventually exchanged for G. Zakharov, a Soviet official at the UN arrested for spying, the charges against him were clearly fabricated. On the issue of nuclear testing, the Soviet deadline passed uneventfully, but the Soviet Union announced that it would end its unilateral moratorium following the first test of the United States in 1987.

In December 1987 Gorbachev made his first visit to Washington. It ended successfully with the signing of an agreement on the elimination of medium-range nuclear missiles, and with an invitation to the American president to visit Moscow the following summer. Gorbachev also began to make some major policy changes. The first concerned the Soviet war in Afghanistan. Though Soviet officials in general – at least when discussing the issue with foreigners – were reluctant to make any concessions on the continuing occupation, it had begun to arouse interest in the media, and among activists such as Sakharov. An action taken at the latter part of the Brezhnev regime (December 1979) hardly inspired much faith in a leader who had overtly rejected all aspects of Brezhnev's policy. In addition the war was a continuing drain on Soviet resources and manifestly unsuccessful. In July 1986, Gorbachev had announced the departure of six Soviet divisions from Afghanistan by the end of that year. On 8 February 1988, he declared that the departure of the army from the small border nation could begin on 15 May if an agreement could be signed in Geneva before that date.

Ultimately, an agreement was signed on 14 April. The Soviet Union agreed to begin removing its troops over the next nine months, with a starting date, as agreed, on 15 May. The last troops would leave by 15 February 1989. Almost immediately, the Soviet media began to criticize the decision to enter the country more than nine years earlier. Writing in *Literaturnaya gazeta* (18 May 1988), Vyacheslav Danishchev commented that the decision to invade Afghanistan was caused by mistakes and the general incompetence of the Brezhnev administration. There were in May 1988 some 115,000 Soviet troops in the war-torn country. On 25 May, the Soviet authorities revealed that 13,310 Soviet troops had died during the conflict, with 35,478 wounded. The figures, given the length of time that had expired, were not particularly high, but they omitted disease and drug addiction victims, and local losses of the Afghan population were very high. Thus the decision seemed a logical one, but it was nonetheless an admission of failure, and one unlikely to appease the families of Soviet soldiers who had died in the war. In ending the conflict, Gorbachev removed one of the last obstacles to developing a much-improved relationship with the United States. The international world now had evidence that in Gorbachev it had encountered a Soviet leader who was not restricted to rhetoric and willing to make fundamental changes of policy. The period of 'Gorbymania' in the West was about to begin.

Analyzing Gorbachev's first three years in power, Terry McNeill observed that the Soviet leader had recognized the importance of mutual security issues, that he continued to propagate the idea of Europe as a common home, and that his attitude to the West was less confrontational than that of his predecessors, a 'live and let live' policy. McNeill listed three basic premises as comprising Gorbachev's foreign policy. The first was that the Soviet leader recognized that the capitalist system was unlikely to collapse; the second, that a healthy economy rather than a powerful military was the single foundation for world power; and third, that the slow but massive military build-up conducted under Brezhnev had achieved little. The Americans had countered with rearmament and programs such as SDI, along with competition in the developing world and increased spending that the Soviets could not match (McNeill, 1988, pp. 3–4). He might have added an essential fourth, namely engagement. As a leader, Gorbachev was constantly exploring issues and differences with Western leaders, and the Americans in particular.

Architects of Soviet foreign policy

To what extent did his advisors influence these policies? The appointment of Shevardnadze as Foreign Minister, to replace Gromyko, was clearly a critical factor. It was he who insisted on the renewal of ties with Washington. Shevardnadze, however, was inexperienced and needed guidance in his first months in office. One of the strongest supporters of a new Détente was Aleksandr Yakovlev, with his long years of residence in the West (1973–83). Yakovlev's case was a fairly typical one of an outspoken hardliner transforming into a supporter (perhaps even the main advocate) of Glasnost, and his view of the world was one of multi-polarity rather than one divided between two Super Powers. Above all, however, it seems fair to say that Gorbachev created his own foreign policy, using the powers that he wielded first as General Secretary of the CC CPSU and later as Soviet president. It is more accurate to perceive this policy as one of sudden, sometimes inspired, initiatives rather than a long preconceived plan to bring an end to the Cold War. One should also bear in mind that throughout his term in office, and partly through his own machinations (as noted below) his authority steadily declined so that by 1990–91, it was only in the foreign policy sphere that he maintained any serious credibility as a world leader.

The years 1988–89 were the high point of Gorbachev's foreign policy, starting from the summit with Reagan in Moscow on 29 May–2 June 1988 when the two leaders discussed a wide variety of issues from discussions on the Strategic Arms Limitations Treaty (START), human rights, and regional conflicts. In the following month, Gorbachev visited Poland where he acknowledged that there were unfortunate 'blank spots' in the history of the two countries – implicitly the massacre of Polish officers in 1940 at Katyn and other locations – and in October, West German Chancellor Helmut Kohl paid his first official visit to the Soviet Union. On 6 December, Gorbachev went to New York to speak at the United Nations. There he shocked his audience by declaring his intention to reduce the Soviet armed forces by 500,000 troops over the next two years. He also announced the forthcoming removal of the Soviet army and military equipment from Central Europe and Mongolia. It was a remarkable performance that led to a mini-personality cult of the Soviet leader in a most unexpected venue: New York. Everywhere Gorbachev went crowds of admirers greeted him.

Likely these foreign visits, particularly to the United States, provided some much needed relief from the unrelenting tedium and difficulties of domestic politics. Henceforth, Gorbachev rarely missed an opportunity for travel abroad, often at seemingly inopportune times. That he was indefatigable and robust is only too evident. But the period inaugurated a phenomenon of a Soviet leader manifestly more popular abroad than at home. His popularity, however, rested on his conciliatory tactics, which, in turn, appeared to undermine his standing as the head of the world's major Communist Party in his home country. The questions were: how far was Gorbachev prepared to go in dismantling the military structure built up for the Cold War conflict? At what point would the Soviet Union cease to be a military threat or, conversely, resolve to crack down on dissident republics or renege on international agreements that appeared to bring it no conceivable advantages?

The year 1989, an epic year in international politics, was marked by extensive travel for the Soviet leader. In April, he went to Cuba, and after declaring his 'unbreakable friendship' with the island Communist state he immediately went to visit an old friend, British Prime Minister Margaret Thatcher, an early admirer of Gorbachev. The following month, US Secretary of State James Baker arrived in Moscow, at which time Gorbachev proclaimed the unilateral removal of 500 tactical nuclear weapons from Eastern Europe. The Americans could hardly keep pace. On 12 June, Gorbachev flew to West Germany. In early July he was in France, prompting French president Mitterand to issue an appeal to the countries of the west to support Perestroika. At the Council of Europe, Gorbachev reiterated his desire for a common European home. A major breakthrough in the Cold War was in the offing. The only apparent obstacle was the SDI program.

Eastern Europe

The situation in Eastern Europe by this time had begun to change rapidly, catalyzed by the apparent wave of tolerance in Moscow, which lessened considerably the fears of Soviet intervention. Neither Gorbachev nor Shevardnadze was willing to apply the Brezhnev Doctrine. The question was how far the USSR would allow changes to occur among the crumbling Communist governments. On 6 October, Gorbachev arrived in East Berlin for celebrations marking the 40th anniversary of the GDR, where he stood alongside Communist leader Erich Honecker to watch a parade. Gorbachev seems to have been ambivalent on the issue of a divided Germany. He warned Honecker, an inveterate hard-line Communist, of the urgent need for reforms in the GDR, but he also emphasized the necessity of preserving the postwar borders of Europe. Within less than a month, the Berlin Wall had fallen. Changes occurred rapidly in the East European 'satellite' states. Todor Zhivkov's regime in Bulgaria collapsed on 10 November, and in Czechoslovakia and Hungary there were new governments in place by the end of the same month. In Romania, the removal of the Ceaucescu regime turned violent and culminated in the execution of the former leader and his wife.

The Poles had already made similar changes with the Solidarity union becoming the most important catalyst of political change. The new Polish prime minister, T. Mazowiecki, visited Moscow in late November, and he and Gorbachev again reiterated the need to maintain the existing European borders. Mazovetsky then paid a visit to Katyn. In a period of euphoria in Eastern Europe, Gorbachev's reputation was high, not as the architect for change, but because he adopted the role, on behalf of the Soviet Union, as a bystander. On 1 December, Pope John Paul II, a patriotic Pole, received Gorbachev in the

Vatican and arranged for the restoration of diplomatic relations between the Roman Catholic Church and the USSR. Amid the fundamental regime changes in the former satellite states, however, lay the issue of a united Germany, one that had preoccupied the Soviet Union since 1955. Would the new Germany exist within or outside NATO? If it joined the military alliance then the balance of power on the European continent would change sharply. The Soviet Union, in effect, would be renouncing its role as a superpower and reversing its policies introduced since the end of the war.

Gradually, the rapidly changing European situation forced the Soviet leader to modify his stance. Initially, Gorbachev appeared prepared to accept the future unification of Germany as long as the amalgamated state remained outside NATO. In taking such a position he was adhering to a Soviet stance that dated back to the mid-1950s. In January and early February both GDR Premier Hans Modrow and West German Chancellor Helmut Kohl visited Moscow. Before discussions began with Modrow, Gorbachev stated that a union of the two German states was now probable but that the process must be gradual and not undermine international stability. On several occasions, including 6 March 1990, the Soviet leader declared that the Soviet Union would not accept the participation under any conditions of a united Germany in NATO, since the strategic balance of power in Europe would be altered. All four Allied powers from 1945 took part in the decision to unite Germany: the Soviet Union, the United States, Britain, and France. The formula thus became known as 2+4 (the two German states and the four allies).

Gorbachev could only stall or delay the inevitable. On 17 May, he halted the departure of Soviet troops from the GDR, but two months later, following another visit of Kohl to Moscow, he finally gave in, and allowed the new Germany to join/remain in NATO. The growing impotence of the Soviet Union in international affairs was evident. The move also reflected an internal conflict between the main architects of Soviet foreign policy. On the one hand there was Gorbachev and what has been described as his 'team of internationalists': Aleksandr Yakovlev, Georgy Shakhnazarov, Georgy Arbatov, and Anatoly Chernyaev; and on the other hand was the CC's International Department headed by Valentin Falin and his First Deputy, Boris Fyodorov. The latter two figures had vested interests in Germany: Falin had spent seven years in Bonn during the 1970s, and Fyodorov, a GRU intelligence officer, was a specialist on the country. Both felt that Gorbachev had surrendered too easily when faced with pressure from the Americans.

Earlier, in January 1990 both the Hungarians and the Czechoslovaks demanded the removal of Soviet troops from their territory. The future of the Warsaw Pact was now at stake. The East Europeans were no longer willing to remain in what they saw as an obsolete organization. On 7 June 1990, the seven countries of the Pact met in Moscow to review its role in the changed Europe. Hungary announced its intention of leaving the alliance before the end of 1991. In late February, the states in the Pact resolved to disband its military structures, and declared that as of 31 March, it would cease its existence, thus ending peacefully a military alliance first put into place in 1955, and symbolically on the occasion of the admission of the West German state into NATO. In one sense, the Soviet leader was in no position to dictate events and had decreasing room for maneuver. From the Western perspective, the dramatic end to the Cold War owed everything to Gorbachev. Yet as noted, his actual initiatives were minor.

Ending the Cold War

In the meantime, the warming relationship between President George Bush and Gorbachev, initially tentative, was beginning to pay major dividends. They held a second summit meeting in the United States from 30 May to 3 June 1990 (by that time Gorbachev was more than happy to return to USA to escape the political tensions in Moscow). The two leaders signed a statement on chemical weapons and agreed to cut back strategic weapons. At that point the main items to be resolved included a growing political tension in Lithuania (discussed below) and the German question. In late July, President Bush travelled to Moscow and the two leaders signed the START Treaty on 31 July, a major breakthrough in Soviet–US relations. What might have been the peak of Gorbachev's very personal foreign policy, however, was undermined and partly sullied by overwhelming political and economic problems at home. Bush, for example, also held a private meeting in the Kremlin with the new Russian president, Boris Yeltsin, who refused to appear in public with Gorbachev and Kazakh leader Nazarbayev. This meeting provided implicit recognition to the growing power of Yeltsin and the RSFSR. Bush also gave a speech in Kyiv, advising Ukrainians, among other things, of the dangers of embarking on a course of 'suicidal nationalism.'

As noted at the beginning of this chapter, the Soviet regime was not brought down by foreign policy or the arms question. On the other hand, the foreign policy adopted by Gorbachev, which involved rapprochement with the Western Powers, along with the decision to abandon the Brezhnev Doctrine, while instituting a more tolerant atmosphere vis-à-vis the countries of Eastern Europe, did lead indirectly to the overthrow of the satellite Communist governments. It is debatable how far Gorbachev could have applied force in any single case – one recalls the reluctance of Khrushchev to invade Poland in 1956 during a Polish leadership crisis because of fears of getting embroiled in a protracted military conflict. And of all the countries that were removing obsolete and out-of-touch governments, Poland was the most sensitive, thanks largely to the large Polish Diaspora in the United States. The change of governments in Eastern Europe transformed fundamentally the postwar structure, though not the postwar borders other than in Germany.

In turn, the new independence of these countries from Moscow served to encourage the republics of the Soviet Union to seek more authority.

Lastly, it is pertinent to ask the question, given the worldwide acclaim for Gorbachev as a result of his Nobel Peace Prize and his lasting prestige as an international statesman, whether his foreign policy owed more to design than to an awareness that it was no longer practicable to try to maintain Soviet military control or ideological leadership (which meant increasingly little outside the confines of regional leadership apparatchiks) in the face of growing popular opposition. The Gorbachev leadership was the first in Soviet history that never threatened or carried out some form of military intervention, with the exception of the two brief interludes under Andropov (1982–84) and Chernenko (1984–85). The Soviet leadership was more moderate and more tolerant, but also espoused policies that were realistic for the times. It simply could not afford to continue an expensive and futile war in Afghanistan. Though intervention in Eastern Europe might have been possible in theory, by late 1989, the divisions and upheaval within the Soviet Union rendered the East European crises no more than an unwanted diversion from domestic strains. By this same time, the overriding issues were twofold: the ruling structure of the country and the nationalities question. Initially the links between the two were not clear-cut.

CHAPTER THREE

THE NATIONAL QUESTION

THE SUBMERGED DILEMMA

The national question might be described as a 'submerged' dilemma. The foundations of the Soviet Union in late 1922 represented essentially a compromise between the large Soviet Russian republic and much smaller non-Russian entities – initially the Ukrainian, Belarusian, and Transcaucasian republics. In the 1920s, this compromise, created by Lenin, consisted of a policy that was termed 'national in form, socialist in content.' It began with an experiment in the development of non-Russian cultures, and a fairly permissive environment that saw a gradual 'indigenization' and development of national elites. In the non-Russian republics, this new development was particularly advanced in the Ukrainian and Belarusian Soviet Socialist Republics, the territories of which were also increased at the expense of Russia. By the late 1920s, the policy was reversed under Stalin, and a new policy of centralization, and attacks on what were perceived as 'bourgeois nationalism' in the republics was instituted. By the late 1930s, extensive purges destroyed national elites, while industrial development under the new Five-Year Plans – replacing Lenin's more tolerant New Economic Policy that had given more scope to private farmers – brought the devastated rural population to the towns. By 1939, the Soviet Union had expanded from an original four to twelve republics, encompassing a huge area from the European heartland to the Caucasus and Central Asia.

In several cases, especially in Central Asia and the Caucasus, these republics crossed tribal boundaries. Large enclaves of minority groups were included in the titular republic of others. Ostensibly they had joined the Soviet Union on a voluntary basis and were committed to the Union. In 1940, however, based on the August 1939 non-aggression pact between Nazi Germany and the Soviet Union, Stalin also installed military bases in the three Baltic States – Estonia, Latvia, and Lithuania – which had gained their independence from the postwar settlements that followed the First World War. In the summer of 1940, the Soviet regime annexed all three republics and set up Soviet Socialist republics. Compared to some other territories occupied in the same period, and particularly eastern Poland, and compared to the results of the attempt to annex territories from Finland, which resulted in a costly war, the takeover of the three Baltic States, with their relatively small populations, did not constitute a dangerous step for an expansionist government. After all, the states had formerly been part of the Russian Empire. The incorporation of the Baltic States increased the number of Soviet republics to fifteen. In contrast to earlier USSR expansion, however, the annexation did not receive recognition from the United States.

In the postwar years, there were various attempts to address the 'national question' by the Soviet leadership. In the Brezhnev period, there was hope for a 'merger' of nations and the creation of the elusive entity called 'The Soviet Man.' In reality, there were few prospects for such a development outside the confines of the three Slavic republics and the northern regions of Kazakhstan, in which Russians made up the majority of the population. In any case, from the 1930s Soviet nationalism was superseded by Russian nationalism in official propaganda, and the glorification of many events in the Russian past. In the Baltic States, large migrations of ethnic Russians, particularly into Estonia and Latvia, raised fears that the indigenous population would soon become a minority in its own republic.

The Russian language was regarded as the intra-national language of communication between the republics. By the 1970s it was also difficult for an individual to make much progress in a career without a good knowledge of Russian. In some republics, such as Belarus, Russian had begun to replace the national language as the one spoken by the majority of the population. This situation was concealed by the official census, but it was evident to most observers. Even in Ukraine, a majority of the population spoke Russian as its first language. In short, when Gorbachev came to power in the spring of 1985, there was little that remained of Lenin's original conception of the Soviet Union. The republics in some respects had made significant gains in promoting local cadres to leadership positions and even control of the ruling Communist Party. But there appeared to be little hope of their ever exercising their constitutional right to secede from the Union. Russia was the leading republic, but paradoxically the one without a separate structure for its party organization. Thus even in Russia there were many who felt that the current structure did not favour ethnic Russians.

Gorbachev was perhaps a leader who might have been expected to play a role in the inauguration of a new nationalities policy. He heralded from the Caucasus, an area in which dozens of national groups lived side-by-side. He could hardly have been unaware of some of the real and potential defects of earlier policies. And yet there is little indication, even from his memoirs, that he had any clear conception of how to deal with the national question. Crises developed quickly, particularly in the Caucasus and in the Baltic States and in part because of his uncertainty as to how to respond, the situation got out of control. As early as 16 December 1986, riots broke out in the Kazakh capital of Alma-Ata, when Gennady Kolbin, an ethnic Russian, replaced the First Party Secretary, Dunmukhamed Kunaev. The riots may have owed something to local resentment of the growing number of Russians settling in Kazakhstan. In the following summer, a problem dating to the late war years resurfaced. The Crimean Tatars held a demonstration in Red Square, demanding the right to return to their homeland, from which Stalin had deported them in 1944–45, along with several other nationality groups, for alleged collaboration with the foreign invaders.

NAGORNO-KARABAKH

Though Gorbachev did not create the dilemma of the Tatars or Russian settlement in Kazakhstan, he did bring about the conditions under which protests might take place. Because of the more tolerant atmosphere of Glasnost, old ethnic tensions began to resurface. The Armenians were among the first to make use of the new freedom of expression. Their protests centred on the autonomous oblast of Nagorno-Karabakh (Karabagh), which had been part of Azerbaijan since 1923, and in which some 75 per cent of the population was made up of ethnic Armenians. It seemed plausible to many Armenians that this territory should now be reunited with the Armenian SSR. Further, some felt that the Azeris had kept the territory deliberately underdeveloped. On 11 February 1988, the first of numerous demonstrations to incorporate Nagorno-Karabakh into Armenia began, with thousands marching in the Armenian capital of Erevan. Gorbachev decided to hold a special Central Committee session to address the issue. On 20 March, the Nagorno-Karabakh oblast committee of the Communist Party voted overwhelmingly to rejoin Armenia, thus putting pressure on Moscow to respond decisively. In response, in late February in Sumgait, Azeris slaughtered the local Armenians, leaving more than thirty dead.

The Nagorno-Karabakh story henceforth is one of civil war, violence, and intolerance, with the Union government attempting and failing several times to take a stand, or to mediate between the two sides. By the summer of 1988, the Armenian authorities had demanded that the territory be annexed to Armenia. Azerbaijan refused. In July, the oblast itself announced its secession from Azerbaijan and that it was reuniting with Armenia. However, the USSR Supreme Soviet repealed this decree. Armenians and Azeris began to clash in various towns by the fall and winter of 1988. Then on 7 December, a massive earthquake destroyed the Armenian town of Spitak, and most of Leninakan, killing 25,000 people and bringing about a national emergency. For a brief time, this national tragedy overshadowed the conflict over Nagorno-Karabakh. In January 1989, the Moscow government declared direct rule over the disputed territory, a situation that lasted until the following November, but the fighting only became more intense. By this time, both ethnic groups had formed their own national movements. In Armenia's case it was directed against the corruption of local Communist leaders; in that of Azerbaijan, the People's Front consisted of both intellectuals and extreme elements. In neither case was there any willingness to accept decisions on high from Moscow.

By early 1990, the conflict had escalated to one that crossed several borders. In Baku, there were attacks on Armenian homes. After some 300,000 Armenians protested about attacks on Armenians in Azerbaijan at a public demonstration in Erevan in January, the Soviet government proclaimed an emergency in several parts of the Turkic republic. Soviet security forces were sent into Baku on 19 January and came into conflict with members of the Azerbaijan People's Front. At least 80 people were killed in this skirmish. On the following day, the new Azeri party leader Viktor Polyanichko and Prime Minister Ayaz Mutabilov met with Gorbachev in Moscow to discuss the presence of Soviet troops in Azerbaijan. Iran was also brought into discussions about conflicts across the border. The Azeris in general were incensed at the Soviet presence and the People's Front called for a republican-wide strike. The Moscow government, in turn, maintained that it had entered Azerbaijan in order to prevent a coup d'etat by the People's Front. By this time Soviet warships had begun a blockade of the port of Baku.

The violent conflict continued throughout the duration of the Soviet Union though at varying degrees of intensity. On 17 February 1990, the Armenian Supreme Soviet declared that the decision by the Soviet government to make Nagorno-Karabakh part of Azerbaijan had been illegal. The territorial war between the two Caucasian ethnic groups signified the disintegration of central control. Although some 17,000 Soviet troops had forced their way into Baku, there seems to have been no long-term policy other than to prevent the People's Front from taking power. Neither the Azeris nor the Armenians were satisfied with the response of Moscow to their situation. Before long, the Azeris began to deport Armenians by force from Nagorno-Karabakh. In addition the Nakhichevan Autonomous Republic declared in January 1990 that it had seceded from both Azerbaijan and the Soviet Union, and called on countries such as Turkey and Iran, in addition to the United Nations, to protect its territory.

What could Gorbachev and the Moscow government have done? More than a decade later, there is no clear answer to this question. By this time, ethnic affairs had begun to monopolize the attention of the Soviet government and the situation in the Baltic States (see below) took priority. Gorbachev felt obliged to respond to the attacks on Armenians but lacked the will for a wholehearted application of force. Ultimately, extremist elements on both sides came to the forefront and a compromise was thus rendered more difficult. Either the Soviet forces had to be strong and determined enough to maintain order, or else the central government should have demanded a regional resolution of the conflict. The resort to violence, however, was a direct consequence of Glasnost and new attention of indigenous elites to both their future and simultaneously to their real or imagined historical legacies. The latter question had been submerged for years beneath official rhetoric of the fraternal friendship of the Soviet peoples. In the late 1980s its manifestations were ugly and one-sided, with both sides feeling that their interests and rights had been violated.

THE BALTIC STATES

Though very different in their history and religion the three Baltic States acted very much in unison during the late 1980s. More than any other part of the Soviet Union they had a clear idea of their goals which, for the most part, signified national independence and renunciation of the August 1939 Nazi–Soviet Pact through which they had been incorporated into the Soviet Union. According to the 1989 census, Lithuania had a population in that year of 3.7 million, Latvia 2.7 million, and Estonia 1.6 million. The indigenous populations in each case were approximately: 3 million Lithuanians in Lithuania, 1.4 million Latvians in Latvia, and 1 million Estonians in Estonia. In the latter two republics, as noted above, the native populations were in some danger of becoming a minority in their own republics as a result of the large influx of Slavs, particularly to the cities. The Baltic States generally enjoyed a higher standard of living than other parts of the Soviet Union and used the lax atmosphere of the Gorbachev years to push for their national rights.

The first notable demonstration occurred in all three states on 23 August 1987, which was the 48th anniversary of the signing of the Nazi–Soviet Pact, hardly a major numerical anniversary! All three republics also led the movement to create national or popular fronts in support of Perestroika, which took place between April and November 1988. In mid-September of this same year, Estonia tested the reaction of the Soviet authorities by proclaiming Estonian to be the state language of the republic. Two months later, the Estonian Supreme Soviet declared that its laws took precedence over the laws of the USSR, which provoked an angry reaction in Moscow. In mid-May 1989, the movements held a Baltic Assembly in Tallinn, which discussed united action to promote the economic and political sovereignty of the three republics. In Lithuania, the relatively strong Communist Party split into two: a larger group under Algirdas Brazauskas that declared itself to be independent from its all-Union counterpart; and a pro-Moscow faction led by Algimantas Naudziunas. It was on the largest of the three republics that the Soviet authorities placed their focus, particularly in view of the unprecedented decision of leading Communists to break from Moscow.

Gorbachev first sent his new ideological chief, Vadim Medvedev, to Vilnius, to be followed by a personal visit, also in January 1990. Before Gorbachev's arrival, thousands of Lithuanians demonstrated in support of independence. Gorbachev, who traveled with the chief editor of *Pravda*, Ivan T. Frolov, met with Brazauskas, but failed in his mission to persuade the breakaway party members to return to the fold (Gorbachev, 1995, pp. 571–3). A key element in the dissension between Vilnius and Moscow was Article 6 of the 1977 Soviet Constitution, which guaranteed the Communist Party the leading role in society, and several demonstrations occurred demanding the erasure of this clause. By 11 January 1990, both the Lithuanians and Latvians had removed this provision from their constitutions. Around the same time, Brazauskas won the election as Chairman of the Lithuanian Supreme Soviet with an overwhelming proportion of the vote.

By mid-February, the Supreme Soviets of all three republics had adopted declarations in favour of moving toward independence – in the case of Latvia, Russian delegates had voted overwhelmingly but unsuccessfully against such a motion. In the USSR Supreme Soviet, the Baltic deputies proposed the creation of a Commission to discuss their secession from the Soviet Union. Up to this point, the Baltic States appeared to be moving smoothly toward independence. In late February, the Sajudis party won 71 seats in the elections to the Lithuanian Supreme Soviet, giving it a slight majority even before a second round to decide the 45 remaining seats. The Lithuanian Supreme Soviet then introduced a political gambit by issuing the declaration of the immediate independence of Lithuania on 11 March, even before the second round of voting began. By a vote of 124–0 it decided to re-approve Lithuania's 1918 declaration, which had rendered it independent from Soviet Russia. The assembly elected as its chairman Vytautas Landsbergis, leader of the Sajudis. A few days later, the parliament elected a new government led by Prime Minister Kazimiera Prunskiene, with Brazauskas as her deputy.

In retrospect, this move was bound to infuriate Moscow and give the impression that something underhand had taken place. The declaration was made one day before the opening of the new Congress of People's Deputies in Moscow. Presumably, then, the deputies in Moscow were to be presented with a fait accompli. Landsbergis declined an invitation to come to Moscow and explain the decision. Gorbachev declared that it was his duty to defend the rights of the people of Lithuania. The Moscow Congress rejected the decision in Vilnius, and Soviet laws continued to be valid in the republic. Wrangling then followed over the status of Lithuania. Landbergis began to insist that any negotiations must be on an equal basis between two 'heads of state.' Gorbachev, in contrast, began to describe the situation as an 'illegal coup.' Meanwhile the decision took on an international status given the prior lack of recognition of the United States of the Baltic States as part of the Soviet Union.

The United States wisely declined to get involved. Jack Matlock, addressing six Sajudis delegates at Spaso House in Moscow, maintained that full diplomatic recognition from the United States could only be given if the Lithuanians could demonstrate control over their territory (Matlock, 1995, p. 231). At the same time, the Americans made Gorbachev aware that they would not look kindly on any acts of military aggression against the break-away republic. On 15 March, the Moscow Congress rejected the declaration and gave Landsbergis three days to respond to the decision. The situation now became very tense. Lithuania sent a delegation to Moscow at the required time to reaffirm the declaration of independence. The Soviet government, however, was dissatisfied. Several Supreme Soviet deputies requested that Gorbachev take a decisive response, and assert direct control over Lithuania from Moscow. Gorbachev demanded that the Lithuanians give up all weapons to the Soviet authorities and heightened its border regime. A tense standoff then prevailed for several months.

Though Estonia and Latvia did not advance toward declarations of independence quite so rapidly – largely because of the presence of substantial Slavic minorities – there is no question that both republics were equally anxious to sever ties with Moscow. Estonia convened an unofficial parliament on 12 March 1990. Exempting the Communist Party, the parliament was made up of deputies of various political leanings. It issued a request for the revocation of the 1940 decision for the annexation of Estonia into the Soviet Union and for the immediate departure of Soviet troops on Estonian soil. The Estonian Popular Front won almost 50 per cent of the deputies in the Estonian Supreme Soviet in the elections in spring 1990 and was easily the largest faction. As in Nagorno-Karabakh, the Soviet reaction to events was slow and uncertain. No doubt the Baltic separatists had been encouraged by the lack of reaction in Moscow to the downfall of Communist regimes in Eastern Europe in 1989. Matters were complicated by the changing political situation in Moscow, which gradually weakened the Gorbachev regime. As early as 1989 there were signs that it was losing its grip on the USSR. By late 1990, however, Gorbachev had formed a political alliance with some of the more hard-line politicians and resolved to take firmer action to prevent the loss of the Baltic States.

These actions proved to be disastrous for the future of Soviet rule in the Baltic States, with heavy-handed actions in both Lithuania and Latvia. For Gorbachev, whereas Brazauskas represented a difficult but perhaps manage-able opponent, Landsbergis was little more than a provocateur. The Soviet leadership decided first of all to issue an order to special troops to round up young Lithuanians for the Soviet army. By 7 January 1991, Soviet tanks had crossed the border into Lithuania, armed with paratroopers. Further military vehicles arrived the next day. On 8 January, Prime Minister Prunskiene resigned following protests against rises in food prices and the Supreme Council's decision to suspend the decree that had introduced them. According to Gorbachev there were demands from the republic that Moscow should step in and restore order (Gorbachev, p. 576). On 11 January a Committee of National Salvation (CNS) formed, ostensibly as an alternative to the break-away government of Landsbergis who, declared Gorbachev, refused to make any compromises.

Why had the Committee of National Salvation been formed? The Soviet version is that it was set up to support presidential rule directly from Moscow. When it had tried to approach the Lithuanian parliament, however, hooligans attacked its members and 28 people had to be hospitalized. The CNS reportedly had tried in vain to stop Lithuanian television from issuing anti-Soviet broadcasts. Soviet police chief Boris Pugo maintained that most of those who had approached the TV tower were also physically attacked with sticks and rods. Therefore CNS members appealed to the Soviet government for 'military assistance.' The attempt to impose direct rule from Moscow was proving more difficult than anticipated. At this point, a decision was made to restore order using Soviet troops, and to take over government buildings in Vilnius.

Subsequently, no single person would admit responsibility for what followed. Soviet troops occupied several buildings. While some buildings were guarded by local Lithuanians, an attack before dawn saw the troops seize the radio station and TV tower, killing 13 Lithuanians and wounding over 150. Pugo declared that an order to use force had not come from Moscow. Gorbachev maintained that he knew nothing about the assault until afterward – an astonishing admission from the then Soviet president. The Soviet authorities ultimately blamed a local commander for the situation getting out of hand (Foye, p. 1). Response in Moscow was mixed. The Soyuz group in the USSR Supreme Soviet supported presidential rule over Lithuania, whereas the Interregional Group bemoaned the excessive use of force. Democratic Russia organized protest marches in Moscow and Leningrad; and Boris Yeltsin, whose government later signed bilateral treaties with the Baltic States recognizing their sovereignty, declared the assault 'an offence against democracy.'

Perhaps from the Soviet perspective, the deaths had not been anticipated. But policy remained consistent and was applied also to Latvia at the same time. On 20 January, Black Beret troops attacked the Latvian Ministry of Internal Affairs, killing four bystanders and injuring ten others. Under pressure from the Russian government, Gorbachev promised an inquiry into these events. At the same time he had evidently chosen to apply a policy of firmness backed by force with regard to the Baltic States. At least one of his advisors (Chernyaev) could not comprehend the Soviet president's desire to keep the Baltic States in the Soviet Union at all costs. OMON troops began to attack border checkpoints in Latvia and Estonia, often beating up local border guards.

Following the attack on Vilnius, the Lithuanian Supreme Council opted to hold a vote on whether the republic should become an independent state. This vote was to take place on 9 February 1991, and Latvia and Estonia decided to follow suit on 3 March. Gorbachev responded that such elections had no legal basis. In these elections all three republics received convincing support for independence, even among the Slavic citizens. In Lithuania, with nearly 88 per cent of the electorate taking part, over 90 per cent voted in favour (over 2 million people). In Latvia and Estonia, the participation was also over 80 per cent in each case, with the vote in favour 73.7 and 77.8 per cent respectively, i.e., considerably higher than the proportion of the indigenous populations. The resort to force had failed. Moreover, it had catalyzed the movement to sever ties with the Soviet Union, assisted by the almost universal condemnation of the Soviet assault on Vilnius.

In conclusion, regarding the Gorbachev regime's handling of relations with the Baltic States, it perhaps faced an impossible situation. The Baltic States had no wish to remain in the Soviet Union and only an invasion could have prevented their course of action. Gorbachev was at least partially correct when assessing the tactics of Landsbergis, and even more astute politicians like Brazauskas could not ignore public sentiment. Gorbachev could conceivably have 'lost' the Baltic States without destroying the Soviet Union. Compared to events in the former Yugoslavia, the violence applied was very limited. The shock of 13 deaths effectively ended any serious assault and damaged considerably Gorbachev's international reputation. For many outside observers, it appeared inconceivable that the winner of the Nobel Peace Prize could have resorted to force. Either the Soviet leader had reached the limits of his tolerance or else he had lost control over his troops. Neither option provided much ground for confidence in the Soviet president.

Equally significant are the links between the Baltic populations and the non-Russian republics, particularly in the European part of the Soviet Union. These contacts led to the development of 'copycat' popular movements and to declarations of state sovereignty across the Soviet Union in the summer of 1990. The role of Russia will be treated separately below, but it altered the political situation when Russia itself was divided on a policy of force to prevent the Baltic States seceding from the Soviet Union. An open media also ensured that the events in Vilnius and Riga reached the Soviet population quickly and often without any embellishment from censors. Thus the Baltic States set the pace for other Soviet republics and tested the limits of Moscow's tolerance and above all its will to respond with force when the situation got out of hand. Gorbachev by 1991 had come up with a solution of sorts (discussed below), namely a referendum on a renewed Union that would allow more authority to the republics.

Such ideas provided little incentive to republics that believed their incorporation into the USSR had occurred through violence and collusion with Nazi Germany. Very quickly after the coming to power of Gorbachev, in the Baltic States pre-war flags had appeared in the streets and national anthems were restored. Focusing on the means of their annexation and on Article 6 of the Soviet Constitution, it was possible to bring change rapidly in the conditions of Perestroika. Crucial also was the lack of appeal of the Soviet Union, which appeared to be bereft of ideology, willing to abandon its commitments in Eastern Europe and the developing world, and gradually casting off its rigid Communist control. Gorbachev was on good terms with the United States, the country that refused to recognize Soviet control over the Baltic States. Moscow responded with discussions and then through the application of limited force. But the government had been seriously weakened through the economic crisis and political reforms, and it had lost its monopoly over the media. The Baltic States represented physically only a small part of an empire built up by Stalin, but they were also the harbinger of great changes.

GEORGIA, UKRAINE, AND BELARUS

The situation in Georgia, the third republic in the southern part of the Caucasus, was more peaceful than that of its neighbours in the early years of Gorbachev's leadership. On 9 April 1989, however, Soviet troops inexplicably attacked a large peaceful march in support of Georgian independence, killing about 20 people. The attackers advanced with sharpened spades, but a majority of the victims died from asphyxiation, a result of inhaling chemicals contained in gas canisters. This single action motivated many Georgians to support a movement toward independence. Georgia also had to deal with several minority claims for autonomous or independent status, including Abkhazia (the demonstration on 9 April was directed in part against Abkhazian secession) and South Ossetia by early 1990. After South Ossetia proclaimed itself a Union republic, heavy fighting occurred between Georgians and Ossetians, especially near the Ossetian capital of Tskhinvali. In a March 1991 referendum, almost 99 per cent of the Georgian population supported independence, in a heavy voter turnout. The next month, the Chairman of the Georgian Supreme Soviet, Zviad Gamsakhurdia, provided the parliament with a text for independence, which would be introduced gradually over the next five years.

Gamsakhurdia soon began to suspect that Soviet troops were helping the Ossetians in their conflict with Georgia. By 12 April, the Soviet government had suspended rail and sea shipments to Georgia. Gamsakhurdia subsequently became president in an election of May 1991 in the first democratic election of a republican leader. For some time, however, civil conflict engulfed Georgia. As in the Baltic States, the Soviet government tried initially to restore order, but once the Georgians began to strike in protest at what they saw as Soviet aid to the breakaway South Ossetians, it became plain that there was little to be gained from prolonged discussions with Gamsakhurdia. A romantic and flawed figure who soon began to display dictatorial tendencies, Gamsakhurdia was overthrown in 1992 and subsequently killed in the fighting that continued in this republic after the end of the Soviet Union. His replacement was Shevardnadze.

In Ukraine, the second largest of the Soviet republics, the Communist Party was traditionally strong. Ukrainian party leader, Volodymyr Shcherbytsky, had been installed in 1972 to replace Petro Shelest. The latter, while supporting aggressive Union policies such as the Soviet invasion of Czechoslovakia, had appeared sympathetic toward Ukrainian nationalist sentiment. From 1972 onward, Ukraine (together with Belarus) appeared to be the most stable of all republics. Some critics have referred to Shcherbytsky as a hardliner. The term seems inappropriate; he was rather a traditional Communist leader. He would support the interests of Ukraine insofar as he thought appropriate and without causing tensions. Unsurprisingly therefore, Gorbachev thought it wiser to retain his services after March 1985, even though Shcherbytsky was unresponsive to the new policy of Perestroika. As a valuable agricultural and critical industrial part of the USSR, Ukraine of all the republics had to be kept free of subversive influences.

Gradually the Communist Party of Ukraine came under pressure to make changes. Its role following the Chernobyl disaster was particularly inglorious. Several party members had fled from the scene; Shcherbytsky evidently removed his family members from Kyiv before proceeding with the annual May Day parade of 1986. After Chernobyl, an environmental movement called the Green World came into existence. In 1988, three party members and well-known literary figures – Ivan Drach, Dmytro Pavlychko, and Volodymyr Yavorivsky – founded the Popular Movement in Support of Perestroika (Rukh). In November 1988, the two new groups, in support of greater awareness of the environment and popular reform, took part in the first major demonstration in Kyiv. But it attracted no more than 10,000 people, and when the demands became political, the police switched off the microphones.

The Communist leaders vilified the Rukh, but it flourished, partly because it appeared to be closer to the policies espoused in Moscow than those of the Ukrainian party. In September 1989, Shcherbytsky retired with full honours (he died the following January) and Volodymyr Ivashko replaced him. Within a few months, however, Ivashko agreed to become Gorbachev's deputy in Moscow, an action that was regarded as a betrayal by many party and non-party members in Ukraine. (Curiously the Kyiv party boss, Hryhory Revenko, did a similar thing, agreeing to move to Gorbachev's team in Moscow.) Thereafter, the CPU split between the rank-and-file party under Stanislav Hurenko and a parliamentary majority group led by ideological secretary, Leonid Kravchuk. This latter branch was more attuned to the changing circumstances in Ukraine and eventually was to find common ground with Rukh. By 1989–90, Ukraine became more assertive, led by protesters from the more nationally conscious western regions. This change came about partly through de-Stalinization and a greater awareness of the recent past. For example on 22 January 1990, a human chain formed from Kyiv to L'viv to mark the anniversary of the declaration of independence in 1918. The CPU membership declined substantially in 1990, losing some 220,000 members under the unpopular Hurenko. Rukh, by contrast, was growing, and had a reported 632,000 members by early 1991 (perhaps one-third the size of the CPU at this same time). In this same year, the Supreme Soviet adopted Ukrainian as the state language of Ukraine and in July, Ukraine declared state sovereignty.

In neighbouring Belarus, popular discontent was evident by 1990, mainly as a result of anger at corruption among the party leadership. Communists dominated the Belarusian parliament after the elections of 1990, while the opposition was able to muster only 32 out of 400 seats. The Belarusian Popular Front (BPF, *Adradzhenne*), which emerged from the Martyrology movement headed by Zyanon Paznyak, embraced several issues at once – the cause of Chernobyl victims, atonement for the crimes of Stalin, as manifested by the discovery of a mass burial ground at Kurapaty, in the northern suburbs of Minsk, and the revival of the Belarusian language and culture, in addition to historical memories. In Belarus, progress for the popular movement was even more difficult than in Ukraine and the BPF had to hold its founding congress in Vilnius, Lithuania in June 1989. In 1990, however, Belarusian was adopted as the state language, and the BPF was able to hold a demonstration of 100,000 in central Minsk on 25 February 1990. When the Communist Party leader Efrem Sokolov attempted to address the crowd, his voice could not be heard over the noisy heckling. By April 1991, the republic was subject to an impressive strike movement, which demanded the legalization of private property, the end of party influence in the workplace and the sale of its assets to Chernobyl victims, as well as new elections to the Belarusian Supreme Soviet.

In other republics, the gradual disintegration of the centre did not bring in a new era of unity and independence. Instead, virtual civil war situations developed in Moldavia and Tajikistan. In January 1990, the mainly Slavic population of Tiraspol Raion voted in favour of self-government and the establishment of a Dnestr Autonomous Republic that would include this region. In Dushanbe, Tajikistan protesters demanded the removal of the Armenian population from the city in February 1990 and the transfer to the republic of the cities of Samarkand and Bukhara, which were considered ancient centres of Tajik culture. Elsewhere in Central Asia, in June 1989, at least 100 Meshketian Turks died in conflict with Uzbeks. The contrast between the political and economic demands of the European republics is apparent. In the Caucasus and Central Asia, ethnic and territorial differences took precedence. The CPSU, however, did not distinguish between its constituent republics in such terms. How far and in what ways its members considered the national question is evident from a CPSU Central Committee Plenum of September 1989.

THE PLENUM ON NATIONAL POLICY, SEPTEMBER 1989

The Plenum is notable for being the clearest indication of the party's attitude to the national question in the Gorbachev period. The meeting was prompted in part by the rapid changes taking place in Eastern Europe and the need to update the party's policy to meet new conditions. Most of the proceedings were recorded in *Pravda* (24 September 1989). It began with a review of the past, praising Lenin's original policies of national self-determination for the republics and regions, along with the input of all nationalities into the victory in the Great Patriotic War. At the same time, 'mistakes' and 'short-comings' had been evident, particularly Stalin's deportation of peoples during and at the end of the war, ungrounded repressions of organizations and individual citizens for their nationalistic views, and various excesses of the Soviet administrative-command system. These latter transgressions included industrial development that harmed the natural environment and demographic migrations that sometimes changed the ratios of the local population and new immigrants.

How could the party improve the situation? The Federation, according to this overview, had to be improved both in political and economic terms. This could be done by expanding the rights of various autonomous national formations within the Union, along with recognizing the equal rights of all peoples, and the free development of the languages and cultures of nationality groups. There must be mutual respect of one another's historical traditions and national differences. The Union had to be developed on a voluntary basis because 'There are no powerful republics without a powerful union, and no powerful union without powerful republics.' How was power to be divided between the centre and the republics? The role of the former was to be confined to legal powers over 'essential' political and economic development, security, and defence, along with the coordination of foreign policy.

The Union republics, on the other hand, should control remaining issues and be able to choose their own form of self-governance. Citizenship was to be based on a broad perspective, so that citizens of a republic were automatically citizens of the Soviet Union. The document advocated a special system for the Russian Federation, since it contained such a large number of autonomous regions. It advised a two-house parliament so that all national groups might gain fuller representation. The Plenum had debated the question of a new Union Treaty – later to become an obsession of Gorbachev – to replace the one issued in 1922, which was still in effect. Autonomous republics, oblasts and districts required an expansion of their rights and responsibilities, especially concerning natural resources, environmental protection, and the development of ethnic languages and cultures. Special protection had to be given to the small peoples of the North, Siberia, and the Far East. On languages, the indigenous groups should be entitled to have their own language designated as the state language of the republic, while there should be support for Russian as the main language of international communication.

Lastly, the national republics and autonomous regions must be given greater representation at the state level through the establishment of a state department for nationality issues and national relations (in addition to the existing Council for Nationalities within the USSR Supreme Soviet). This policy had originally been recommended at the 19th Party Conference. Regarding supervision of nationality policy, the Plenum maintained that changes were necessary in order that the younger generation was raised in the spirit of 'socialist internationalism.' This archaic term was not to be regarded as a negation of national rights, but rather as a decisive form of opposition to manifestations of nationalism and chauvinism (how the line was to be drawn between national development, nationalism, and chauvinism was not made clear). Flexibility was the key factor, according to the overview, and no universal solution was possible to individual questions pertaining to national issues.

Though the document offered little that was objectionable, it still seemed to perturb many participants. Sokolov, the Belarusian First Party Secretary, for example, asked whether the right of the republics to self-determination was of an absolute nature: 'It should be taken into account,' he said, 'that all republics have responsibilities with respect to others and the entire country.' On the other hand, the platform on the division of responsibilities between the Union and the republics, in Sokolov's view, was not well thought out. Union ministries would still likely take the most important decisions leaving little leeway for the republics to act. Why not then, he asked, restrict the centre's duties to those industries that were critical for the entire country, such as the fuel and power industries, metallurgy, chemicals, defence, some of the transport industries, and environmental protection? He condemned destructive strikes, and felt that Communists should not be participating in them. A. Masaliev, the party leader in Kirghizia, also noted that some of the intelligentsia supported rallies and strikes, and even appealed to capitalist countries for support. Their goal, in his view, was to overthrow the Soviet system.

In Ukraine, secretary of the CPU Central Committee Yury Yelchenko offered a warning about the 'extremist nationalist aspirations' that were leading to dangerous social discord and negative economic and political repercussions in some parts of the republic. He felt that the experience of the first years after the revolution had to be recalled: nationalism was nationalism, chauvinism was chauvinism, and counter-revolution was counter-revolution! In some cases, national movements were putting forward anti-socialist principles, based on 'bourgeois-nationalist values.' The chief culprit in Ukraine, he declared, was the Rukh, and particularly its adherents in the western regions of the republic and in Kyiv. Their goal was to take power and then to bring about 'national isolation.' Thus the goal of issuing laws to abolish extremist organizations, issued by the Plenum, was particularly appropriate in this case. Yelchenko's view was fairly typical of the Plenum and reveals that among the party elite the outlook had not changed much by September 1989.

What is also evident in these discussions is the vague but delineated link between economic problems and the growing national movements. Among others, Brazauskas raised this point, as a prelude to a demand for economic independence for the republics. The party leaders clearly wanted more power for the republics because therein lay their power bases. But they did not wish to become overwhelmed by a tide of new national movements that would sweep them from office. They also had considerable difficulties in bridging the gulf between Union and republican jurisdiction. How was a new Union to work if the republics took full responsibility for their economies, and how far could the power of the centre be reduced without rendering it completely ineffective? These kinds of questions help to explain confusing remarks, such as those provided by Kazakh party leader Nursultan Nazarbayev, who declared initially that 'our real enemy is strict centralization' and then went on to say that while he favoured economic power for the republics, 'political independence must not exceed constitutional stipulations.' He also warned of 'destructive nationalist forces' and stressed the necessity of the Communist Party remaining united.

The Chairman of the Presidium of the RSFSR Supreme Soviet, V. Vorotnikov, stated the obvious fact: 'For some time now we have underestimated the depth of the ethnic processes,' which, he believed had occurred in part because of the weakening of the party's ideological influence. In his view, it was the party's duty to address this predicament and come up with a solution. Others similarly seemed to think that the situation could be resolved by legislation alone. If there were laws, for example, to stop ethnic protests or against conflict based on ethnic grounds, then the Soviet Union might find a way out of the ethnic conflicts that had arisen. R. Nishanov, from the position of Chairman of the USSR Supreme Soviet Council for Nationalities, believed that the catastrophic scale of inter-ethnic conflict in the USSR had been caused by the decline of spirituality and the absence of laws that would restrict committing of crimes on ethnic grounds. Presumably then, a crackdown on such manifestations might have ended national protests!

The discussion is instructive in that it illustrates the direction and limitations of the party's position on the national question well into the period of Perestroika. This debate preceded the 28th Party Congress in July 1990 and focused on what had become, along with the economy, the chief problem for the Gorbachev administration. From all the comments, one is left with only the vague notions of providing economic sovereignty within the Union, of giving certain rights to the republics. Gorbachev evidently listened. At the Congress, new statutes made all republican first party secretaries ex officio members of the Politburo – a move that came too late, as by this time the authority of the Politburo had been reduced considerably – and the raising of the status of the Council of the Federation from consultative to policy-making by Gorbachev.

By 1990, the situation in the national republics had changed irrevocably, spurred by the progress of the Baltic States. From the Caucasus to Central Asia, the republics had begun to gain power vis-à-vis Moscow, and this power would be jealously guarded by national elites. In all cases, these elites had gained their authority through the Communist Party, and subsequently began to identify more with republican than with central interests. This was a logical development. To do otherwise would have been to fall behind in the process of decentralization. In the summer of 1990 therefore, all the Union republics declared economic sovereignty, the control over their natural resources and the right to make decisions concerning their individual economic development. It would be difficult henceforth for all-Union ministries based in Moscow to ride roughshod over the republics, whether this was in the formulation of economic plans or the location of a new nuclear power station. Ironically, the acquisition of power by the republics – which as yet was by no means complete or certain – occurred at the same time as the economic crisis in the USSR as a whole. The strikes that had occurred in the country, such as those of the coal miners, were not motivated by national or ethnic interests. Yet they came to have a resounding impact on the national question.

Between the spring of 1988 and the spring of 1991, TASS reported, 1,200 civilians had died and 10,000 had been wounded in inter-ethnic conflicts. The total may have been underestimated, since in many cases, particularly in the Caucasus, it was difficult to discern precise figures. The extent of national self-assertion varied in the various republics. In Central Asia, the most significant factor was less national sentiment than control over resources and the existing party structure. The Central Asian party authorities in general were willing to work within a renewed Soviet structure as long as it did not undermine their regional control. At the other end of the spectrum, the Baltic States had effectively withdrawn from Soviet structures by the spring of 1991. Gorbachev's efforts to restrain them had been feeble and had failed. Georgia also no longer regarded itself as bound by Soviet laws. Armenia and Azerbaijan were at war. Both blamed the Soviet government for the protracted conflict over Nagorno-Karabakh. Armenia in particular favored self-determination if not outright independence – the latter brought prospects of hostile neighboring states threatening its existence once Moscow's control had been released.

Tiny Moldavia felt threatened by a breakaway movement in the regions inhabited mainly by Slavs. The question of 'reunion' with Romania had also been raised. For the Soviet leadership, the crucial situation lay at first in Ukraine and Belarus. Gorbachev stated more than once that a USSR without Ukraine was inconceivable. The two republics occupied important geo-strategic locations on the Polish border. Ukraine provided critical industrial and agricultural input for the Moscow center, although its older industries were in decline and its harvests were much lower than at their peak. By the end of 1990, Ukraine had also pushed strongly for greater self-control. In the face of this surge of national sentiment, the central government in Moscow had remained impassive, at times hostile and aggressive, at others vacillating and uncertain. Sudden violent acts, such as those in Georgia and Lithuania, were isolated events. There was no clear-cut attempt to clamp down on protests and demonstrations against the Soviet regime. For all their momentum, however, the national movements required some form of catalyst to transform the system from a Union to one of independent republics. This catalyst appeared in 1991 in the form of the Russian Federation under a new president, Boris Yeltsin. Russia was the final piece of the puzzle, the one that transformed an already complex picture of a weakening center and demanding periphery.

CHAPTER FOUR

DOMESTIC POLITICS,
1989 TO MID-AUGUST 1991

THE CONGRESS OF PEOPLE'S DEPUTIES AND NEW PRESIDENCY

The resurrection of Boris Yeltsin's political career began in 1989. Following his dismissal from his position as Moscow party leader in November 1987, most observers – as indeed the Soviet leadership – considered that Yeltsin's political career was likely over. Gorbachev, perhaps out of sympathy, gave him a minor post as deputy minister for construction. In March 1989, the Central Committee began an investigation of his advocacy of a multi-party system in the Soviet Union. Yeltsin's popularity in Moscow, however, was evident. While the investigation was under way, about 10,000 people demonstrated in his support in the streets of Moscow. Yeltsin also announced that he would be a candidate in the forthcoming elections to the Congress of People's Deputies. Despite official obstructions and harassment, the voters of the Moscow district in which Yeltsin ran voted overwhelmingly for his candidacy, and with more than 90 per cent of the popular vote, his political career began to take off once again.

The elections to the Congress and the establishment of this new organ provided the focal points of the year 1989. The Congress was to be made up of 750 deputies from public organizations and 1,500 from electoral districts, as decided at the 19th Party Conference. To win a seat in an electoral district, a candidate had to receive more than 50 per cent of the vote. Otherwise a second round of voting was to be held. In some districts there were numerous candidates and the incumbent, and often unpopular, party boss for the first time in his career had a serious struggle to win an election. Voter turnout was high – more than 80 per cent – and there were some surprising results across the country. On the other hand, party members were best placed to mount election campaigns in terms of resources and organization, and ultimately they succeeded in winning 85 per cent of the seats in the Congress. Nonetheless, it was the reformers among party members that did best, and there were some embarrassing outcomes for party stalwarts.

Before the new Congress could convene, Gorbachev made another attempt to purge recalcitrant and hard-line members from the Central Committee, forcing into retirement 110 members and candidates. Ryzhkov, a loyal though unimaginative supporter of Gorbachev, became Chairman of the USSR Council of Ministers on 8 June. The former Cold War Foreign Minister, Andrey Gromyko, died on 2 July, thus severing symbolically a link with the Soviet past. Gorbachev also decided that in the regions the positions of party secretary and chairman of the government should be merged. This move would not only reduce the Soviet bureaucracy, but would serve to empower the government as opposed to the party. In line with this idea, the Congress would also elect from its ranks a new Supreme Soviet, which for the first time would have real legislative authority, rather than serving as a rubber stamp for party decrees. It was a means of undermining the authority of the CPSU, and thereby removing obstacles to the goals of Perestroika. The CPSU itself formally relinquished its monopoly on power on 7 February 1990. However, it would be an error to perceive Gorbachev as a radical reformer. Essentially he was at the centre of the political spectrum by 1989, and there were factions that felt that Perestroika had lost its direction and initiative. Some felt even that Gorbachev's behavior at the Congress was still that of an old-style party leader.

Thus the paradox of the Congress is evident. On the one hand, as sessions of the new assembly could be heard on radio and watched on television, the country appeared to be transfixed. Nothing like it had been seen before. Eminent leaders that might appear only in *Pravda* or *Izvestiya* could be seen on a daily basis. Moreover, these people were revealed as all-too fallible, often unable to answer questions satisfactorily. The USSR seemed to be a debating society. But on the other hand, delegates had to go through Gorbachev to get to the podium. When delegates went too far, the banter and sharp admonition from the chairman to stop speaking would interrupt the speakers. Gorbachev's irritation was especially evident when Sakharov came forward to speak. Sakharov focused on controversial topics, such as the Soviet attack on demonstrators in Georgia, and his speeches were rather long-winded. Another speaker to incur Gorbachev's anger was Yeltsin. What had happened, however, was that the new forum eliminated the role of Gorbachev as the sole arbiter of the reform process. From this time onward he had lost control of the direction of the country, though he remained the leading personality. The Congress, and the Supreme Soviet elected by it, took the reform process out of his hands. Henceforth, he could never satisfy all parties and at times petty politics superseded the grander conception of a Soviet Union based on new ideas and the reforms of Perestroika. At the same time it is hard to detect a clear predilection toward a multi-party system or democracy on the part of the Soviet population. Stephen White cites a poll conducted among Soviet citizens in the summer of 1989, in which 27.1 per cent of respondents supported multi-party politics, 25.2 per cent considered that the CPSU was sufficiently diverse in its politics, and 23.1 per cent had no opinion (White, 1990, p. 215).

The more radical deputies, including Yeltsin, Sakharov, Yury Afanasyev, and the economist Gavriil Popov created on 30 July the Interregional Group, made up of 388 members and with a stated goal of moving the country from 'totalitarianism' to democracy. About two-thirds of the IRG came from the RSFSR, which would serve as a pressure group to push through more radical reforms. Yeltsin had failed narrowly to be elected to the Supreme Soviet, but one of the elected members gave up his seat for him. Gorbachev, on the other hand, was elected chairman of the USSR Supreme Soviet with 2,123 votes in favor and 87 against. When the 2nd Congress met in December 1989, Gorbachev tried to remove from the agenda the question of eliminating Article 6 from the USSR Constitution, concerning the leading role of the Communist Party in Soviet society. He thus had already begun to adopt a position holding back the more radical deputies who were trying to push for more radical reforms. In the weekly *Moskovskie Novosti*, chief editor Yegor Yakovlev contrasted the liberal reformers in charge of foreign policy, such as Shevardnadze and Aleksandr Yakovlev, with their conservative counterparts running domestic policy. On 20 January 1990, the Democratic Platform of Communist reformers formed in Moscow. Representing some 55,000 Communists from 13 of the Union republics, 455 delegates assembled in Moscow the avowed goal of establishing a Western-style social democracy at the forthcoming 28th Party Congress in July.

The consequence of this Platform was an organization called Democratic Russia, which had as its main aim political influence in the Russian Federation with the approach of the March 1990 elections to the Russian Congress of People's Deputies (RCPD), along with support for the democratic ideals of the late Andrey Sakharov, removing Article 6 from the Constitution, a regulated market economy, and a new Russian Constitution. There followed a number of rallies in support of Perestroika, including a particularly large one outside the Kremlin, with the participation of 200,000 people on the eve of the Central Committee Plenum. The Plenum itself on 5–7 February resolved to create a presidential system in the Soviet Union. Gorbachev felt that the issue required further discussion, but he maintained that it was time for the Communist Party to relinquish its monopoly on power and fight for its existence alongside other political parties. As always, at the party plenums, Gorbachev would get frustrated with the staunch anti-reformers and embrace more radical slogans. The new presidency promised to provide him with renewed authority, power that to some extent he had relinquished voluntarily by transferring power from the CPSU to the government structures.

The idea to create a Soviet presidency – as opposed to the ceremonial position of Chairman of the Supreme Soviet, usually a sign of demotion in the past – received approval from the Supreme Soviet on 27 February 1990.

Almost immediately, the idea became shrouded in controversy with the decision that the first president was to be elected by the Congress, and successors by universal adult suffrage. As Gorbachev declared at once that he would be a candidate for the post, he avoided the rigors of a countrywide election. One can comprehend the logic of such a decision, especially given the complex and pressing problems facing the country. It did, however, provide ammunition for Gorbachev's rivals subsequently. The new president on paper was an extremely powerful figure, equivalent to the old key post of General Secretary of the party. He could be elected for no more than two five-year terms, but he would be head of state and commander of the armed forces, with authority to declare war or a state of emergency (this latter clause was later withdrawn). In cases of crisis, the president had the authority to introduce direct presidential rule. One limitation was that he could not dismiss the Congress of People's Deputies, though he did have the right to dissolve the Supreme Soviet. Gorbachev, however, still retained the position of General Secretary. How would he resolve this apparent contradiction of power?

The question was especially urgent given the role of the CPSU as an opponent of and indeed the main obstacle to the Perestroika reforms. As long as Gorbachev retained the two key posts his position would remain ambivalent. In early 1990, nevertheless, he was not ready to abandon the party and subsequently he veered between loyalty to old party comrades and those who wished to end the party's monopoly on power. Not until the August 1991 putsch ended did Gorbachev change this stance. Paradoxically therefore he was at the same time the initiator of and impediment to Perestroika, the reform program with which he is associated. Yet the swing in the popular mood was evident from the March 1990 elections, at which the radicals received high portions of the votes in Russia, Ukraine, and Belarus. However, few of the seats were decided in the first round, and in most republics, a second and even third round of voting were necessary to decide the final composition of the assemblies.

After Gorbachev had decided to run for the new presidency, several other names were put forward, including those of Nikolay Ryzhkov, the Chairman of the Council of Ministers, and Vadim Bakatin, the Minister of Internal Affairs. Both declined to run. A Plenum in mid-March therefore approved the single candidacy of the Soviet leader. On 14 March, Gorbachev won the election, receiving 1,329 votes, with 495 against – mainly a result of the opposition of the Interregional Group, which was concerned that Gorbachev was accumulating too much power – and over 350 abstentions. Almost immediately, Gorbachev created a Presidential Council, ostensibly now the most powerful body, replacing the CC CPSU Politburo. Did these events strengthen or weaken Gorbachev as leader? In the short term, they appeared to allow him more room for maneuver, and to distance himself from the desires of the party. In the long term, it was to prove a weaker position than that of General Secretary once Russia elected to go the same route and appoint its own president. The advantages of maintaining power through the party had been the centralization of authority and the hierarchical system of administration. Moreover, the old party system had the advantage of familiarity. Lastly Gorbachev, even when running unopposed, had some 850 votes either against him or abstaining. Thus already within the Congress, he was facing a sizeable opposition. Ominously on 29 May, his rival, Yeltsin, won the election for Chairmanship of the Supreme Soviet of the RSFSR. Russia had also resurrected its Communist Party, in abeyance since the 1920s.

How popular was the new president in the country? It seems fair to say that in the spring of 1990, despite all his difficulties and the increasingly acute economic picture, Gorbachev was quite popular, at least more so than most of his contemporaries. In a poll published in *Argumenty i fakty*, which looked at the leaders of Perestroika and fourteen national figures past and present on a five-point scale, the overall victors in the latter category were Sakharov (even though he had died the previous year) and Lenin respectively. But Gorbachev came second in the former group, whereas the least popular figure of those listed was Ligachev. The ascendancy of Lenin might indicate that the basic beliefs and traditions of the population had not changed fundamentally. But Lenin was being examined more from a historical perspective. The assessment of contemporary leaders suggests that while Gorbachev had made some progress, those surveyed preferred a more radical approach, and the choice of Sakharov illustrated perhaps greater faith in a dissident figure not associated with the party leadership.

THE 28TH PARTY CONGRESS AND AFTERMATH

The notable thing about the 28th Party Congress (2 June 1990) is that it was held at all. The CPSU was in disarray, its members leaving in the hundreds, and its elected leader appeared also to be its chief enemy, particularly concerning its future role in society. Yet the party was far from finished. Gorbachev also allowed his name to be put forward for re-election and won a comfortable victory. His choice as Deputy First Secretary was the former leader of the Communist Party of Ukraine, Volodymyr Ivashko, who was preferred over the ritualistic hardliner, Yegor Ligachev, and won some 80 per cent of the votes. A third candidate, the more militant Communist and leader of the resurrected Russian Communist Party (June 1990), Ivan Polozhkov, withdrew from the race before the Congress began. However, the former organ of power, the Politburo, was deprived of its authority. The most powerful bodies forthwith were to be the Presidential Council (which had been created in March 1990) and the Council of the Federation. The American political scientist George Breslauer notes that three factions had emerged within the party at the Congress: that of Ligachev, which sought to preserve the party's monopoly in Soviet society; that of Yeltsin, which considered that the party must give up its dominant position by eliminating party cells in non-political institutions; and that of Gorbachev, which was both anti-monopolist and anti-abolitionist, maintaining that the party must take its place alongside other political parties and fight for its position (Breslauer, 2002, p. 100).

At the Congress, Gorbachev reacted angrily to several speakers who perceived the collapse of Communism in Eastern Europe as a disaster. He maintained that these regimes had been Stalinist in composition, and declared that he no longer adhered to the Brezhnev Doctrine, which had been used to justify the invasion of Czechoslovakia in 1968. He also emphasized that the traditional Soviet enemy, the United States, was now playing the role of a global partner. Though he had retained the authority to deflect criticism of his rivals, his opponents were now demanding that some of the reformers be removed from the leadership. Aleksandr Yakovlev, for example, resigned from the Central Committee, though he remained a member of the Presidential Council. There was also a dramatic episode in which Boris Yeltsin resigned from the party and, in front of the TV cameras, walked out of the Congress. Sobchak and others followed suit. Yeltsin pointed out, upon leaving, that the Congress was not an important event. The rift in the CPSU was now evident, but caught in the middle of two polarized wings, Gorbachev felt obliged to maintain his party allegiance and position. In retrospect, this decision must be considered one of his fundamental errors, a result perhaps of his illusions about a continuing role for the CPSU in political life.

By late 1990, some of the principal leaders in the Perestroika campaign had left office. One was Eduard Shevardnadze, who resigned as Foreign Minister on 20 December. In an interview with *Moskovskie Novosti*, Shevardnadze stated that he had resigned in fear of military repressions, such as those seen in Tblisi and Baku. Clearly he was also frustrated with Gorbachev's incessant speeches and debates, which superseded the enforcement of laws and reforms. Why did Gorbachev allow Shevardnadze's resignation? This was a minister who was recognized and respected internationally for his role in bringing the Soviet Union out of international isolation, and who had promoted successfully the much-improved relations with the West. Like Yakovlev, Shevardnadze seems to have been sacrificed at the behest of Communist hardliners, and partly because of Gorbachev's desire to retain the support of the military. The latter had suffered several setbacks over the previous year, including the 'loss' of friendly regimes in Eastern Europe and the contraction of the Soviet Union from an imperial giant to a country immersed in domestic problems and unwilling to assert the Soviet role in the world as a military superpower. Liberal reformers were often blamed in the media for this change in status. On the other hand, one of his interpreters has blamed Shevardnadze for deserting Gorbachev at a crucial time (Palazchenko, 1997, p. 243).

Gorbachev meanwhile opted for a dual policy of enhancing his own authority and developing new alliances with more conservative (meaning in this instance traditional Communist) figures. Shevardnadze, upon his resignation, had expressed his fear that there might be a military coup in the Soviet Union. Though his fears proved premature, Gorbachev did seem to be changing direction, increasing power at the top and promoting more traditional Communists to the leading offices. On 21 December, the Congress discussed the leader's program for expanded authority, and four days later, it accepted a constitutional amendment that led to the establishment of a smaller Cabinet of Ministers directly responsible to the president, along with the newly created position of Vice-President. For the latter post, Gorbachev nominated Gennady Yanayev, a colourless figure, who struggled to gain enough votes from the Congress to take up the post. On 26 December, the Congress accepted an increase in the power of the president by a large majority. Notably at this time the largest groups in the Soviet Congress of People's Deputies were the Communists (730 seats) and the Soyuz faction (561), whereas the reformist Interregional Group possessed only 229.

Why had Gorbachev opted for a route that appeared to take him away from the reform program of Perestroika? There were two related reasons. First, it was necessary to increase the power of the central administration vis-à-vis the republics. Second, the Soviet president was facing a power struggle with the Russian Federation. Before discussing these further, it also worthwhile to note that the constitutional changes of December 1990 had altered the USSR's structure by taking the initiative away from the parliament (Congress of People's Deputies) and putting it into the hands of the Presidency, the Cabinet of Ministers and the Security Council. The fourth part of the ruling administration, the Council of the Federation, was less pliable, as several prominent republican leaders, including Yeltsin, remained active therein. Some of the personnel changes implemented by Gorbachev were enforced. In late December, for example, his Prime Minister, Ryzhkov, suffered a heart attack, and had to be replaced. His successor, Valentin Pavlov, who had formerly held the position of Finance Minister, was a selection as uninspired as that of Yanayev. Other members of the Gorbachev team, such as Boris Pugo as Minister of Internal Affairs and Viktor Kryuchkov as the head of the KGB, constituted a new ruling group that differed fundamentally from the reformers who had put together the Perestroika program. Perhaps such choices were logical, given that the Russian Republic leadership had embraced a course of radical reforms that would decentralize the country and take power away from Moscow.

With his additional authority, Gorbachev pressed ahead in the formation of a new team. On 7 March 1991, he asked that the USSR Supreme Soviet approve nine new officials to the Security Council (created in December 1990, and effectively replacing the Presidential Council), including Yanayev, Pavlov, Pugo, Kryuchkov, and Aleksandr Bessmertnykh, the former Soviet ambassador to the United States, who had replaced Shevardnadze as Foreign Minister. Yakovlev, who had been a member of the Presidential Council, was excluded from the new body. With this team in place, Gorbachev began to address the growing threat from the Russian Republic. By late 1990, any former friendship between Yeltsin and Gorbachev had dissipated. Yeltsin had demanded the resignation of the Ryzhkov government at that time, commenting that the RSFSR should be given the right to nominate key positions such as Prime Minister, and the ministers of Defence and Finance in some sort of coalition government, in which he and Gorbachev would share power. Yeltsin's Foreign Minister, Andrey Kozyrev, declared in an interview with *The New York Times* (25 November 1990) that before long, the Russian government would gain control over nuclear weapons located on the territory of the RSFSR. These were ominous threats.

What choices did Gorbachev have? Analysts of this period have tended to focus on the change of direction in Moscow, perceiving an ambiguity in Gorbachev himself. The Soviet president certainly had his faults, as any political leader, but the major one may have been naivety. He continued to believe that a solution lay in some form of compromise that might placate the republics, particularly the RSFSR, and yet leave the Soviet system intact. The structure might evolve from a federation to a confederation or a commonwealth, but ultimately Gorbachev wanted (justifiably) to maintain some authority at the center, and particularly control over key issues, such as defence, foreign policy, and possibly the budget. Yet he was preoccupied constantly with structural changes that were often relatively meaningless: from the Presidential Council to the Cabinet of Ministers, a new Vice-President and a Security Council. Both he and Yeltsin were also vying desperately for the support of the military and control over weapons. Russia had constantly put pressure on the Soviet leadership by announcing ever more radical economic programs, whether these were workable or not. In one respect, Gorbachev had brought these difficulties on himself by his liberal platform and dilatoriness in implementing meaningful economic changes. He also probably underestimated the ruthlessness of his opponents, and was limited by his own narrow outlook, in which the CPSU continued to play some sort of role.

THE REFERENDUM OF 17 MARCH 1991

Gorbachev's response to these dilemmas was for a referendum to answer the question: Do you consider it necessary to preserve the USSR as a renewed federation with equal rights in which the rights and freedoms of an individual of any nationality are fully guaranteed? The Supreme Soviet, on 16 January, approved the date of 17 March for the referendum. The responses from the republics were rapid. On 7 February, the RSFSR voted that several more questions would be added to the ballot papers in Russia, including whether Russia should have its own president, elected by popular ballot, and questions pertaining to the right of private ownership. Yeltsin called openly for Gorbachev to resign on 19 February, maintaining that the Soviet leader was intent on amassing personal power and had brought the Soviet Union to the verge of a dictatorship. The next day the USSR Supreme Soviet condemned Yeltsin's remarks, but it was evident that they reflected a growing concern in Russia and several other republics concerning a return to centralized authority. Democratic Russia held a rally outside the Kremlin on 22 February in support of 'Democracy and Glasnost,' which was reportedly attended by about 400,000 people, most of whom shouted the praises of Boris Yeltsin. The size of the gathering indicates the groundswell of support for the Russian leader. Subsequently, Democratic Russia urged voters to vote 'No' to the referendum question, as a 'Yes' vote would lead in its view to a return to Communist authority.

The republics initiated a more coordinated response on 2 March when the Consultative Council of the Democratic Congress met in Moscow. It included representatives from 22 parties and movements in 11 Soviet republics, led by Democratic Russia, the Ukrainian 'Rukh' and the Belarusian Popular Front. The Council met in the aftermath of the violent events in the Baltic States and it condemned the actions of the central government. Speakers suggested the formation of an anti-totalitarian coalition and a meeting in Moscow, comprising the leaders of republican parliaments to meet on 21 April and found a treaty of commonwealth sovereign states, which would undermine the draft Union Treaty. At this Council, delegates were unanimous in support of Yeltsin and RSFSR Prime Minister Ivan Silayev. The link between Yeltsin and the two Slavic republics, Ukraine and Belarus, was an important one. All three republics claimed to be working in the interests of democracy and against a totalitarian system. The realities were otherwise in that sentiments concealed the power struggle between the two governments of Russia, the USSR and the RSFSR. From the outset, and partly as a result of clumsy reactions to events in the Baltic States, Gorbachev had lost much of the goodwill he had nurtured in republics such as Belarus (which he visited on 26 February 1991) and Ukraine.

On the eve of the referendum in the latter republic, amendments were made to the referendum questions. All Ukrainian voters were to answer two questions: whether they supported the preservation of the Soviet Union, and whether Ukraine should be part of this Union according to the principles of its declared sovereignty in July 1990. In the three Galician regions (L'viv, Ternopil, and Ivano-Frankivsk), however, where national consciousness was highest, a third question was to be appended: whether Ukraine should become a fully independent state. The question added an element of farce to the proceedings in that the third question appeared to contradict the second, and to render the first superfluous, unless these three regions proposed to secede from the USSR and from Ukraine after the referendum. Thus both in Russia and Ukraine, participants in the referendum, significant additions had been made to the referendum that would, if implemented, change the nature of the relationship of these republics with the new USSR. Armenia, Georgia, Moldavia, and the

Baltic States decided not to take part in the referendum, though polling stations were set up in Moldavia and Latvia. Freed of controversy therefore, and in the original form advocated by Gorbachev of one question, the referendum applied only to Belarus (where Communist forces were traditionally strong) and to the republics of Central Asia.

On 8 March, the news agency TASS published the text of the draft Union Treaty, which referred to the republics as 'sovereign and equal states' that could determine their own form of government. Moscow was to retain authority over defence and foreign policy, and the republics (as in the original USSR Treaty of 1922) had the right to secede from the Union. The USSR would become the acronym for a Union of Sovereign Equal States. As the date of the referendum approached, Yeltsin continued his active campaign of rallies and demonstrations, bitterly denouncing the Soviet leadership and demanding Gorbachev's resignation. On 10 March, for example, up to 500,000 people turned out once again in Moscow, a sign of Gorbachev's increasing unpopularity in the capital. No doubt, Yeltsin proved himself more adept even than Gorbachev in dealing with the public. He could speak their language. He also had the significant advantage of being out of the ruling elite and in opposition, blaming Gorbachev for the problems of the country and offering platitudes and slogans regarding his own solution to these dilemmas. It was a masterful performance, but the sincerity of his pronouncements (whether he was promoting democracy or seeking power) can only be a matter for debate.

Just prior to the referendum the newspaper *Sovetskaya Rossiya* questioned whether the post of Russian president was really necessary, commenting that it would place enormous authority in Yeltsin's hands and allow him to destroy the Soviet Union. It noted that the new president would have the power to appoint ministers and diplomatic representatives, and should there be an attack on Russia, he had the right to declare war through his position as the Supreme Commander of the Armed Forces of the Russian Federation. *Sovetskaya Rossiya* was hardly one of the voices of Glasnost and the newspaper had remained solidly within the Communist camp promoting a return to the past and more traditional forms of government. Nonetheless, the article, written by several lawyers, raised some valid points. At the least there were now two contenders for power over the Russian 'space,' and it was difficult to conceive how there could be two leaders in control of different apparatuses in the same city (Moscow). Gorbachev, however, preoccupied with what appeared to be his last chance of preserving the Union, did not mount any substantial opposition to the inclusion of the question of the Russian presidency on the ballot paper.

On 17 March, more than 80 per cent of the electorate took part in the referendum, of which 76.4 per cent supported the motion for a renewed USSR (113.5 million people) and 21.7 per cent voted 'No' (32.3 million people). Table 1 shows the results in the nine participating republics:

Table 1 Selected results of the referendum of 17 March 1991 (percentages)

Republic	Turnout	Percentage in favour
Russia	75.4	71.3
Ukraine	83.5	70.2
Belarus	83.3	82.7
Uzbekistan	95.4	93.7
Kazakhstan	88.2	94.1
Azerbaijan	75.1	93.3
Kirghizia	92.9	94.6
Tadzhikistan	94.4	96.2
Turkmenistan	97.7	97.9

Source: *Izvestiya*, 27 March 1991, p. 3.

On the morning of 17 March, Soviet radio and television urged voters to support the referendum, thus leading some critics to maintain that the procedure was far from democratic. Gorbachev interpreted the results as a sweeping victory for his initiative. Even in the regions where voting was unofficial, the voter turnout had been impressive: over 700,000 went to the polls in Moldavia (population 4.4 million) and 436,000 in Latvia (population 2.7 million). On 21 March, the USSR Supreme Soviet issued a resolution that the results of the referendum would be binding throughout the country. There were however, some anomalies and side effects of the vote. In Ukraine, more people had voted for the second resolution that Ukraine should be a sovereign state than had supported the USSR's preservation, and in the western regions, an overwhelming majority had backed an independent Ukraine. In Russia, meanwhile, 69.86 per cent had supported the idea of a Russian presidency and Yeltsin announced at once that he intended to be one of the candidates.

In his memoirs (Gorbachev, 1995, p. 593), Gorbachev argues that the referendum was a resounding success and brought about renewed hope for a new federation of equal states. Almost immediately, however, there was a confrontation on the streets of Moscow. It occurred because the Soviet leader tried to put a stop to the series of mass demonstrations in support of his rival Yeltsin by imposing a three-week ban (issued by the USSR Supreme Soviet on 21 March) on such events, and bringing Soviet troops to the capital to enforce such a ban. The KGB and the police were also given the task of imposing order in Moscow. One week later, however, the Moscow City Soviet gave the Democratic Russia movement a permit to hold a rally on the day of con-vocation of the Congress of People's Deputies of the RSFSR (henceforth the RCPD). Over 100,000 people duly gathered on 28 March, and walked from Manezh to Tverskaya Street carrying placards in support of Yeltsin. When the

RCPD convened on this same day, Yeltsin put forward a resolution, which was accepted by a vote of 532–286, to defy the ban issued by the USSR Supreme Soviet. Thus less than two weeks after the referendum that appeared to give a new lease of life to Gorbachev, the Russian government had come out openly in opposition to Soviet decrees.

Three days after these tumultuous and tense events in Moscow, over 90 per cent of the Georgian electorate participated in a referendum on independence, and 98.9 per cent supported the motion. Though Georgian leader Gamsakhurdia opted to move toward full independence gradually, the decision was nonetheless a setback for Gorbachev. From the distance of 12 years, there seems to be an element of self-delusion in Gorbachev's perspective. For a month, the Soviet government had bombarded the population with propaganda about the referendum and the concept of a new Union. The voters, however, were somewhat fickle. Voting for a more democratic Union was one thing, but many were not committed to it, and the vote did not alter the political or economic situation across the country. For a new Union to succeed, Gorbachev required the commitment of the republican leaders and a certain amount of self-sacrifice. Certainly, these leaders would be asked to put aside republican aspirations for full independence. Moreover, only 9 out of 15 republics had taken part, and in some cases, as noted, they added questions to the referendum that contradicted the principal one.

On 23 April, Gorbachev began discussions on the new Union agreement with the leaders of the nine republics that had taken part in the referendum at his government dacha at Novo-Ogarevo, just outside Moscow. The meeting became known as the 1+9 agreement. At the Central Committee Plenum that took place on the following day, both Gorbachev and his Vice-President in the Politburo Ivashko addressed the recent demands that he should resign, which had been directed at both his positions of president and General Secretary. A few days earlier at the Second Congress of the Soyuz group, chaired by Yury Blokhin, Colonel Viktor Alksnis had demanded a special CPD session to remove Gorbachev and the Congress called for a six-month state of emergency, during which time measures should be taken to deal with the economic crisis with a moratorium on strikes and suspension of political party activities using the intervention of the Soviet army. Gorbachev stated that it was necessary at the present time that the same person held both leading Union positions in order to prevent a vacuum of power at the top and the possibility of the reversal of democratic reforms. The main opposition at the Plenum came from the troublesome secretary of the Russian Communist Party, Ivan Polozhkov, who just a week earlier had lent his support to Yeltsin, who had faced a similar movement to remove him from the Russian leadership. When a vote took place, Gorbachev easily survived the challenge within the Central Committee. Then, to confuse issues, and on the verge of the Russian presidential election campaign, Yeltsin declared that he had buried his differences with

Gorbachev and that the two must now work together to prevent the disintegration of the Union.

As Yeltsin was on the verge of an important election, a cynic would attribute the most Machiavellian of motives. It was preferable to maintain in power a relatively weak leader as head of the Union, whether through the Soviet presidency or Politburo. Had one of the hardliner opponents succeeded Gorbachev, then civil conflict might well have broken out in Moscow. Though popular among the Russian public, Yeltsin always faced some serious opposition, and the Soviet president was a useful, albeit temporary ally, allowing him, among other things, important access to the media and television, as well as support from the undisputed USSR leader. Westerners often perceived the two leaders as natural partners, defending the gains of Perestroika against Communist opposition. Yeltsin, however, was merely being flexible at a critical juncture. Thus disputes with Gorbachev must be put aside, at least until the Russian presidential election was over. For the Soviet president, such offers were all too rare. Though his memoirs indicate that Gorbachev disliked Yeltsin intensely on a personal level, the two leaders often spoke the same language on Glasnost and Perestroika, differing only on the question of where real power should lie.

TOWARD A NEW UNION TREATY

Six candidates took part in the election for Russian president. They were, in addition to Yeltsin, Vadim Bakatin, the former USSR Minister of Internal Affairs, Al'bert Makashov, the Commander of the Volga-Urals Military District, Nikolay Ryzhkov, former USSR Prime Minister, now recovered from illness, Aman-Gel'dy Tuleev, the Chairman of Kemerovo Oblast Soviet, and Vladimir Zhirinovsky, a relatively unknown populist Russian nationalist. Zhirinovsky's name was added to the list of registered candidates only on 22 May by the RCPD, as initially he had not submitted the required list of 100,000 signatures in support of his campaign. Yeltsin chose Afghan veteran Aleksandr Rutskoy as his running mate, turning down candidates such as Khasbulatov, because of their lack of appeal to the public. In the dashing Rutskoy, Yeltsin surmised, he had harnessed a 'tiger,' someone who in his view would appeal to 'middle-aged matrons' and bring out the military vote. Though he would later regret making this choice (Rutskoy led the parliamentary revolt against Yeltsin in 1993), the decision to appoint Rutskoy was an astute one. Yeltsin's main complaint at the time was that the general would constantly criticize Yeltsin's appearance during the election campaign.

The results of the election appear in Table 2. The turnout was 74 per cent. Yeltsin, with 57 per cent, was the outright winner, and became the first democratically elected president in Russian history. In general, he proved to be more popular in towns than in rural areas, and his overall majority in

Table 2 The Russian presidential election of 12 June 1991

Candidate	Percentage of vote
Bakatin, V.V.	3.4
Makashov, A.M.	3.7
Ryzhkov, N.I.	16.8
Tuleev, A.M.	6.8
Yeltsin, B.N.	57.3
Zhirinovsky, V.V.	7.8

Source: *Izvestiya*, 3 July 1991

urban areas was 70 per cent. He took the victory very seriously, as confirmation by the voters of his right to rule Russia. He also decided subsequently to have his office in the Kremlin, in addition to Gorbachev, which added new doubts regarding the legitimacy of the Soviet government and Gorbachev, the non-elected president of the USSR. After the election, Yeltsin embarked on a triumphal tour of the United States. Upon his return, on 10 July, an inauguration ceremony, which was a virtual throwback to the tsarist past, was held in the Kremlin, attended by 6,000 guests, and with the participation of Patriarch Aleksey II as well as a bemused Gorbachev. The inference again was quite clear. Russia now had dual power and a conflict for authority between the two governments could not be far off.

Observers pondering whether Yeltsin would be prepared to make use of his new powers did not have long to wait. On 20 July, the new president issued a decree banning the activities of political parties and public organizations in entities belonging to the state. The decree instructed the RSFSR Supreme Soviet to prepare a bill that would prohibit political activity in organs under the administration of the USSR: the USSR armed forces, the USSR Ministry of Internal Affairs, the KGB, the Office of the Prosecutor, and the USSR Supreme Court. In brief, Yeltsin was laying claim to authority over Soviet institutions as well as specifically Russian ones. Ten days after his inauguration he had thus made a blatant grab for power. Various authorities condemned the decree, including the USSR Supreme Soviet and the CPSU Politburo, as well as the RSFSR Politburo. Critics proclaimed that not only did it violate Articles 48 and 51 of the Soviet Constitution, but also Article 48 of the RSFSR Constitution, and two articles of the law on public associations. The army evidently opposed the new decree most strongly, but Yeltsin remained convinced that by the end of the year it would be enforced in all regions of the RSFSR.

Just over a week later, Yeltsin further incensed the Soviet leadership by signing an agreement in Moscow with Lithuanian leader Landsbergis, which established new relations between Russia and Lithuania. Each state agreed to recognize the other as sovereign. It was also known that Russia was preparing a new law that would establish 'presidential administrations' in all oblasts and raions of Russia, along with the new State Council that would include the heads of the most important Russian ministries. A Russian Security Council would maintain ties with the USSR and Soviet institutions, and with the Soviet Armed Forces. In brief, then, upon winning the presidency, Yeltsin believed that he had a popular mandate to take over power in Russia. He was not naive, and must have been aware of the challenge these decisions presented to the crumbling Soviet government. The key question perhaps is why he continued to pay lip service to the process of formulating a new Union agreement. Was it to prevent a reaction from Gorbachev, an attempt to convince the Soviet leader that there was still hope for such an arrangement, even while taking measures that doomed it to failure?

Gorbachev meanwhile began to work slowly and methodically toward the signing of the new Union Treaty. His commitment to this course was more dedicated than to his earlier policies. On 24 May, he chaired a meeting to draft the new treaty. In attendance at Novo-Ogarevo were the Prime Ministers and the chairmen of the Supreme Soviets of the majority of Union republics, along with the leaders of the 18 autonomous republics, who debated further an initial draft that had been put together by Gorbachev and the leaders of the nine republics that took part in the referendum. The USSR Supreme Soviet (4th Session) created a Preparatory Committee, which then met on 17 June to complete the draft, but there were some crucial points of contention, including that of payment of federal taxes. On 6 July, the Russian Supreme Soviet approved the draft in principle and the signing took place three days later. Of the nine republics, only Ukraine had yet to sign the agreement (now called the 9+1 agreement in deference to the republics), and put off the debate until after 1 September.

On 12 July, the USSR Supreme Soviet approved the draft Union Treaty by 307 votes to 11, with 18 abstentions. Though the RSFSR continued to raise the thorny question of a Union tax, the issue was avoided with a compromise that no taxation would be imposed without consultation with the republics. In practice this single clause seriously jeopardized the entire agreement, since without a guarantee of income from the republics, the Union was doomed. For Gorbachev it was almost the end of a lengthy period of negotiations that he had conducted in good faith. Whatever his mistakes in the crucial year of 1991, one cannot deny his sincerity and diligence in working toward a new treaty that would replace the one forming the Soviet Union in 1922. On 2 August, he appeared on the television program *Vremya* to speak about the Union Treaty. In truth, he could not provide any definitive information. Russia, Belarus, Tajikistan, Kazakhstan, and Uzbekistan would sign the treaty on 20 August, he announced, with the other republics signing at a later date. Ukraine would be permitted to continue studying the draft copy. Armenia and Moldavia would also provide their decisions later, with the former debating the issue of secession from the Union. Likely all these republics would sign the treaty by September. Georgia and the three Baltic States would be given the option of working out their positions on the treaty.

While these difficult negotiations were in place – doubtless exaggerated in their scope by the optimistic Soviet president – democratic political forces in the country, and Moscow in particular, had formed a new association. On 1 July, there came the announcement of a New Democratic Movement, initiated by several well-known political figures, including Shevardnadze, Yakovlev, the mayors of Moscow and Leningrad, G. Popov and A. Sobchak, radical economists Shatalin and Petrakov, and two key figures from the RSFSR leadership: Aleksandr Rutskoy, Yeltsin's Vice-President elect and running mate during the Russian presidential election, and Ivan Silayev, the Prime Minister of the RSFSR. The new movement declared that it would stand in opposition to the CPSU. Its origins lay in the sentiment that the Soviet leadership had abandoned its democratic and pro-reform course, and had been taken over by traditional and hard-line Communists. The CPSU appeared to be close to defunct, and according to Gorbachev, only 15 million members remained, 4 million having left the party over the previous 18 months.

On 16 August, Aleksandr Yakovlev wrote an interesting article in the government daily *Izvestiya*, in which he argued that a powerful group of Stalinists had taken over the core of the party leadership and that a coup d'etat was being planned. Yakovlev had not abandoned his friendship with Gorbachev, but the pioneer of Glasnost did not think that Gorbachev controlled the party any longer. As we have noted, however, the CPSU was badly weakened by the summer of 1991, though it continued to exist, and Gorbachev had not abandoned it. Had he done so, his authority would have rested solely on his presidency. To many traditionalists, Gorbachev appeared to have lost the plot. He had made numerous concessions to the republics, but these measures had failed because of the arbitrary actions of Russian president Yeltsin, upon winning the 12 June election. Yeltsin was not a sincere negotiator. On 14 August, Gorbachev had a telephone conversation with Yeltsin, and was shocked to learn that the Russian leader had doubts about the wisdom of signing a new Union Treaty. Yeltsin had also abandoned the party at the 28th Congress and issued a ban on its continuing authority in the workplace and in government institutions. The RSFSR had laid claim to authority over the Soviet army and the KGB. Thus, the traditionalists felt, if they were to act against such trends, it was imperative to do so at once, before the signing of the Union Treaty, which would effectively bring about an end to Soviet control over the republics. Gorbachev, however, should not logically have been more than a symbolic target of the plotters when he went for his annual vacation, intending to return to Moscow to sign the Union agreement on 20 August. The real target should have been Yeltsin. That he was not the main victim is an indicator of the persistence of the fiction that real power in the country still lay with the traditional instruments of the party and the KGB.

CHAPTER FIVE

THE PUTSCH AND THE COLLAPSE OF THE USSR

THE PUTSCH, 18–21 AUGUST 1991

Historians and political scientists continue to debate the significance of the putsch that took place in Moscow from 18 to 21 August. Opinions range from those who perceive the putsch as a last-gasp reaction of old party stalwarts against Gorbachev to those who maintain that Gorbachev himself may have been responsible to some degree for the attempted coup. In his memoirs (Gorbachev, 1995, p. 631), Gorbachev notes that when he was informed that five senior officials from Moscow had arrived at his dacha on 18 August, the security officials had allowed them to pass through because two of them, Yury Plekhanov, a KGB Lieutenant-General and Chief of the Main Guard Department, and Valery Boldin, one of Gorbachev's staff assistants, were familiar visitors to the Soviet leader. The other visitors were as follows: Oleg Baklanov, the head of the military-industrial complex; Oleg Shenin, a CC CPSU Secretary; and Valentin Varennikov, the USSR Deputy Defence Minister and chief of the Soviet ground forces. Gorbachev discovered that all the phone lines at the dacha had been disconnected and that his visitors had arrived with an ultimatum. Baklanov informed the Soviet leader that he was to sign a decree declaring a state of emergency, and hand over power to Vice-President Yanayev, to which Gorbachev replied with an expletive. Gorbachev's compound, in an idyllic spot on the Black Sea coast, had been isolated by KGB troops.

Gorbachev at least was given the option of coming to terms with the plotters. There were eight main figures involved in the formation of the 'State Committee on the State of Emergency': Baklanov, Vladimir Kryuchkov, the chairman of the KGB, Prime Minister Pavlov, Boris Pugo, the Minister of the Interior, Vasily Starodubtsev, leader of the USSR Peasants' Union, Aleksandr Tizyakov, president of the Association of State-Owned Enterprises, Yanayev, and Dmitry Yazov, whom Gorbachev had appointed to the position of Defence Minister after the young German pilot Matthias Rust had landed his small plane in Red Square four years earlier. Several figures can be considered supporters of the putsch, including Gorbachev's boyhood friend and Chairman of the USSR Supreme Soviet, Anatoly Lukyanov, Major-General Vyacheslav Generalov of the KGB, Plekhanov, and Varennikov. The position of several other figures, including Gorbachev's CPSU deputy Volodymyr Ivashko, was highly ambiguous. According to Yeltsin, Foreign Minister Bessmertnykh's name should be added to the list of plotters. In brief, the key figures belonged to the KGB, the police, and the army, though it was not clear whether all Soviet troops would remain loyal to Yazov, as well as key figures in the administration of the USSR and the party hierarchy.

The close relationship between Gorbachev and the KGB has been cited as one of the factors in the build-up to the putsch. Several leaders, including Yeltsin, were under KGB surveillance, and Kryuchkov regularly supplied the Soviet leader with printed reports concerning the activities of those being monitored (Dunlop, 1993, p. 193). Gorbachev, it is noted, often made additional notes in the margins of these documents. In this way, the KGB could often convince Gorbachev that certain people were working against him. That Gorbachev believed at least some of these reports is not in doubt. What is in question is the employment of such policies by a leader purporting to espouse democracy. It is essentially a matter of judgment. Most world leaders relied to some extent on the reports of their secret service. Kryuchkov, as was to become evident, had more lofty goals, namely the restoration of the 'old values' of the state and former prestige of the party, KGB, and army. He also believed that he could convince Gorbachev as to the wisdom of such a course. His goal was not necessarily to revert to some form of Stalinist dictatorship, but rather the Soviet Union in its spring 1985 variant. The goals were therefore modest but nonetheless would not be easy to achieve.

On the morning of 19 August, at 6 am, the plotters declared the existence of the new State Committee and announced a state of emergency in the country – the date of the appeal was given as 18 August. Gorbachev had reportedly been relieved of his duties for health reasons, and therefore Yanayev in his stead, and according to the Constitution, had taken over as the leader of the eight-man committee. Almost hourly the State Committee began to issue decrees. First of all the state of emergency was to last for six months and all strikes and demonstrations were banned. Speculators and corrupt elements were to be exposed, and all international obligations of the USSR would be met. Lukyanov perhaps signalled the major reason behind the putsch when he renounced the new Union Treaty, which, he said, did not reflect the results of the March referendum. The laws of the republics, he maintained, should not be given priority over Union laws and thus it was necessary to introduce a new Soviet Constitution. Virtually the entire Cabinet of Ministers of the USSR supported the coup. It was time in their view to restore order. Kryuchkov and Yanayev had taken over the mantle of General Lavr Kornilov when he attempted to overthrow the Kerensky regime in 1917.

The new leaders turned immediately on the 'pernicious' elements of Glasnost, such as newspapers. Only nine newspapers were permitted to exist: *Pravda, Izvestiya, Trud, Rabochaya Tribuna, Krasnaya Zvezda, Sovetskaya Rossiya, Moskovskaya Pravda, Selskaya Zhizn*, and *Leninskoye Znamya*. Excluded from this list were the main initiators of Glasnost, such as *Moskovskie Novosti* and *Ogonyok*, whose editor, Vitaly Korotych, elected to remain in the United States, evidently believing that the reaction had come to stay. Not all the newspapers on the official list complied with the wishes of the insurgents. *Izvestiya*, for example, did not appear on 19 August, and its edition of 20 August included the statements made in opposition to the putsch by Yeltsin. By 9 am on the 19th, tanks had appeared on the streets of Moscow and occupied key positions on squares and by government buildings. Though the KGB had watched Yeltsin's house, they did not arrest him, inexplicably. Thus on the first morning of the putsch, the Russian leader travelled into Moscow by car and held a press conference at the White House, the location of the Russian government. In his speech, Yeltsin declared that the putsch was an act of madness and demanded the return of Gorbachev.

The failure to arrest Yeltsin was perhaps the main error of the plotters, but there were many others. Most of the world watched the events in Moscow on CNN, and the drama began to degenerate into a comedy-farce. Outside the Kremlin, protesters began to gather, eventually joining hands to prevent the movement of tanks. Tank drivers were admonished by old ladies or by young women with flowers. At 1 pm, Yeltsin climbed atop a tank and demanded a restoration of constitutional rule. Growing more confident, he appealed for a general strike to protest the unlawful deposing of Gorbachev, while those at the White House received feeds from radio stations operating surreptitiously or from the BBC or Radio Liberty. Yeltsin's speech did contain an interesting point: he had issued a presidential edict, which emphasized not only that the putsch was an illegal action, but also that the plotters were guilty of treason under the criminal code of the RSFSR. He also stated that as president of Russia, he was taking control of all territory of the Russian republic. Two hours after his first comments demanding the return of the Soviet president, he had used the instruments of power in Russia to defend his position. It was to be a significant turning point in the demise of the USSR.

At 5 pm, a shaking Yanayev held a press conference at the Soviet Foreign Ministry, and screened live across the country. He stated that the country had suffered a catastrophic slide and that there were now multiple centers of power (presumably Moscow and the republics). Gorbachev would eventually return to office, but he was exhausted and needed some time to recuperate. It was an unconvincing performance, and even by the evening of the first day of the putsch, it was evident that the plotters had little public support. The army appeared to be half-hearted and the leaders lacked confidence to enforce their will. By this time the crowd at the White House had grown considerably in size. Elsewhere in the country, Soviet troops and tanks occupied key positions in the Latvian capital of Riga, and took over the administration of the police, as well as TV and radio stations. There appears also to have been a plan to take over the recalcitrant (from the plotters' perspective) West Ukrainian city of L'viv, although it was never implemented.

As the day dawned on 20 August, the opposition, led by Yeltsin, began to gain in confidence. Troops of the renegade 14th Army under General Aleksandr Lebed, declared their loyalty to President Yeltsin and took up positions at the White House. Yeltsin sent an ultimatum to Lukyanov, chairman of the USSR Supreme Soviet, demanding the dissolution of the Emergency Committee as well as a personal meeting with Gorbachev in the presence of Yanayev. He would accept the fact of the Soviet leader's illness only after a medical inspection by doctors affiliated with the World Health Organization. Yeltsin demanded that all troops should be removed from Moscow and Leningrad. With another presidential edict, he declared his control over all armed forces on the territory of the RSFSR, and refused to accept any orders given by Yazov and Kryuchkov. The legality of such decrees, on both sides, would present an interesting debate for lawyers. Though he invoked Gorbachev's name on every occasion, the Russian president had elevated Russian laws over Soviet ones, and by taking control over the army – he also stipulated the formation of a Russian Guard – the defiance of Yeltsin had now been transformed into a straightforward power struggle for control over the Russian 'space' in the Soviet Union.

It need hardly be added that the international community did not perceive of the putsch in such a way. It was defined rather as a struggle of democrats against reactionary Communists, people who wanted 'to turn back the clock' and restore a system that retained some of the vestiges of the Soviet past. Because of Yeltsin's pronouncements and partly through wishful thinking, many observers equated Yeltsin and Gorbachev as fellow strugglers against the plotters, which, to some extent, they were. But over the course of a few days the balance of power in Russia changed dramatically. For a brief time, as Dunlop suggests (Dunlop, pp. 253–5), the putsch posed real dangers for the Soviet state and for the gains made by Perestroika. But once it became evident that the Emergency Committee was reluctant to apply force to enforce its decrees, the putsch's failure was only a matter of hours away. It became a glorious public occasion, a manifestation of support for Perestroika and democracy, but behind the scenes, the Russian government prepared the way for taking control over Russia, no matter what occurred in the other republics.

Yet Yeltsin moved diplomatically at all times. At 3.15 pm on 20 August he spoke to US President George Bush, who expressed support for Yeltsin and Gorbachev. British Prime Minister John Major, in a later telephone conversation, promised Yeltsin 'decisive action' should the White House be attacked. Moldavia, Georgia, and Kazakhstan strongly opposed the coup. Ukraine and Belarus adopted a more cautious attitude, not committing themselves to either side initially. By the evening, Pavlov was reported to be suffering from high blood pressure. Yanayev, in a conversation with Yeltsin, agreed to call off plans to attack the White House. There was a serious incident just before midnight, as troops and demonstrators clashed on the Moscow Garden Ring Road. Protesters tried to block the road with overturned buses, and, as tanks broke through the barricade, three young men were crushed to death. At the White House, another protester died in the early morning of 21 August when he tried to enter a military vehicle. Thereafter the Emergency Committee began to lose its nerve, and tanks began to leave the area of the White House at 1.30 am. By mid-morning, the CPSU, in the form of Ivashko, had condemned the putsch, and ordered that Yanayev must speak with Gorbachev. The Russian Supreme Soviet put together a team of six people to travel to Crimea and meet Gorbachev. Members of the Emergency Committee were already on their way to the same location in the presidential plane. Another edict issued from the office of Yeltsin announced that all enterprises on Russian soil were now under the jurisdiction of the Russian government.

From the perspective of Gorbachev, the events were a harrowing experience. He refused to talk to the Emergency Committee representatives, now regarded as traitors (Kryuchkov, Yazov, Lukyanov, and Ivashko) until all communications at the dacha had been restored. Once they were in operation, he made telephone calls to Kazakh president Nazarbayev, Yeltsin, and President Bush. He relates his relief at seeing the arrival of representatives of the Russian (as opposed to the Soviet) government – Rutskoy, Silayev, Bakatin, Primakov and others. Only when the Russian leaders had arrived did he agree to talk, in their presence, to one of the plotters, Lukyanov, along with Ivashko, whose role in the putsch remains uncertain. In the early hours of 21 August, Gorbachev and his family arrived at Moscow's Vnukovo airport on a plane that also carried some of the plotters. It was reported that Gorbachev's daughter Iryna had suffered a nervous breakdown, and his wife Raisa looked ill. The condition of Gorbachev's family, and the Soviet leader himself, is the most convincing refutation to those who theorize that Gorbachev was either behind the putsch or a sympathizer. Doubtless the plotters offered him an opportunity to lend his support to their actions, but it was never very likely that it would be forthcoming.

In Moscow by this time, several members of the Emergency Committee had been arrested, including Kryuchkov, Tizyakov, and Yazov. Pugo was on the run and there were rumours that he had committed suicide (these were later confirmed). Before noon on 21 August, Yanayev and Baklanov were taken into custody, and Starodubtsev had left Moscow. At noon a Rally of Victors was held at the Russian White House before a delirious gathering of more than 100,000. Moscow Mayor Popov called for the resignation of the Soviet government, and requested that Gorbachev should now abandon the Communist Party. Outside the Lubyanka, another crowd tried to remove the statue of Feliks Dzerzhinsky, the first head of the Soviet secret police, and perceived as the founder of the KGB. Though they did not succeed, the statue was taken down later in the day.

Crowds everywhere chanted the name of Yeltsin and condemned the organizers of the putsch: the KGB and the CPSU. Gorbachev had already removed Yazov from control of the army and replaced him, with General Mikhail Moiseyev. He opted to retain Bessmertnykh, and gave Leonid Shebarshkin the position of KGB chairman. He also fired his chief of staff, Boldin, for his part in the plot, appointing in his stead Hryhory Revenko, the former party leader of Kyiv Oblast. Yeltsin was incensed at some of these appointments, warning Gorbachev that Moiseyev, Bessmertnykh, and Shebarshkin were unacceptable. At his behest, the Soviet leader soon revoked these decisions, replacing the three above with General Yevgeny Shaposhnikov, Shevardnadze, and Vadim Bakatin respectively. At a press conference, Gorbachev discussed the conditions of his captivity. He also thanked Yeltsin for his defiance and promised to remove hardliners from the CPSU. Gorbachev looked haggard, and was still uncertain which of his subordinates had remained loyal and which had joined or sympathized with the plotters. He also appeared unaware of how the balance of power in Moscow had changed during his absence.

On 23 August, the impact of the events became more evident, particularly during a speech given by Gorbachev to the RSFSR Supreme Soviet. His audience was happy to hear praise for the role of Yeltsin, but reacted angrily when Gorbachev declared that the CPSU contained not only plotters but also loyal and faithful members. After Gorbachev also defended the USSR Supreme Soviet, Yeltsin insisted that the Soviet leader read out the minutes of the meeting of the USSR Cabinet of Ministers, during which most members had supported the Emergency Committee. Was Gorbachev himself involved? He denied it strongly. Many did not believe him. Yeltsin also suspended all activities of the Russian Communist Party henceforth. Gorbachev agreed to approve all edicts issued by Yeltsin over the previous three days (an unwise action, though dictated by pressure), and he revealed that he and the Russian president had decided to assume each other's powers should either one of them be unable to carry out their duties for whatever reason. Gorbachev thus accepted the equal power of the RSFSR government in August 1991; for Yeltsin it was recognition of his growing authority in Moscow.

The first major casualty of the failed putsch was the CPSU. An investigation of the party headquarters revealed numerous compromising documents. Clearly the party could no longer continue its former existence. Gorbachev, however, was reluctant to take such a definitive step and even at this stage praised socialism. Dunlop maintains that Gorbachev's views had not changed since 1987 when he had first introduced the Perestroika reform program, and that he felt the need to balance political forces in order not to suffer the same fate as Khrushchev in 1964 (Dunlop, 1993, p. 259). On 24 August, Gorbachev resigned as head of the CPSU. He also called for the dissolution of the party and a ban on party cells in the army, KGB, and police (all of which had been carried out already on the territory of the RSFSR by Yeltsin). The other immediate target of post-putsch decrees was the KGB. Bakatin was named as its new leader, while Viktor Barannikov took over as Minister of Internal Affairs. Bakatin began to dismantle the organization at once, though it was to retain some of its basic duties as an intelligence agency.

An edict of Yeltsin also curbed newspapers that had been favoured by the leaders of the putsch (with the exception of *Izvestiya*, which had supported the Russian president). The Russian president's Control Department carried out an investigation of the regions, making the appalling discovery that some 70 per cent of Russia's regions had either sided with the Emergency Committee or resolved to await events before deciding which forces to support during the putsch. Three oblast governments had backed Yeltsin, along with the administrations of the cities of Moscow and Leningrad. Communist Party committees in Russia were strongly in favour of the plotters and none had supported Yeltsin. The revelations were an indicator that had the putsch extended beyond the major cities into the regions, it may have been successful. They also illustrated the limitations of the power of Yeltsin (and for that matter Gorbachev) outside Moscow. On the other hand, this research did not assess the degree of support for the plotters among the general public. Traditionally, regional party committees would follow orders from the centre. The events of August 1991 were unlikely to solicit any different reactions. On 29 August, the USSR Supreme Soviet banned the activities of the CPSU in all regions of the USSR (the vote was 283 to 29) and froze all its assets because of its role in the failed putsch. It was not a total ban. The Komsomol dissolved itself only on 28 September, though the organization had been in deep decline for some time.

What did occur directly after the failure of the putsch was an immediate transition of the national republics to independence. The putsch directly catalyzed this process, which may have been protracted otherwise. Whereas Yeltsin had used the occasion to take over power in Russia, the republics elected to withdraw from a centre that was now discredited and clearly had wished to reverse the reforms of previous years. On 24 August, as a result of a compromise between reformed Communists and the Rukh deputies in parliament, Ukraine declared independence, subject to a national referendum on 1 December, a date that would also see the election of the first Ukrainian president. In Minsk, the name of the republic was changed from the Belorussian Soviet Socialist Republic (BSSR) to the Republic of Belarus, and under the leadership of the chairman of the Supreme Soviet, Stanislau Shushkevich, a former Vice-Rector of the Belarusian State University, Belarus declared independence on 25 August. It also suspended the Communist Party of Belarus. On 24 August also, the RSFSR recognized the independence of Latvia and

Estonia (it had recognized that of Lithuania earlier). Moldavia declared independence on 27 August. Though the republics of Central Asia and Kazakhstan remained in the USSR for the time being, the Union was greatly reduced.

Why had these republics – particularly Ukraine and Belarus – taken such a course? Ostensibly they declared independence because they had little option. Their ruling Communist parties were no longer recognized in Moscow. Indeed, not a few Communist leaders had adopted uncertain attitudes toward the Moscow putsch. In order to remain in office, many of them quickly played the 'nationalist card.' In truth, these republics, especially Ukraine, had already made significant strides toward independence by August 1991. They had not established the prerequisites of an independent state, such as state boundaries, currencies, foreign and defence ministries, nor were they accepted by the international community. But their leaders had perceived that there was a vacuum of power in Moscow. It was rapidly being filled by Yeltsin and the leaders of the RSFSR. But what was the relationship of the RSFSR with the republics of the USSR? Would these republics become subordinate to the Russian state? Such a course was inconceivable. It can be posited therefore that one reason for the rapidity of the declarations of independence in Kyiv and Minsk, was fear of coming under the control of the emerging new Russia.

The attitude of the new Russia to the republics and to its own regions is illustrated by its response to the changing situation. As Gorbachev reverted once again to his hope that a new Union agreement could still be signed, Ruslan Khasbulatov, acting chairman of the Russian Supreme Soviet, informed the USSR Supreme Soviet that the Russian regions (including the autonomous republics, such as Tatarstan, Chechen-Ingushetia, and Yakutia) could sign the Union agreement as members of the RSFSR team. Yeltsin's press spokesman, Pavel Voshchanov, stated that Russia had the right to discuss border issues with all republics other than the three Baltic States. His comments, which were unlikely to have been issued without the backing of President Yeltsin, were echoed by Moscow mayor Popov, who maintained that there should be 'negotiations' over territories such as Crimea, Odesa, the Dnestr region, and northern Kazakhstan. At the least therefore, Russia would question the territorial boundaries of Ukraine, Moldavia, and Kazakhstan.

What did Russian want? Yeltsin, in theory, had not abandoned participation in the negotiations for a new Union Treaty, possibly because he hoped thereby to retain a strong Russian voice in the affairs of the other Union republics. This voice would not be heard if Russia passively accepted the new declarations of independence. The Baltic States, to be sure, had to be abandoned for diplomatic reasons (though the case of ethnic Russians living there would be taken up by Yeltsin later). It would be misleading to attribute all the actions of the Russian president in this period to political goals. He was often inconsistent, sometimes seeming to wish to work with Gorbachev, and at other times against him. The major issue was the Union. While it existed, Russia was the key player, and as long as the Union republics and regions took part in it, then Russian authority, and that of its president, was enhanced.

Gorbachev was now a leader with a receding constituency. Boldly he soldiered on in an increasingly meaningless exercise: the signing of a new Union Treaty. He was irritated by international recognition of the independence of the three Baltic States. His ideal, even now, was to retain the Soviet Union and all 15 republics. On 29 August, the USSR Supreme Soviet withdrew the special powers it had given to the president in 1990, a move made to prevent future coup attempts, but diminishing Gorbachev's role still further. Yeltsin's truculence and power grabbing was also a source of annoyance to the Soviet leader. Gorbachev told the USSR Supreme Soviet that it was time that Yeltsin stopped interfering in Union affairs. Such interventions had been acceptable during the emergency, but now they should be ended. But on the very same day that Gorbachev made these comments (28 August), Yeltsin issued an order that all transactions involving precious metals and stones had to be approved by the Russian authorities. By this time Russia had also taken control of the USSR Finance Ministry, as well as the State Bank and Bank for Foreign Trade. Were these measures legal? After the putsch, no one questioned any more the right of Russia to take away authority and control from the Moscow center.

ADMINISTRATIVE CHANGES

The USSR began to make some administrative changes in its dwindling circle of power. On 29 August, the USSR Supreme Soviet appointed a new Security Council that included the leaders of the nine republics involved in the Union Treaty, as well as Bakatin and Primakov (members of the original council), and familiar names from the earlier years of Perestroika, such as A. Yakovlev and Ryzhkov. Also included were mayors Popov and Sobchak, and Revenko. Shevardnadze declined to join it. On 1 September, an Extraordinary USSR Congress of People's Deputies convened, on the instruction of the USSR Supreme Soviet, and introduced several new structural changes. These included a Council of 20 deputies from the USSR and the republics, a new State Council, that would include the USSR president and the republican leaders, and an Inter-Republican Economic Committee, again with representation from all republics. The key organ, according to Gorbachev, was to be the USSR State Council, which would take over from the Security Council as the main decision-making body. In late September, Gorbachev also established an advisory body called the Political Consultative Council, again composed of trusted figures from Perestroika (Popov, Sobchak, Aleksandr Yakovlev, Yegor Yakovlev, Bakatin, Ryzhkov). However, these measures would remain in place only during what was termed the 'transitional period.' This period would end with the signing of a new Union Treaty. During maneuvers reminiscent of those of Kerensky prior to the Bolshevik Revolution of November 1917, Gorbachev persisted with his singular goal: to bring to a conclusion the new treaty, according to the mandate he had received from the voters in March 1991, all the changes that had occurred during the interim notwithstanding. He had retained his former energy and drive, and because of them had been able to convince doubtful republican leaders that it was worthwhile to continue the endless discussions. One serious problem remained: Yeltsin was no longer committed to the enterprise.

THE FAILURE OF THE UNION TREATY

On 1 September, Gorbachev announced that he and the leaders of ten republics had agreed to sign a treaty on a Union of Sovereign States. In addition, the ten would also sign an economic agreement. The new addition was Georgia, which decided to take part in the drafting of the new treaty. Ukraine, on the advice of the leader of parliament, Leonid Kravchuk, also took part. Gorbachev considered that the treaty was now his 'top priority.' The USSR CPD and the USSR Supreme Soviet agreed to continue in session until the new treaty was signed, and a new USSR authority was established. At the same time, Russia continued to take control of important resources and centers. For example, in mid-September, it nationalized all energy resources on Russian territory: oil, natural gas, hydroelectric and nuclear power stations. As oil and gas exports were important earners of hard currency, the move further undercut the financial stability of the Moscow center. On 21 September, a referendum of secession from the USSR took place in Armenia, and received the support of 99 per cent of voters, with a turnout of more than 95 per cent. The Armenian parliament duly ratified these results. The question was how seriously the empowered republics would take the new negotiations. What powers would be left to Gorbachev and the USSR?

By early October, Gorbachev had circulated the latest version of the Union Treaty to the republics. There was no longer any mention of exclusive powers for the Union government or a federation, and the new entity was referred to as the Union of Sovereign States (USS). On 12 October, Gorbachev appeared on television to announce that within three days he and republican leaders would sign a new treaty for an economic community. He expressed his hope that Ukraine would support this community rather than an independent state. In the event, this treaty was signed on 18 October, and established a common economic space. Three republics declined to sign it: Ukraine, Moldavia, and Azerbaijan, and all the republics still required the approval of their parliaments before the treaty was finally accepted. After Russia had signed the new Economic Community Treaty, Yeltsin stated that it was binding, and Russia would no longer contribute anything to the central budget, other than what was cited in the agreement. Gorbachev now began to seek his main goal: a political treaty that would provide a new basis for the Union.

On 14 November, at a meeting of the USSR State Council, the leaders of the seven republics still ostensibly committed to a new Union Treaty announced that they were ready to sign a newly revised version for what was now called a 'confederative union of sovereign states.' The USSR president would still command the armed forces, including nuclear weapons (the Ministry of Medium Machine Building and the Ministry of Atomic Energy), and represent the country abroad. Earlier Yeltsin had also removed the Ministry of Finance from the jurisdiction of the USSR. On 25 November, the long saga appeared to be reaching its final stages. Gorbachev arranged for a press conference to announce the Treaty, only for Yeltsin to baulk at the last minute, declaring that he wanted more powers allocated to the RSFSR and less for the center. One wonders how much less power the center could have been deprived of and still survived! By this time, the future of the Union Treaty hinged on the results of the referendum on independence in Ukraine to be held on 1 December (see below).

YELTSIN CONSOLIDATES HIS POWER

The republics were beginning to pick and choose the areas in which they would cooperate. When a new USSR Supreme Soviet met in Moscow, for example, on 21 October, only delegates from seven republics (Russia, Belarus, Kazakhstan, and the Central Asians) attended. Azerbaijan and Moldavia sent observers. Ukraine, Georgia, and Armenia did not feel it necessary to send their delegates. In Russia meanwhile, centralization was under way in the main decision-making bodies. When the RCPD began a new session in Moscow on 28 October, Yeltsin put forward his own name as the new Prime Minister (Silayev, surprisingly having moved to the USSR administration) and asked not only for additional powers to introduce reforms, but also for a ban on any further elections in Russia until 1992. In addition, both the president and the Russian authorities arrogated themselves the right to overrule any Soviet laws that appeared to impede the reform process. The appointment on this same day of Khasbulatov as Chairman of the Russian Supreme Soviet solidified the Yeltsin team. As the head of a team of reformers, Yeltsin appointed Deputy Prime Minister Yegor Gaidar, who was in control of 13 Russian ministries involved in the new radical economic policies that would introduce shock therapy into Russia.

In November, Yeltsin strengthened his position further in the long, unannounced struggle for power with the Soviet center. On 6 November, he signed an edict that prohibited all activities of the CPSU and Russian Communist Party on the territory of the RSFSR. He also appointed himself officially the new Prime Minister of Russia and Gennady Burbulis as his First Deputy. The RSFSR Council of Ministers became ipso facto the government of Russia.

To ensure that he had allies in addition to the Baltic States, he engineered perhaps his most cunning and vital move to date: an agreement on collective security and defensive strategy with Ukrainian Prime Minister Kravchuk. Russia now agreed to recognize the existing borders of Ukraine, though the issue of Crimea and the Black Sea Fleet was to reappear in later years, causing considerable tension between the two republics. Now, no matter what the result of the Ukrainian referendum, Yeltsin was sure of a firm ally in Kravchuk in his bitter conflict with Gorbachev. In this same month, he took over the Soviet mint and cut off funds from Russia to about 80 Union ministries, which therefore had to be closed down, releasing into the ranks of the unemployed thousands of bureaucrats.

Yeltsin also chose to ignore the draft Union Treaty by extending his authority into the few areas assigned to the Union. These included foreign policy, as Russia took over the Foreign Ministry. Gorbachev retained full control of defence and railways, but Yeltsin began to share with him control over nuclear weapons. Most important was the issue of funds. As Russia took over Union banks, it also rejected the agreements that the USSR had signed with the IMF and World Bank, and agreed to deal with Soviet debts. The USSR's existence now depended on the support of Russia. However, for the center, all was not yet lost. Yeltsin lacked the moral authority and the international standing of Gorbachev, built up over the years of Perestroika. However, it was not necessary for any public acknowledgement of the power struggle. Slowly but inexorably, Russia was squeezing the life out of the Soviet Union. On 15 November, Yeltsin took control over the Soviet gold and diamond industries, and placed the office of the State Prosecutor under the jurisdiction of the Russian government.

In late November, several more measures solidified Russian authority. The KGB was banned and re-instituted as the Agency of Federal Security. On 28 November, a Law on Russian Citizenship, issued by the Russian Supreme Soviet, took precedence over existing Soviet laws. It also applied to more than 25 million Russians living outside the boundaries of the Russian Federation, and to more than 20 million exiles that had left Russia since the revolutions of 1917. Finally on 30 November, in a meeting with Chairman of the State Bank Viktor Gerashchenko and Gorbachev, Yeltsin took control over the Union budget (by now in an impossible situation as few funds were incoming) and announced that he would continue to manage it until the end of the year. The inference was obvious. After December 1991, there would be no further need to cater to a Soviet center or to a USSR president.

THE BELAVEZHA AGREEMENT

On 1 December, residents of Ukraine went to the polls for a vote on independence. Since the announcement of an independent Ukraine on 24 August, the situation in the USSR had changed dramatically. The center had declined to a feeble entity, whereas the revitalized Russian Federation had begun to assert its power. For Yeltsin, the result was probably immaterial. An interesting though limited question is what would have happened had Ukraine decided to remain part of the Soviet Union? Would Yeltsin have tried to assert power over the republic as he had with the Gorbachev administration? The question proved immaterial once the results were announced, and more than 90 per cent of Ukrainian residents approved independence. In reality, they had little choice if they were to retain control over their affairs and extricate the republic of 52 million from the quagmire of Russian and Soviet politics. Even in Russian-speaking and ethnic Russian areas, a clear majority favored independence. On the same day, Kravchuk won the election for Ukrainian president, defeating several rivals on the first ballot with more than 57 per cent of the vote, a notable achievement for a former CPU ideological secretary who had remained at least equivocal during the period of the Moscow putsch. Magnanimously, Gorbachev sent a telegram of congratulations to Kravchuk on 4 December. Only St Petersburg mayor Sobchak commented, pointlessly, that Russia would immediately raise territorial claims on Ukraine if the republic refused to join a political union with Moscow. On 1 December also, Nazarbayev, the only candidate on the ballot paper, won the election as president of Kazakhstan, the start of long years of self-aggrandizement and accumulation of power in that republic.

On 4 December, Gorbachev and Yeltsin held a private meeting to discuss the results of the referendum in Ukraine. Gorbachev was genuinely aggrieved at the vote, commenting later on television that he could not imagine a Union without Ukraine. For Yeltsin, the vote spelled the end of the increasingly futile attempts at a new Union Treaty, a process in which he had offered only half-hearted support at best. Communications were now under way between Belarusian parliamentary leader Shushkevich, Yeltsin, and Kravchuk. According to Shushkevich (as recorded in a personal interview in December 1998), the original plan was to invite all three leaders, in addition to Gorbachev, to the hunting lodge at Belavezha, a vast park in the Brest region (a favorite hunting resort of former General Secretary Brezhnev), to resolve remaining differences. Yeltsin, however, declared that he would attend only on condition that Gorbachev did not participate. Since Yeltsin was considered a vital player, Shushkevich agreed to this demand. The result was a meeting that Gorbachev subsequently regarded as secretive and a betrayal, particularly given his recent conversation with Yeltsin.

Over two days and many toasts, the three leaders and their associates resolved to form a loose association called the Commonwealth of Independent States. Shushkevich's view was that all three leaders were satisfied with the results: Belarus and Ukraine had an agreement from the leader of Russia to recognize the independence of their states; Yeltsin had succeeded in forming a new entity in order to remove Gorbachev and end the existence of the Soviet

Union. Nazarbayev later expressed his annoyance at having been excluded from the meeting. Yeltsin, in his turn, has argued that the three negotiators had tried to make contact with the Kazakh leader while he was flying over Moscow, but failed. Then, says Yeltsin, Gorbachev 'got to him' and Nazarbayev decided not to come (Yeltsin, 1994, pp. 115–16). It is an unconvincing explanation. The Belavezha agreement was held in secret and great haste, and there was never a serious effort made to include the Kazakh leader. One could argue that it was unnecessary given that those at the hunting lodge were leaders of three of the original states of the Soviet Union. But this line of thinking can only take one so far: the three leaders had not explained their meeting either to their publics or their parliaments.

The day after the meeting, in Moscow, Gorbachev met with Yeltsin and Nazarbayev in the Kremlin to discuss the formation of the CIS. Gorbachev was happy that Ukraine had taken part in discussions, but he maintained that the three leaders had no mandate to decide the fate of the Soviet Union. The Chairman of the USSR Supreme Soviet Council of the Union, Konstantin Lubenchenko, also remarked that the Belavezha agreement lacked any legal foundations. On the other hand, a Russian legal expert, Sergey Shakhray, declared that the republics were merely taking back the powers removed from them by the Treaty of 1922, when all three, together with Transcaucasia, were responsible for the formation of the Soviet Union. Since Transcaucasia had split into three republics subsequently, it had no right to take part in such a meeting, but the three founding states did have such a right. A counter to this statement would be that Shushkevich, at least, lacked a popular mandate in Belarus, though both Yeltsin and Kravchuk were now democratically elected presidents. On the other hand, the USSR was still recognized as an international entity, and Gorbachev had acquired a significant reputation outside the country. Perhaps what incensed Gorbachev the most was that the three leaders had informed US President Bush of proceedings before Shushkevich called Moscow to inform the Soviet president.

On 10 December, the parliaments of the three Slavic states approved the Belavezha agreement to form the CIS. In Belarus and Russia's case the vote was overwhelming, but there was significant opposition in Ukraine, where only 288 out of 367 delegates approved the agreement. For some Ukrainian deputies, the formation of the CIS appeared to contradict the recent ratification of independence. Nor had Kravchuk asked for the approval of his parliament beforehand. The Russian parliament now formally abrogated the 1922 Treaty, and Yeltsin remarked that it had no choice, given the refusal of the Soviet leader to give up the idea of a strong central power. At the USSR Supreme Soviet in Moscow, Russia and Belarus lowered the status of their delegates to observers. On 13 December, the leaders of the five Central Asian states agreed to join the CIS on condition that their existing borders would not change or be questioned. This was the prelude to a meeting in Alma-Ata of eight republics (excluding the three founders of the CIS and Georgia), which resulted in a decision to join the CIS. Ukraine now began to reconsider its premature decision at Belavezha, and Kravchuk decided that it would only join the CIS provided that it was a loose association and did not seek to create a new confederation or state. In practice, though the CIS did receive immediate world attention, it never worked fluidly as the newly independent republics gave priority to domestic interests rather than inter-republican cooperation. The purpose of the formation of the CIS was to destroy the Soviet Union, and remove Gorbachev from office, two tasks that it achieved within a matter of weeks.

Gorbachev was left with few options following the announcement of the CIS. His long months of negotiation with the republics had been rudely curtailed by the actions of the three Slavic leaders, and particularly Yeltsin. On 16 December, the Russian Supreme Soviet declared that it would soon move into the Kremlin rooms of the USSR Supreme Soviet. The next day, Gorbachev and Yeltsin held a two-hour meeting during which the former admitted that he had no options other than to resign as Soviet president and accept that by the end of the year, the Soviet Union would cease to exist. Russia took control of the strategic nuclear arsenal and the armed forces peacefully on 25 December. On this same day, Gorbachev appeared on Central Television to address the public. Just prior to his appearance, he had spoken with President Bush and informed the US president of his decision to step down, and urged him to recognize the CIS. Two days earlier he had held a similar conversation with Britain's John Major. On television, Gorbachev stated that he had carried out a historic task of taking a totalitarian state toward democracy, but that he was strongly opposed to the dissolution of the USSR and had remained committed to a multi-national state. It was brief, poignant last hurrah, but it was sufficient to infuriate the Russian leader.

The last days of Gorbachev's leadership dissolved into a petty vendetta. Officially he had been permitted five days to move out of his Kremlin office, but on 27 December, Yeltsin and colleagues arrived in the early hours, took over the office, and emptied a bottle of whiskey in celebration. In similar fashion, Gorbachev was evicted from his presidential home and dacha, though he did secure a 'retirement package' from Yeltsin. It was a shabby and unprofessional treatment of a long-time colleague and it reflected the personal nature of the struggle between Gorbachev and the man he had elevated from his Siberian party stronghold. What was the need for such haste? Gorbachev describes Yeltsin's anger at the speech the former made on television. That same evening a formal ceremony transferring power to the Russian Federation was scheduled to take place in the Kremlin. Yeltsin and his entourage did not appear, and instead chose to eject Gorbachev from the building two days later like a common interloper (Gorbachev, 1995, p. 672). Twelve years on, Gorbachev's insistence on a Union State based on the March 1991 referendum appears to have been a misguided and forlorn hope. There is no doubting, however, the dignity and grace with which he left office, following conversations with world leaders (Kohl, Mitterand, Major, Bush) who revered and respected him. It represented the difference between a statesman (Gorbachev) and a vindictive politician intent only on gaining power and defeating a rival (Yeltsin). It had taken Yeltsin six months to gain supreme power in Moscow after the Russian presidential election. Gorbachev, in truth, should have resigned much earlier than he did.

On 26 December, the sixty or so deputies remaining in the USSR Supreme Soviet voted to dissolve the assembly, though in fact the assembly lacked a quorum. The RSFSR on this same day became known as the Russian Federation. Russia also took over the seat of the USSR at the UN, and Soviet embassies worldwide became ipso facto Russian embassies, an action that perhaps illustrated the predominance of Russia within the Soviet Union. On 31 December, the Soviet flag on the Kremlin was lowered and replaced by the Russian tri-coloured, white-blue-red flag. One of the world's most powerful states, and the country most responsible for the defeat of Hitler's Germany, had fallen in a virtually bloodless change of power, and to the disbelief of many of its citizens and the world at large. How had it happened? Was it a tragedy or a relief, the failure of a great experiment initiated by Lenin, but abused by Stalin, and brought to a conclusion by the Leninist student Gorbachev?

CHAPTER SIX

WHY DID THE SOVIET UNION COLLAPSE?

Historians will no doubt continue to debate the main causes of the collapse of the Soviet Union for many years. Certainly, very few analysts predicted it, and many denied that the Soviet Union, and Gorbachev in particular, were even in a crisis. There was a tendency in the West to focus on Russia to the detriment of the republics, or else to perceive the Soviet Union as a country that could be comprehended from the perspective of Moscow, first and foremost, which led to the relative neglect of the views in the national republics. There is also a point of view that the end of the USSR signalled the conclusion of the long Cold War conflict between the Soviet bloc and the West, resulting in a victory for the latter. Certainly the United States emerged as the world's only global power, a situation that changed the way in which decisions were reached and, temporarily at least, reduced the authority and influence of the United Nations, a body established as a result of wartime treaties. But this did not necessarily signify that the West was responsible for the collapse of the Soviet Union. Quite the contrary, the Soviet Union, despite the rigours and pressures of the arms race, did not suffer economic collapse at the peak of that competition. It fell apart at a time when relations with the West had improved to an unheard-of harmony with strong personal friendships between the leaders of the former Cold War enemies. It occurred at a moment when those same Western leaders were anxious that it should remain in place (under Gorbachev's leadership) as the most stable alternative.

If the Cold War loss theory fails to convince, then so does the idea that Gorbachev himself destroyed the Soviet Union by undermining the authority of the Communist Party. That Gorbachev was frustrated with the obstinacy of the party and its opposition to his Perestroika program is evident, but he was reluctant to sever ties with the organization that he had followed throughout his career and that had brought him to power. Only after the failed putsch of August 1991, and then with the greatest hesitancy and only at the behest of Yeltsin, did Gorbachev agree to the suspension of party activities. However, the structural reforms carried out by Gorbachev after 1989 did weaken the party considerably, creating a vacuum of power in the Soviet structure. Though it was filled in part by the new Congress of Deputies and the USSR Supreme Soviet, neither had the sort of authority formerly wielded by the party. Instead, the new Soviet president became the key figure, but Gorbachev's authority within the Union was limited by the fact that he had not won his position through a national election. Had he done so, he would likely have been victorious. Moreover, the creation of an empowered as opposed to a ceremonial president was soon to be emulated by the republics.

Gorbachev's authority in his early years was unquestioned. Those who maintain, as Yeltsin did, that he was trying to build up too much central power through the presidency miss the key point. As party leader, Gorbachev already had substantial authority. He became frustrated because members of the party did not wish to follow his lead in all directions, particularly in a radical economic reform program, but in that respect, he had an opportunity to take firm steps and declined to do so. Essentially, Gorbachev was a cautious leader, and he often saw his role as one of intermediary between various factions, keeping in mind Khrushchev's removal for being too impetuous and alienating both the army and KGB. More so than his predecessors, Gorbachev was a charismatic figure who was at home in front of a TV camera and confident in making public appearances (though many of these were staged with a handpicked audience). He did not need cue cards or prompting, and often he made pronouncements without warning his advisors or close associates. On the other hand, those analysts who have maintained that Gorbachev introduced democracy into the Soviet Union (or Russia) are also going too far. True, he established institutions that enhanced the power of the government and began to curb the omnipotence of the Communist Party. There is no doubt also that the chief opponents of Perestroika were the leaders of the Soviet nomenklatura. But Gorbachev's goal was always to strengthen and augment the power of the Soviet Union, not to destroy it. Everything else he sacrificed for that ultimate goal. In August 1991, the plotters would not have gone ahead had they not believed that at some point, Gorbachev would come over to their side, albeit as a weakened president. Like any leader he had his faults, but did these faults lead inevitably to the end of the Soviet state?

In his meticulous study, George W. Breslauer provides both a 'harsh' and 'generous' evaluation of Gorbachev's leadership strategy. Dealing here only with the former, one notes this analyst's focus on several key factors: the weakness of his national and economic policies; his refusal to come to terms and work with Yeltsin; and his change of direction in the Fall of 1990 when he replaced liberal reformers with hardliners who would subsequently mount a putsch against him (Breslauer, 2002, p. 292). Gorbachev failed to recognize, Breslauer notes, that 'Yeltsin and the radicals were the wave of the future.' To the above might be added the criticism of Shevardnadze that Gorbachev had a tendency to become involved in endless debates, or Yeltsin's that Gorbachev did not like to admit to making mistakes (Yeltsin, 1994, p. 117), Khasbulatov's comment that he mixed personal and family suffering with political events (Khasbulatov, 1993, p. 183), as well as the disturbing remark of Anatoly Chernyaev that during six years of working for Gorbachev, the Soviet leader never once thanked him for his efforts (Chernyaev, 2000, p. 245) – a small point, perhaps, but one that demonstrates Gorbachev's lack of ease with his peers and subordinates. He had few close friends and one might even say that he did not get along well with people.

This point is worth a small digression. As a man from a kolkhoz family who became a member of the Soviet intellectual elite, Gorbachev might be considered a success story. Yet his background and personality alienated him from those whose support was essential to his survival. The average worker and peasant did not take his words very seriously, particularly after constant repetition without material changes around them. They also did not like Gorbachev's elevation of his wife Raisa to a public figure. Her taste for expensive clothes and public occasions was deeply resented. Never before had a Soviet leader seemed to 'share' his office with his partner. Conversely, Soviet intellectuals never accepted Gorbachev either as a member of their circle. He spoke Russian with a southern accent and made frequent grammatical errors, some of them eliciting jokes and ridicule. In this sense, Gorbachev lacked a social standing. Neither workers, nor peasants, nor the intellectual elite accepted him as one of their own. He lacked a constituency and, as we have seen, he did not develop close friendships.

Gorbachev's most important failure was not to reconcile the results of Glasnost with the rise of the national question in the Soviet Union. Problems in the republics surfaced almost immediately upon his taking office and were only exacerbated by the more tolerant atmosphere within the media and the development of civic life at all levels of society. In the Baltic States, protests focused on the illegality of the Nazi–Soviet Pact. Arguably, Gorbachev could have negotiated the departure of the three Baltic States from the USSR and still maintained the Union. His hesitation ensured that the initiatives of Baltic leaders, and particularly the Popular Fronts, filtered down to the other republics. Observed from a distance there is a remarkable similarity about developments in the European states of the USSR: protests against nuclear power and environmentally damaging industries; the formation of Popular Fronts; de-Stalinization and democratization of the media; splits in the Communist parties between a pro-Moscow and a regional faction; declarations of state sovereignty, etc. Aside from the three Baltic States, was there any possibility of secession in these republics in the earlier years of Gorbachev's leadership? The answer is still unclear. The Georgians were alienated by a brutal act of the Soviet militia in 1989. Western Ukrainians had taken Ukraine along a route that might ultimately end in a quest for independence, but they were not representative of all Ukrainians. Elsewhere in Ukraine there was a general feeling of dissatisfaction but it lay more with the mismanagement of the economy and the decline of living standards than with issues related to independence or national self-assertion.

The rise in national sentiment in the republics received a significant boost from the downfall of Communist regimes in Eastern Europe, and from contacts with the Soviet leadership in Moscow. In the first instance, Gorbachev's abandonment of the Brezhnev Doctrine sounded the death knell for decrepit governments that in some cases, Poland and East Germany for example, were almost devoid of popular support. When the USSR did not respond to the regime changes – indeed in the case of the GDR it appeared that a regime change was favoured – then the Soviet republics could act with more confidence. Many of them could join in with genuine enthusiasm during the denunciations of Stalin and the rehabilitations of many of those purged during the Stalinist era. These actions went much further than in the Khrushchev period, and given the openness of the media, they gave rise to questions about the legitimacy of Soviet power, and to the role and leadership of Lenin, the most sacred part of Soviet doctrine. Gorbachev, ostensibly a devout follower of Lenin, was irritated by some of the liberties taken by newspaper editors. In early 1991, for this reason, the Soviet authorities renewed censorship over TV and radio with the abolition of 'Gostelradio' and its replacement with a new company under Leonid Kravchenko. No doubt Gorbachev was under pressure to place similar restrictions on the media.

Yet at the same time he was also anxious to maintain his international standing and the good relations he had developed with world leaders. That same priority also affected his relationship with the Baltic States, the occasional ham-handed forays into Vilnius and to the border regions notwithstanding. There could be no major crackdown on the Baltic States or other republics because such an action would endanger the Soviet leader's enormous international prestige. This is perhaps why, to the incredulity of some Western observers, Gorbachev feigned ignorance of what actions had been taken, limited though they might have been. Arguably, the half-hearted assaults were more damaging to the Soviet leadership in the long term. They left the impression of indecision and a lack of will on the part of Gorbachev. Yet tensions were often high. In Kyiv in 1991, for example, there was genuine tension and fear of a reaction in Moscow to the democratic, pro-independence movement in Ukraine. These fears were not necessarily identified with Gorbachev, but rather with some of his new associates, particularly Kryuchkov, Yazov, and Pugo.

The culmination point of the rise of the republics was the referendum of March 1991. Yet the results of that referendum continue to be debated. Gorbachev's own definition was both narrow and self-deluding. There was never a mandate for a strong central power. The vote for a revised Union meant different things to different people. When additional questions were added to the ballot, they produced contradictory results. The voters wanted sovereignty and they wanted independence; they also voted for a revised Union. There could be no better indication of an immature electorate, unused to making major decisions and for whom an election had for many years been no more than a ritual. However, republican leaders were anxious to expand the areas under local control. Regional power thus took precedence over purely national issues. In August 1991, these regional leaders played the nationalist card to ensure their survival, but the significance of the devolution of power from Moscow to the republican capitals should not be underestimated. Nor should one neglect the general sentiment, in areas like Eastern Ukraine, for example, that economic recovery and higher living standards might be more sustainable through independence than through a new version of the Union.

Much then depended on Gorbachev's personal relations with republican leaders. His most loyal allies were the heads of the republics of Central Asia, which had become virtual satraps, highly corrupt, and with local leaders enjoying privileges reminiscent of the worst excesses of the Brezhnev years. Elsewhere he was on less solid ground. Nazarbayev seems to have trod a careful path between Gorbachev and Yeltsin, while ensuring that his own power base became stronger. Gorbachev could make little progress in the Baltic States, even with the leaders of the pro-Moscow branches of the local Communist parties. He seemed on more solid ground with Ukraine and Belarus, but after August 1991, the situation in these republics changed dramatically. Why were Kravchuk and Shushkevich, for example, prepared to exclude him from the discussions at Belavezha? And how far did Gorbachev himself change toward the end of his period in office? Why was he willing to cast off his original team of reformers in late 1990, appointing people to high office – Pugo, Pavlov, etc. – that were clearly not supporters of the Perestroika reforms and that were opposed to granting significant power to the republics? Was he duped by the regular and misleading KGB reports supplied to him by Kryuchkov?

This book has argued that it was Gorbachev's relationship with Yeltsin that proved to be the most significant factor in the ultimate fall of the USSR. Yeltsin may not have had a long-term program to bring about the downfall of Gorbachev or the Soviet Union. Like his rival, he also had used the party apparatus to rise to prominence. On occasions, they appear to have had similar goals. But Yeltsin possessed a ruthlessness and willpower that was lacking in the Soviet leader. As was demonstrated in the attack on the Russian parliament building in October 1993, Yeltsin had no qualms about taking drastic action should the situation warrant it. In the late Soviet period, the rise of Yeltsin coincided with a festering national problem. The turning point was the decision to hold an election for a Russian president. In contrast to the situation in the other republics, a strong USSR could not co-exist alongside a strong RSFSR. The two things were incompatible. Yet some Russians also felt that they had not benefited from the Soviet experience, and even that the federal nature of the Union in some respects actually discriminated against Russians – hence the apparent need to re-establish a Russian Communist Party and Central Committee. For the Soviet authorities, the creation of such structures in Russia should have come as a warning. With the creation of a presidency and the announced intention of Yeltsin to run in the election, the die was surely cast. Dual power had not worked in 1917 and it could not work in 1991. What Russia was doing, under the leadership of Yeltsin, was undermining the Union agreement of 1922. In fact, the Russian concept of a federation that would be composed within rather than outside Russia was very similar to that advanced by Stalin in the early 1920s, one that Lenin had firmly rejected.

Russia's assault on the Soviet center also coincided with a period of economic crisis that had resulted from a number of factors: inefficient state companies, half-hearted but disruptive economic experiments, widespread strikes and demonstrations during working hours, environmental concerns about a number of industries and nuclear power stations all combined to bring the economy first to a standstill and then to a sharp decline. As Russia began to withdraw payments to the Soviet budget in 1991, and then to take over key sectors of the economy, particularly energy, gold, and diamonds, there were simply insufficient funds reaching the Union coffers in Moscow. It is hard to perceive these actions as anything other than calculated to bring about the collapse of the center. However, it does not necessarily signify that Yeltsin had such a goal in mind from the outset. Indeed, he had a number of personal battles to fight first, particularly in his own constituency of the Russian Federation, where the revived Russian Communist Party posed an immediate threat, and there was significant opposition to Perestroika. Until the summer of 1991, it was by no means clear that the Gorbachev administration and the Soviet Union only had a few months of existence remaining. Most factors indicated a protracted struggle and given Gorbachev's record, few observers doubted that he would last the course.

Other factors then combined to transform the situation. One was the Soviet leader himself, who had begun to run out of original ideas and to lose the faith of Soviet citizens. There had been a surplus of plans, debates, schemes that were not carried out, changes of direction, new organs of power, efforts to give meaningful authority to the Supreme Soviet, along with constant complaints from the Soviet leader that his reforms were being held back by those unwilling to contemplate radical changes. Most of these complaints lacked real substance. The truth was that Gorbachev himself had no precise plan or campaign. Like his predecessors he became obsessed with slogans rather than actions. Had Gorbachev resigned in 1988 or early 1989, he likely would have been remembered as an ambitious reformer, foiled in his efforts by hard-line Communists. But as one new unfinished reform ran into another, and neither the Cabinet nor the USSR Supreme Soviet gave the president their full support and backing, it appeared to many within the USSR that the core of the problem might be the Soviet leader himself. Yet his standing, particularly outside the country, was such that few dared to take action against him. The alternatives to Gorbachev in power, frankly, appeared to offer even worse prospects.

The event that brought matters quickly to a head was the failed putsch of August 1991. The creation of an Emergency Committee seemed to emanate from the same forces that had published the famous letter of Nina Andreeva in the newspaper *Sovetskaya Rossiya*, i.e., from those who wished to maintain the system of neo-Stalinism, replete with past glories of the war, and heroes such as Lenin and Stalin. Behind the putsch stood the KGB, part of the army, the internal police, and the leaders of the Communist Party. The USSR Supreme Soviet offered more limited support. Even the leaders of the Russian regions were in favour of the new leadership. Over the course of two days, however, it became plain that the Emergency Committee had little or no public support. Frantically, its members turned to Gorbachev as their last hope, but he rejected them quite firmly. The drama was soon to become a tragicomedy, as drunken *apparatchiki* eventually realized their campaign had failed and began to flee from Moscow. There seems no reason in retrospect to doubt that Gorbachev acted both bravely and nobly during these days. Surprisingly though, not even confinement in his Foros dacha convinced the Soviet leader that it was time to renounce the agencies of Soviet power: the party and the KGB. In his memoirs he expresses his relief at seeing the arrival of the leaders of the RSFSR. Only then did he know that his safety and that of his family were assured. But when he returned to Moscow, he did not recognize how fundamentally the situation had changed, declaring before the Russian parliament that he did not wish to engage in a 'witch hunt' (Khasbulatov, 1993, p. 171).

The failed putsch did much more for the reputation of Boris Yeltsin than that of Mikhail Gorbachev. It was Yeltsin who emerged a hero, who defied the tanks of the putschists, and who communicated with the Russian people and with foreign leaders. He postured as the symbol of democracy against the forces of reaction and totalitarianism, a light in the darkness, the only hope for the future. Polls conducted at the time (cited in *Pravda* on 12 September 1991) indicate that after the failed putsch, the popularity rating of Yeltsin soared to 91 per cent, the same sort of rating enjoyed by his counterpart George Bush after the victory over Iraq in the Gulf War (or for that matter, that of his son, George W. Bush, after the defeat of Iraqi forces in 2003). Even the dour Khasbulatov enjoyed a rating of over 80 per cent and Russian Prime Minister Silayev 77.7 per cent. Gorbachev's figures hovered between 50 and 60 per cent. The Soviet leader's popularity rose after the putsch, but not substantially. Ten days on, another poll was taken, and over 30 per cent of those polled thought that it was time for Gorbachev to retire. Similarly a survey conducted of 1,236 members of the adult population of the RSFSR,

Ukraine, Belarus, and Kazakhstan and published in *Izvestiya* on 5 September 1991 responded as follows to the question: Whom do you consider the most popular political activist: Yeltsin 45.5 per cent, Gorbachev 19 per cent, Sobchak 13 per cent, Bakatin and Yakovlev 3 per cent. In short, through the events of 19–21 August, Yeltsin eclipsed Gorbachev as a popular figure.

At the same time, and partly behind the scenes, Yeltsin used the drama of the time to accumulate power and then to usurp control over Moscow and the Kremlin. Given the nature of the putsch, it would take a team of legal experts to work out the legality or illegality of Yeltsin's decrees during these days. Gorbachev, at least, was ready to forgive and forget them until he realized that they were never intended as temporary measures. Thus there was a coup within the putsch, during which the Russian president, Yeltsin, took over power from Gorbachev. He was hardly an interloper because he was the elected RSFSR president and the hero who had foiled the Emergency Committee of Kryuchkov and his colleagues. The two events: the rise of Russia (to use Dunlop's term) and the Yeltsin 'coup' signified the end of the Soviet era. It took several related steps to achieve this end: the transfer of ministries and resources from Union to Russian control, the disbandment of the CPSU, and the prevention of the new Union agreement, ultimately through the Belavezha meeting. While Gorbachev sought to preserve the Union, Yeltsin, his nemesis, sought to destroy it.

The Russian takeover of power in Moscow, alone, would have been sufficient to end the existence of the Soviet Union. In theory, Gorbachev might have used the army or the police to assert his control. There have been claims that Gorbachev attempted to apply exactly these forces in early December in an attempt to maintain (or regain) power by force. If so, he does not seem to have made a sustained or carefully thought-out strategy. The first question was whether these troops would be loyal to him in a campaign against Yeltsin; and second, whether Yeltsin was indeed the real enemy. The experience at Foros would not have led naturally to such a conclusion. To the end, Gorbachev seems to have hoped that Yeltsin would eventually assent to the new Union and be prepared to accept some form of Union control, at least over foreign policy and defence. It was a forlorn wish. There are several occasions between 1985 and 1991 when Gorbachev might have resorted to force. To his credit, and despite the humiliations he suffered in the last two months of his leadership, he never placed personal power above his goals for the Soviet Union. Doubtless, he was at times pompous, self-important, often with an eye on his future place in history and his legacy, but in the final analysis he showed commendable restraint.

There were additional events that compounded Gorbachev's dilemmas. The chief of these, it can be posited was the 'loss' of Ukraine to the Union after 24 August. This event was not foreseen either by the Soviet or Russian leadership and it occurred by chance, as a result of an unexpected compromise between national democrats and reformist Communists in the Ukrainian parliament. Without Ukraine, all leaders agreed, there could be no future for the USSR. Ukraine was the heartland, the granary, and the location of several key industries. It was also the nurturing point for many Soviet leaders: Kaganovich, Khrushchev (who had lived and worked in Ukraine though born near Kursk), Brezhnev, Shcherbytsky, and others. Ukraine was a founding member of the Soviet Union. Its capital Kyiv was regarded by many Russians as an integral part of their history and the center of the medieval principality of Kievan Rus'. Thus even Yeltsin and alleged democrats like Sobchak made angry and disparaging threats toward Kyiv at the news of Ukrainian independence. The notion of a referendum was thus a brilliant maneuver by the Ukrainian parliament. It gave Moscow leaders the illusion that there was still some hope and time to change the Ukrainians' minds, and it prevented any kind of premature military action from Moscow against Ukraine, a danger that seems far-fetched today but was very much in the minds of the Ukrainian leaders.

Yeltsin, a brilliant political strategist, used this time well. From a potential foe of Ukraine, he became its best friend, signing a new agreement recognizing its borders and then working around the table with Kravchuk and Shushkevich to come up with a new agreement, the CIS. With all due respect to the Belarusians, they did not figure as major players in this conundrum. Yeltsin used the new alliance with Ukraine as an instrument with which to send Gorbachev to his final defeat. The CIS, in truth, could never have been more than a temporary phenomenon. Kravchuk recognized this fact belatedly. But that was never the point. Through the CIS, Yeltsin rendered Gorbachev's position meaningless. The latter became the Emperor with no clothes, the president without a state, with even his power base of Moscow being taken away from him without a shred of remorse. Yeltsin not only used his powers as president; he appointed himself Prime Minister and banned further elections, ruling instead by presidential edict. For the last two months of the USSR's existence, there were few controls over Yeltsin's authority. He could rule as a virtual dictator in Russia, and he was also the main player in relations with the republics. With no means with which to respond to this political *fait accompli*, Gorbachev resigned quietly although, as noted, even the dignity of being given time to clean out his office was not permitted him. The observer cannot help but be struck by the very personal struggle between these two figures and how between them they brought about the downfall of the Soviet Union. Had they chosen to work together there is no logical reason why it should have collapsed when it did. But this was asking too much of Boris Yeltsin.

The nature of the fall of the USSR can thus be described as a revolt or coup from within: the takeover of the Soviet state by the RFSFR. It did not fall as a result of the Cold War and the arms race, or the backlash against the putsch of August 1991. It occurred in part because of the rise of the national republics against the center, heralded initially by the dramatic impact of Glasnost on the Soviet media and the revival of civic life. It happened also because of the removal of Communist regimes in Eastern Europe and Gorbachev's refusal to counter their fall with the use of force. Gorbachev surely was contemptuous of most of these regimes, which had no popular mandate. It occurred also because of the economic collapse of 1990–91. But the critical event was the rise of a new Russia under Yeltsin, and the ambitions of the Russian president, which led him to power – fuelled partly by bitterness at his past treatment by Gorbachev and his more hard-line associates, such as Ligachev. That it was a revolt from within rather than a civil conflict is also evident from the composition of the post-Soviet leaderships: all the newly independent states had former Communists as leaders. Some, such as Belarus's Alyaksander Lukashenka (elected in July 1994) openly bemoaned the collapse of the Soviet Union as an 'act of treachery.' Others, such as some of the Central Asian leaders, came to power in the late 1980s and remain in office at the time of writing. As a Ukrainian government official commented to me in Kyiv in the summer of 2003, perhaps rhetorically: 'The main question [concerning 1991] is how all the Communist leaders were converted into nationalists.' They became nationalists because it became expedient for them to do so and in order to retain power despite the collapse of the Soviet state. The only leader who did not emerge from the ruling party structure, Georgia's Gamsakhurdia, was soon deposed as a power-hungry renegade.

Lastly, the legacy of Gorbachev is much debated. The former president's standing remains much higher outside his homeland than within. Communists regard him as the man who 'lost' the Soviet empire and destroyed the Soviet Union (they also consider Yeltsin in a similar light). Gorbachev, in retrospect, took on too many tasks and lacked long-term vision. Like all leaders he was somewhat egocentric, and in foreign policy, at least from a Soviet or Russian perspective, he may have conceded too much too quickly to the Western powers, particularly the United States. And yet, and as the memoirs of writers like David Remnick illustrate eloquently, the period of Perestroika was one of great hope and excitement in Russia, a time of the opening of society, investigation of the past, and a sincere attempt at making the Soviet Union a democratic state and one that was the focal point of a genuine federal Union. That it failed cannot be blamed entirely on Gorbachev, though he made perhaps more than his share of blunders. Ultimately, whereas he and his close associates maintained a somewhat blinkered vision of a Soviet future and coveted the achievements of the Soviet past, they were superseded by a narrower vision, economic mayhem, and the re-emergence of the new Russia. Ten years of confusion were to follow under the erratic leadership of Yeltsin. As Lenin also found, it was easier to take power than to rule.

PART FOUR   DOCUMENTS

The death of Konstantin U. Chernenko on 10 March 1985 marked the end of the rule of the Brezhnev 'Old Guard' in the Soviet Union. Rising to power through a role as Brezhnev's clerk, Chernenko was arguably the least effective of all Soviet leaders. The ritualistic wording of the Plenum of the party Central Committee was by now familiar to all Soviet citizens. Chernenko was the third Soviet leader to die in office since November 1982. Yet without much ado, the announcement of a new Soviet leader was included in the commemorative speech about Chernenko's life.

Information Report on the Plenum of the Central Committee of the Communist Party of the Soviet Union

On 11 March there was held an Extraordinary Plenum of the Central Committee of the Communist Party of the Soviet Union.

The Politburo of the CC entrusted Comrade M.S. Gorbachev to open the Plenum.

In connection with the passing away of the General Secretary of the CC CPSU, Chairman of the Presidium of the Supreme Soviet of the USSR, K.U. Chernenko, the Plenum's participants honoured the memory of Chernenko with a minute's silence.

The Plenum noted that the Communist Party of the Soviet Union, all the Soviet people mourned the tragic loss. The life has ended of one of the leading party and state activists, a patriot and an internationalist, an indefatigable fighter for the triumph of the ideals of Communism and peace on Earth.

To the very end, the entire life of Konstantin Ustinovich Chernenko was devoted to the Leninist party, to the interests of the Soviet people. . . .

K.U. Chernenko devoted much attention to the perfecting of developed socialism, to resolving the huge task of economic and social development, increasing the welfare and culture of the Soviet people, to the further rise of the creative activity of the masses, the improvement of ideological work, strengthening discipline, law, and order.

K.U. Chernenko provided a great example in the further development of multifaceted cooperation with the fraternal republics of socialism, the realization of socialist economic integration, the consolidation of the position of socialist partnership. Under his leadership, firmly and consistently were carried out the principles of peaceful co-existence with states of different social strata, was given a decisive rebuff to the aggressive designs of imperialism, was introduced a tireless struggle for . . . the elimination of the threat of nuclear war, for procuring the reliable safety of peoples.

As the apple of his eye, K.U. Chernenko maintained the unity of our Communist Party, the collective character of the activities of the Central

Committee and its Politburo. He always strived so that the party at all levels operated as a united, harmonious, and fighting organization. . . .

The Plenum underlined that in these sorrowful days, Communists, all Soviet people still more tightly gather around the Central Committee of the Party and its Politburo. . . .

The Plenum examined the question about the election of the General Secretary of the CC CPSU.

At the behest of the Politburo with a speech on this question spoke Politburo member A.A. Gromyko. He introduced a proposal to elect as General Secretary of the CC CPSU Comrade M.S. Gorbachev.

As General Secretary of the Central Committee of the CPSU, the Plenum unanimously elected M.S. Gorbachev.

Then at the Plenum spoke the General Secretary of the CC CPSU Comrade M.S. Gorbachev. He expressed profound gratitude for the faith shown in him by the Central Committee of the CPSU, and noted that he well understands the great responsibility of his position.

Pravda, 12 March 1985, p. 1.

DOCUMENT 2   **BIOGRAPHY OF THE NEW SOVIET LEADER**

As was traditional, Pravda *followed the announcement of a new leader with his biography. The passage indicates that Gorbachev's background provided little to suggest that a new type of leader had come to power or that great changes were in the offing.*

Mikhail Sergeevich Gorbachev

Mikhail Sergeevich Gorbachev was born on 2 March 1931 in the village of Privol'noe, Krasnogvardeisk Raion, Stavropol region into a peasant family.

Soon after the Great Patriotic War of 1941–45 at the age of 15 he began his toiling activities. He worked as a mechanic at a Machine Tractor Station. In 1952, he joined the Communist Party. In 1955, he completed Moscow State University ('Lomonosov', Law Faculty), and in 1967 – Stavropol Agricultural Institute with the speciality of an agricultural economist.

From 1955, M.S. Gorbachev was involved in both Komsomol and party work. He worked in the Stavropol region: as the First Secretary of the Stavropol City Committee of the VLKSM [Komsomol], deputy leader of the section of propaganda and agitation, and then Second and First Secretary of the regional Komsomol.

In March 1962, M.S. Gorbachev was advanced by the party organization of Stavropol territorial-production collective farm-state farm administration, and in December of this year approved as the leader of the section of party organs of the regional party committee.

In September 1966, he was elected First Secretary of the Stavropol City Committee of the party. From August 1968, M.S. Gorbachev worked as the Second Secretary, and in April 1970 he was elected the First Secretary of the Stavropol Regional Committee of the CPSU.

M.S. Gorbachev has been a member of the Central Committee CPSU since 1971. He was a delegate of the 22nd, 24th, 25th, and 26th congresses of the party. In 1978 he was elected a secretary of the CC CPSU, in 1979 a Candidate Member of the Politburo CC CPSU. In October 1980, M.S. Gorbachev was advanced from a Candidate to a full member of the Politburo CC CPSU. He was a deputy of the Supreme Soviet USSR, 8th–11th sessions, the chairman of the Commission on Foreign Affairs of the Council of the Union. He was a deputy of the Supreme Soviet of the RSFSR, 10th–11th sessions.

Mikhail Sergeevich Gorbachev is a noted activist of the Communist Party and Soviet state. In all posts entrusted to him by the party he has worked with initiative, energetically and selflessly transmitted his knowledge, the rich experience and organizational talent of bringing to life the policies of the party, wholeheartedly serves the great cause of Lenin, the interests of the working people.

For his service to the Communist Party and the Soviet state, M.S. Gorbachev has received three Orders of Lenin, orders of the October Revolution, the Toiling Red Banner, the 'Badge of Honour,' and medals.

Pravda, 12 March 1985, p. 1.

DOCUMENT 3 **GORBACHEV OUTLINES PERESTROIKA**

Gorbachev's Perestroika program appeared in 1986–87. He described it as less of a program than a collection of thoughts. The passage reveals his reverence of Lenin and also the nebulousness of the policy.

In the West, Lenin is often portrayed as an advocate of authoritarian methods of administration. This is a sign of total ignorance of Lenin's ideas and, not infrequently, of their deliberate distortion. In effect, according to Lenin, socialism and democracy are indivisible. By gaining democratic freedoms the working masses come to power. It is also only in conditions of expanding democracy that they can consolidate and realize that power. There is another remarkably true idea of Lenin's: the broader the scope of the work and the deeper the reform, the greater the need to increase the interest in it and convince millions and millions of people of its necessity. This means that if we have set out for a radical and all-round restructuring, we must also unfold the entire potential of democracy.

It is essential to learn to adjust policy in keeping with the way it is received by the masses, and to ensure feedback, absorbing the ideas, opinions, and advice coming from the people. The masses suggest a lot of useful and interesting things which are not always clearly perceived 'from the top.' That is why we must prevent at all costs an arrogant attitude to what people are saying. In the final account the most important thing for the success of perestroika is the people's attitude to it. . . .

Perestroika is the all-round intensification of the Soviet economy, the revival and development of the principles of democratic centralism in running the national economy, the universal introduction of economic methods, the renunciation of management by injunction and by administrative methods, and the overall encouragement of innovation and socialist enterprise. . . .

Perestroika means priority development of the social sphere aimed at ever better satisfaction of Soviet people's requirements for good living and working conditions, for good rest and recreation, education and health care. It means unceasing concern for cultural and spiritual wealth, for the culture of every individual and society as a whole.

Perestroika means the elimination from society of the distortions of socialist ethics, the consistent implementation of the principles of social justice. It means the unity of words and deeds, rights and duties. It is the elevation of honest, highly-qualified labor, the overcoming of leveling tendencies in pay and consumerism.

This is how we see Perestroika today. This is how we see our tasks, and the substance and content of our work for the forthcoming period. It is difficult to say how long that period will take. Of course, it will be much more than two or three years. We are ready for serious, strenuous and tedious work to ensure that our country reaches new heights by the end of the twentieth century.

We are often asked what we want of perestroika. What are our final goals? We can hardly give a detailed, exact, answer. It's not our way to engage in prophesying and trying to predestinate [sic!] all the architectural elements of the public building we will erect in the process of perestroika.

But in principle I can say that the end result of perestroika is clear to us. It is a thorough renewal of every aspect of Soviet life; it is giving socialism the most progressive forms of social organization; it is the fullest exposure of the humanist nature of our social system in its crucial aspects – economic, social, political and moral.

> Mikhail Gorbachev, *Perestroika: New Thinking for Our Country and the World.*
> New York: Harper & Row, 1987, pp. 18–19, 21–22.

DOCUMENT 4   **THE ANNOUNCEMENT OF THE DETAILS OF THE CHERNOBYL ACCIDENT**

The failure of the Soviet authorities to report in detail the immediate results of the Chernobyl disaster was one of the major reasons for the loss of faith in central control over the industrial resources of the republics. This terse statement was provided almost one week after the accident.

From the Council of Ministers of the USSR

Throughout the day on 30 April at the Chernobyl atomic power station, work has continued to realize complex technical measures.

Radioactivity on the territory of the station and in the immediate vicinity has been reduced by 1.5–2 times.

Work is being introduced to decontaminate polluted areas adjacent to the territory of the atomic power station.

Aid to the injured is continuing, including the 18 people who are in serious condition.

There are no foreign citizens among the injured.

Pravda, 2 May 1986, p. 2.

DOCUMENT 5   **POLITBURO LEADERS VISIT THE CHERNOBYL AREA**

Prior to the arrival of Politburo members Ryzhkov and Ligachev, the local authorities at Chernobyl had evacuated a zone of only 10 kilometres' radius around the destroyed fourth reactor unit. The arrival of two very senior members of the Politburo (the Prime Minister and the Secretary for Ideology) was an indicator of the seriousness of the accident, though it was surprising to some that Gorbachev himself did not visit Chernobyl. Though the zone of evacuation was extended to 30 kilometres thereafter, the tone of the official reports remained constant, assuring readers that the accident had basically been contained.

Evacuation of the Region of the Chernobyl Atomic Power Station

On the 2 May, member of the Politburo CC CPSU, Chairman of the Council of Ministers of the USSR N.I. Ryzhkov and member of the Politburo CC CPSU, secretary of the CC CPSU, E.K. Ligachev visited the region of the Chernobyl atomic power station. Together with the Government Commission, leaders of the CC of the Communist Party of Ukraine and the government of the Ukrainian SSR, party and Soviet organs of Kyiv Oblast and the town of Chernobyl measures for the liquidation of the effects of the accident at the fourth power unit of the AES, normalization of the situation in the adjacent rayon, and the provision of aid to the local population were introduced.

It was noted that work for the liquidation of the accident and the elimination of its consequences is being carried out in an organizational manner with the application of the necessary means. A decision has been accepted about additional measures to accelerate the development of work.

Comrades N.I. Ryzhkov and E.K. Ligachev visited settlements to meet with workers temporarily evacuated from the region of the AES, took interest in the organization of their welfare, supply, and medical services, schools and kindergartens.

In the visit took part member of the Politburo of the CC CPSU, First Secretary of the Communist Party of Ukraine, V.V. Shcherbitsky, Chairman of the Government Commission, Deputy Chairman of the Council of Ministers USSR, B.E. Shcherbina, Chairman of the Council of Ministers of the Ukrainian SSR, A.P. Lyashko, and the First Secretary of the Kyiv Oblast Committee of the CPU, G.I. Revenko.

(TASS)

Pravda, 4 May 1986, p. 2.

DOCUMENT 6   **SOVIETS DENOUNCE THE US PROGRAM OF SDI**

The Strategic Defence Initiative of the United States (the so-called Star Wars program) proved to be the stumbling block in relations between the United States and the Soviet Union in the early years of Gorbachev. This excerpt illustrates the deep divisions between the two sides and is a good example of the sort of Cold War rhetoric emanating from Moscow in early 1987.

'In A Hurry.'

In a speech at the National Press Club in Washington a few days ago, Defense Secretary Caspar Weinberger pushed strongly for the earliest possible deployment of space weapons by the United States.

Earlier, reports the Washington Post, the head of the Pentagon and his trustiest subordinates, including General G. Abrahamson, who heads the SDI programme, and Assistant Secretary R. Perle, held a kind of seminar in the White House for President Reagan. With the help of schematic drawings and diagrams, they attempted to prove to the President that an 'initial' system of space weapons could be deployed as early as 1994.

The 'star wars' supporters were clearly in a hurry. Pentagon officials, arms manufacturers and ultraright-wing organizations have mounted a vigorous campaign in favor of 'crossing the Rubicon' more quickly – proceeding from research and design work in the area of space weapons to actually deploying such weapons in space.

Why the hurry? The answer to this question is provided by one of the pillars of the US extreme right, Attorney General Edwin Meese. SDI enthusiasts, he says, are in a hurry to move on to the practical implementation of their plans so that 'future administrations cannot destroy this programme.' That puts it quite candidly.

They are also hurrying because in the American Congress, where there was already serious opposition to the most militaristic aspects of administration policy, criticism of SDI has grown even further since the recent midterm elections, which gave the Democrats a victory. For SDI, to use the words of Democratic Senator Al Gore, is nothing but a formula for 'an even greater acceleration of the arms race and an end to any sort of sensible efforts in the area of arms control.'

It is difficult to disagree with such an opinion. A start on the deployment of space-system components will undermine the ABM Treaty and dash people's hopes for a reduction in strategic arms. It is common knowledge that it is Washington's stubborn unwillingness to confine work on SDI within laboratory walls that was one of the main obstacles to reaching the important decisions in Reykjavic that would have opened the way to a nuclear-free world. Yet another attempt by the Pentagon to stab the people's hopes in the back – that is the only way to describe the Washington hawks' efforts to impose on the US their plans for making an early start on the deployment of space weapons.

Gennady Vasilyev

> *Pravda*, 21 January 1987, p. 5, cited in *The Current Digest of the Soviet Press*,
> Vol. 34, No. 3 (1987): 14.

DOCUMENT 7   THE DENUNCIATION OF YELTSIN AT THE OCTOBER 1987 PLENUM

Maverick politician Boris Yeltsin offered a critique of Perestroika at the Central Committee Plenum in October 1987. Dismayed at what he termed 'the adulation of the General Secretary' and the machinations of Yegor Ligachev within the Politburo, Yeltsin announced his intention to resign from this ruling body. The response was a sustained attack on Yeltsin, then the party secretary for the city of Moscow, that had a profound and lasting impact on his political career.

When I was mentally assessing the situation, wondering what arguments would be advanced to refute my remarks, wondering who would speak, I imagined that no really big guns would be wheeled up and that nobody whom I regarded as a friend would attack me. But when it started in earnest – when, eyes ablaze, people came up to the rostrum who had long worked beside me, who were my friends, with whom I was on excellent terms – I found it extremely hard to bear their betrayal. I feel sure that these people are now ashamed to read the invective they hurled at me. But what's said is said and cannot be unsaid.

As speech followed speech, the tone became largely demagogic. They all added up more or less to the same message: Yeltsin is an expletive, a four-letter word. Words were repeated, epithets were repeated, labels were repeated. How I endured it, I don't know. . . .

On November 9, I was taken to the hospital with a severe headache and chest pains. I had suffered a physical breakdown. I was pumped full of medicines, mostly tranquillizers, which relaxed my nerves and muscles. The doctors forbade me to get out of bed and kept giving me drips and injections. . . .

Suddenly, on the morning of November 11, the telephone rang on my special Kremlin line, plugged into telephone exchange number 1. It was Gorbachev, and he spoke as if he were calling me not in the hospital but at my dacha. In a calm voice he said: 'You must come and see me for a short while, Boris Nikolayevich. After that, perhaps we will go and attend the plenum of the Moscow City Committee together.' I said I couldn't come because I was in bed and the doctors wouldn't let me get up. 'Don't worry,' he said cheerfully, 'The doctors will help you to get up.'

I shall never be able to understand that. In all my life I have never heard of anyone, whether a worker or a manager, being dragged out of a hospital bed to be dismissed. It is simply unheard-of. . . . However much Gorbachev may have disliked me, to act like that was inhuman and immoral. Why was he in such a hurry? I wondered. Was he afraid I might change my mind? [. . .]

I was thus barely conscious when I appeared at the Politburo. I was in the same condition when I arrived at the plenum of the City Committee. All its members were seated when the entire top brass of the party entered the hall and took their seats on the presidium, like a row of waxwork dummies, while the full complement of this plenary meeting stared back at them, as frightened and mesmerized as a rabbit looking at a boa constrictor.

What do you call it when a person is murdered with words? Because what followed was like a real murder. After all, I could have been dismissed in a sentence or two, then and there, at the plenum. But no; they had to enjoy the whole process of public betrayal, when comrades who had been working alongside me for two years, without the slightest sign of discord in our relations, suddenly began to say things that to this day my mind refuses to absorb.

Boris Yeltsin, *Against the Grain*. New York: Summit Books, 1990, pp. 195, 199, 200–201.

DOCUMENT 8   **PLENUM OF THE CPSU CENTRAL COMMITTEE, OCTOBER 1987**

The October 1987 plenary meeting was the first for which a stenographic record was published afterward. The following excerpt demonstrates further the isolation of Yeltsin and the limits of Glasnost at this time. It provides an example of both the collectivism of the leadership when faced with a challenge and the rigidity of outlook among prominent leaders. The speaker is Volodymyr Shcherbytsky, First Party Secretary of Ukraine.

Now what is it that Comrade Yeltsyn [sic] disagrees with? Either he disagrees in substance with the line toward *perestroika* and the evaluation of the state of affairs and the immediate tasks as outlined in this report. Or perhaps he is afraid of the difficulties to come. This too might well be the case. In short, I support all the comrades who spoke before me and summed up Comrade Yeltsyn's [sic] speech as being politically immature. I think the Moscow communists, the Moscow comrades present here at the Central Committee's plenary meeting, must likewise be disappointed with Comrade Yeltsyn's [sic] speech. And they must feel embarrassed for their secretary who, let us put it bluntly, put on such a bad show today. Maybe it was an ill-conceived step taken under some wrong impression . . . .

Now I cannot pass over Comrade Yeltsyn's [sic] erroneous statement to the effect that two years have passed and the results remain unfavorable, especially in the economy (he said nothing about the social sphere). Indeed, there are many difficulties, of which Mikhail Sergeyevich spoke and of which Nikolai Ivanovich Ryzhkov spoke at the Supreme Soviet session. But it is wrong to say that the tide of the people's mood, that is political enthusiasm, is ebbing. I agree with Comrade Murakhovsky, who called this sentiment defeatist. I don't think it applies to Moscow in any measure. And how can Comrade Yeltsyn [sic] know what the situation is like in other regions? Perhaps from Moscow News. (Laughter.) He has no other grounds for a statement like this. Further he says that if another two or three years pass – that is, what Mikhail Sergeyevich spoke about, and of course this is the optimal period, and it may last more or perhaps more can be done in less time, depending on how things go, this even depends on next year's harvest, not only on our work – then, Comrade Yeltsyn [sic] says, the party's prestige may even totter. I think that is a totally wrong, defeatist statement.

Regarding the people's attitude to *perestroika*, we know of it well. Alexander Yakovlevich Kolesnikov spoke of it today for the miners. And Mikhail Sergeyevich spelled out what needs to be done, how to do it, what difficulties lie ahead and what difficult tasks need to be accomplished. I think we all agree with him. (Applause.)

Political Archives of the Soviet Union, Vol. 1, No. 1 (1990): 112.

DOCUMENT 9 **GLASNOST IN THE MEDIA**

The following is an unpublished letter to the magazine Ogonyok, one of the pioneers of Glasnost. It is a fairly typical request for the media to spend less

time focusing on the problems of the past, and concentrate on current prob-
lems and improving the mood of the people. It illustrates the way in which
Glasnost helped to undermine the principles on which Soviet society was
based.

SMALL FIRES

Dear Editors:

Thanks to *glasnost*, the mass media have told us a great deal about the past.
We learned about the persecution of talented people, who either were victims
of repressions or were forced to emigrate abroad, but still remained patriots
of their country. We found out a lot about the genocide carried out by the
'Father of All Peoples,' about the significant mistakes made before and during
the Great Patriotic War, and the truth about the Afghanistan war. We learned
about environmental problems, although sometimes too late (the Chernobyl
tragedy, for example); we learned the truth about the poisoning of our food,
etc., etc. How could the mood of the people be good after all that?

M.S. Gorbachev, whenever he meets with the people, always asks this
question first: 'How is your mood, comrades?' And everybody always answers
in chorus: 'Good!' All that's missing is a 'hooray.'

It seems to me that people who really want the best for our country could
not talk that way. How am I supposed to be in a good mood if I find out
that my grandfather was a victim of the repressions and died and was then
posthumously rehabilitated; if my father ended up a disabled veteran of the
Great Patriotic War; if my children can't get competent medical care; if they
eat dirty food and breathe polluted air; if I am an assistant professor and my
working hours are twice as long as those of my Bulgarian colleagues, but my
salary lower; if after work I have to stand in line all the time for everything,
but I still have to remember that I am a woman too. If M.S. Gorbachev can be
critical of himself ('Yes, there were and will be mistakes under *perestroika*;
you cannot avoid them'), why must we deceive ourselves? We go to absolutely
absurd lengths with our lies. A peasant woman is asked (on the TV programme
'Glance'), 'What kinds of groceries do they sell in your stores!' Answer:
'Bread; it'd be nice to have a little sugar.' 'And do you think you are living
well?' Answer: 'Yes.' This raises the question: if we are living well, if our
mood is good, what more do we want?

This is what made me write to you. It is no accident that M.S. Gorbachev
always asks his question about the people's mood first. Any psychologist will
tell you that the people's mood is the engine of progress. It's good that the
door to the past has been opened. Thank you to the government for taking
this step and to the journalists who wrote the truth. But, unfortunately, after
reading and seeing all these things, normal people can't be in a good mood. I
think that even Mikhail Sergeyevich's mood isn't always good, because there

are plenty of obstacles in *perestroika*'s path. But he has faith, and that faith should be transmitted to the people. And, it seems to me, one of the most important tasks for the press now is to do all it can to change people's mood for the better, so that 'small fires' of hope for the future will ignite.

To accomplish this, I think less time should be spent on the *past*: much is already clear, journalists are already beginning to repeat themselves. More emphasis should be placed on those new buds – those which are offering something fresh and progressive – so that people will at least have the hope that in the future their grandchildren will be better off. Of course, it will be tough going for you journalists on this road; we Russians have one bad quality – saying no at first to everything new and progressive. But I think this is the tack that the press should take.

One of the most courageous peoples on earth, one of the most talented peoples on earth, should live better. We have earned that right!

L.A. Matokhnyuk
Kiev
Received by *Ogonyok*, May 15, 1989
Unpublished

> *Voices of Glasnost: Letters from the Soviet People to* Ogonyok *Magazine 1987–1990.*
> London: Kyle Cathie Ltd, 1990, pp. 269–71.

DOCUMENT 10   **KGB ON ACTIVITIES OF SAKHAROV**

The KGB under Kryuchkov constantly sent Gorbachev appraisals of the activities of organizations or individuals that it considered dangerous to the interests of the state. Sakharov was a favourite target.

To Comrade M.S. Gorbachev, CC CPSU:

About the political activities of A.D. Sakharov

The propagandistic support from abroad, the possibility to express his views publicly, the uncritical appraisal of the activities of A.D. Sakharov in the Soviet mass media have allowed him considerably to strengthen his authority among circles of the scientific and creative intelligentsia.

Though he gives a positive evaluation of the ideas of Perestroika, he has not changed his entirely negative attitude to the experience of socialist construction in our country. . . .

V. Kryuchkov,
Chairman, KGB

8 December 1989, No. 2482-K/OV.

DOCUMENT 11   THE EMERGENCE OF THE NAGORNO-KARABAKH CRISIS

Nagorno-Karabakh was the first major issue to confront Gorbachev in the area of national policy. Gradually it developed into a major conflict between two significant parts of the southern Caucasus, Azerbaijan and Armenia and led to serious disturbances in the major towns: Yerevan, Baku, and Sumgait. The Soviet failure to respond adequately to the new crisis only exacerbated problems in the national republics.

APPEAL BY THE AZERBAIJAN COMMUNIST PARTY CENTRAL COMMITTEE, THE PRESIDIUM OF THE AZERBAIJAN REPUBLIC SUPREME SOVIET AND THE AZERBAIJAN COUNCIL OF MINISTERS.

Dear Comrades!

The situation that has arisen dictates the need for a new appeal to you. . . .

In recent days, the situation [regarding Nagorno-Karabakh] has again begun to foment; rumors and various kinds of speculation have become more frequent, engendering unhealthy attitudes and hampering further normalization of the situation in our republic. On May 16, a rally of young people, higher-school students and representatives of the intelligentsia was held in Baku. The people who gathered were given an attentive hearing by members of the Bureau of the Azerbaijan Communist Party Central Committee.

We understand and sympathize with people's natural uneasiness, their desire to know more about the situation evolving in Nagorno-Karabakh, our republic and the Armenian Republic, and to get answers to the questions disturbing them. But this must not occur in an atmosphere of nervousness or keyed-up emotions, nor through 'rally-style democracy'; these are fraught, as we have all seen, with unpredictable consequences. The questions posed by the rally participants have been reviewed carefully. Immediate action will be taken on several of them. But it must be kept in mind that some questions were posed whose solution requires thorough study and a certain amount of time.

The present anxiousness among some of the population has been caused, in particular, by events that took place in certain towns in the Ararat District of the Armenian Republic on May 11, where incidents occurred among local inhabitants. There were injuries, but no deaths. Party and Soviet agencies are taking steps to normalize the situation. The USSR Prosecutor's Office is conducting an investigation of each of the incidents. You may rest assured that the guilty parties will be found and called to account to the full extent of the law. . . .

Bakinsky Rabochy, 18 May 1988. Cited in *Current Digest of the Soviet Press*, Vol. XL, No. 23, 1988.

The unprovoked attack of the Soviet military on a demonstration in Tblisi might be considered a turning point in the relationship between the Moscow government and the republics. Gorbachev officially denied any knowledge of the event. In this document, Defence Minister Dmitry Yazov is at pains to point out that General Rodionov and General Kochetov's decision to inter-vene – and with such disastrous consequences – was taken by the Communist Party of Georgia.

'A Military Coup is Impossible: Defence Minister D. Yazov answers questions.'

On June 3, film makers met General of the Army, Dmitry Yazov.

After a short opening address the Minister answered questions about the April 9 tragedy in Tblisi. Dmitry Yazov noted that he knew Transcaucasia well since he had served there. He felt he didn't have the right to assess anyone's action while investigations were going on and a commission of deputies was being set up. 'Anything I say to justify or accuse someone,' said the Minister, 'will lose its significance if [the] commission comes to a differ-ent conclusion.' But he pointed out that the investigation was not the final instance and that the verdict may be pronounced only by the court.

Yazov also said that he had received several telegrams from Patiashvili (former First Secretary of the Communist Party of Georgia), including one dated April 7, with a request to impose a curfew. 'I answered that I wasn't authorized to settle that issue and told them to decide for themselves . . .'. But, for a curfew, troops are needed. The 328th Regiment back from Afghanistan was sent to Tblisi. Its main task was to guard the Government House, post, telegraphs, and the prison in Rustavi.

Regarding the use of gas, the General of the Army said it was established that none of the dead was a victim of poisoning. Samples were taken from the walls of schools, he said, and a substance was detected resembling chlorofoss, which is used in preparations against cockroaches. There are no such sub-stances in Cheryomukha, he said. Present in the hall was an expert from the Military Medical Academy who could have answered in greater detail. But the Minister suggested that passions should not be flared and that we should wait for the results of the commission. The hall didn't insist.

When asked how General of the Army Kochetov turned up in Georgia, Yazov explained that Kochetov was on an inspection mission in Leninakan, where his army is building 18 houses and two schools. When passions were running high in Georgia, he went to Tblisi at the Minister's request to 'help Rodionov look into the matter.'

To the question whether General Rodionov was directly subordinated to the Central Committee of the Communist Party of Georgia, D. Yazov replied that he is a member of the Bureau of the Georgian Central Committee. 'The decision to clear the square was passed by the Central Committee of the Communist Party of Georgia, said the Minister. "I didn't give any command," the Minister declared. The decision to impose a curfew was passed by us at noon on April 9.'

Natalya Gevorkyan.

Moscow News, No. 24, 11 June 1989, p. 2.

DOCUMENT 13   THE LITHUANIAN QUESTION

Of all the problems facing the Soviet Union in the nationalities sphere, Lithuania was the most pressing. The growing rift between Moscow and supporters of Lithuanian independence is evident here, along with a lack of comprehension for such sentiments in the Soviet leadership.

Many a dramatic page in Russian history has been linked to Lithuania. Recent history has been no exception. On Lithuanian territory, many of the issues affecting the future of the whole country were first put to the test. It was a battle for people's hearts and minds. . . .

Besides the political arguments there were possibly weightier practical ones. . . . [But] not a word was said about the considerable privileges granted for political reasons to the Baltic States by the Soviet government since the initial post-war years. Thanks to these privileges and, of course, to greater productivity, their standard of living had always been higher than in other regions of the Union. Few people have given serious thought to that balance. Listening to the speeches of the Sajudis propagandists, not only Lithuanians but people of other nationalities living in Lithuania were fired by the idea that they would live much better once they had shaken off the obligation to 'pay tribute' to Moscow. . . .

I considered it of the utmost importance to understand what was going on in Lithuania and to see whether those who favored complete secession could be persuaded to change their minds. In January 1990 I undertook a fact-finding trip there, on which I was accompanied by the chief editor of *Pravda*, Frolov, who had by then been elected a Central Committee secretary. At Vilnius Airport we were met by Brazauskas and Burokavicius, Central Committee secretary of the Communist Party of Lithuania 'based on the CPSU platform', as well as other officials. The details of that journey are engraved in my memory. We were met everywhere with friendliness and good-will, but virtually from my initial talks with the population of the Lithuanian capital on Lenin Square to the moment of my departure, the sole topic of discussion was the secession of Lithuania from the USSR. . . .

At a factory where the work-force consisted of 30 per cent Lithuanians, about the same percentage of Poles, 20 per cent Russians, Belorussians, etc., all these arguments were, I believe correctly understood. It was also comparatively easy to arrive at a mutual understanding in talks with the peasants, whose down-to-earth common sense enabled them to visualize the adverse consequences of a break with Russia.

It was a different matter altogether with the artistic and academic intelligentsia I met at the Vilnius Press House. There, I am afraid, I was unable to make any contact with my listeners, since most of them were adamant supporters of secession. Before and after that meeting I had repeated encounters with educated, well-disposed people, tolerant by nature, who nonetheless failed to respond to the most weighty and irrefutable arguments because they were obsessed by a fanatical determination to act in accordance with what had become their creed.

Mikhail Gorbachev, *Memoirs*. New York: Doubleday, 1995, pp. 571–3.

DOCUMENT 14   **THE DEBATE ON THE UNIFICATION OF GERMANY**

The discussion of whether a unified Germany should be a member of NATO, the Warsaw Pact or refrain from joining either association reflected the declining position of the Soviet Union in world affairs. As this extract demonstrates, Gorbachev was in no position to counter the suggestions of US president George Bush and ultimately supported the American position unequivocally. It might be recalled that the ostensible reason for the formation of the Warsaw Pact in 1955 was West Germany's entry into NATO.

Gorbachev summarized the steps behind our 'concept' for Germany as follows:

- 'Yes, a sextet.' We'll focus on Kohl, but without ignoring the SPD [the German Socialist Party of West Germany – DRM]. Invite Modrow and Gysi [Gregor Gysi, the new Chairman of the German Socialist Unity Party, the SED – DRM].
- Forge closer relations with London and Paris. ('Maybe I'll go there myself just on account of this issue, spending a day in each capital.')
- Have Akhromeyev [Sergey F. Akhromeyev, chief of the general staff of the USSR – DRM] prepare for the withdrawal of our troops from the GDR ('This is more a domestic than foreign issue; we have 300,000 there, of whom over 100,000 are officers with families that we have to find some place for!')

But the concept that we thought we'd agreed upon – one that proceeded from a recognition of the inevitability of German reunification – wasn't easily realized. In early May, when Shevardnadze was getting ready for the first meeting of the '2 + 4,' there was a very heated discussion at the Politburo.

Gorbachev made a speech whose central point was that there was absolutely no way we could let a reunified Germany be in NATO. 'I'll even go so far as breaking off the Vienna talks as well as those on Strategic Nuclear Forces,' he said, 'but I won't let this happen.'

A milder position paper had already been signed by Shevardnadze, Yakovlev, Kryuchkov, and others. But at the Politburo, except for Shevardnadze they all kept quiet. And my opinion wasn't solicited there. The next morning I wrote a memo to Gorbachev. My main point was to ask how some Politburo members – lacking information on matters outside their particular area of expertise, and not even aware of the latest developments – still discuss and decide such a critical issue? As a result of this, their understanding of the German issue had been shaped by Ligachev's shout: 'NATO is nearing our borders!' This is nonsense. It's reasoning from the mentality of 1945. It's the false patriotism of a mob. Germany will be in NATO anyway, and again we'll find ourselves trying to catch up with the train after it's left the station. Instead of outlining our conditions for agreement in a concrete and determined manner, we're asking for failure. And from the results of the first '2 + 4' meeting – where Shevardnadze had to fall back on vague generalities – it became clear that we lost by refusing to sign the document that had been rejected at the above-mentioned Politburo meeting.

Kohl and Baker were quick to take advantage of it. They declared the '2 + 4' meeting 'historical,' after which 'there will be no obstacles to unification' (Kohl's words). Moreover, the press depicted Shevardnadze as attempting to separate the European process from that of Germany's reunification. Gorbachev tried to 'catch up with the train' during his visit to the United States in late May. The German question was discussed a number of times, and not without tension. Bush even stated once: 'We have a fundamental disagreement here.' Gorbachev was insisting that Germany should be in NATO and the Warsaw Pact at the same time. Bush considered this unacceptable. Then they found a compromise formula, and I quote from their conversation of May 31:

> *Gorbachev:* Then let's word it as follows. The United States and the Soviet Union support a unified Germany deciding for itself which alliance it will be a member of – taking into account the results of the Second World War – prior to concluding an overall, final agreement.
>
> *Bush:* I would suggest a slightly different version. The United States expresses unqualified support for the membership of a unified Germany in NATO. However, if Germany itself makes a different choice, we'll respect that and not raise any objections.
>
> *Gorbachev:* I agree. I accept your formulation.

Anatoly Chernyaev, *My Six Years with Gorbachev*, translated and edited by
Robert English and Elizabeth Tucker. University Park, Pennsylvania:
The Pennsylvania State University Press, 2000, pp. 272–3.

DOCUMENT 15   THE PRESIDENTIAL COUNCIL

The short-lived presidential council was an unsuccessful effort to replace the
Politburo. Its demise was a result in part of the hierarchical leadership style of
Gorbachev and resulted in the departure of some of the leading figures of
Perestroika.

The transformation of the party's general secretary into the president of the
USSR was not a smooth process. His management style, and many of the
methods and habits he had acquired over many years as party secretary in
Stavropol and Moscow, followed him into the office of chief executive. He
needed some kind of structure similar to the Politburo, in which he could
make statements, issue orders, and consider issues requiring his attention,
particularly legislation on national problems. Apparently Yakovlev suggested this idea, which, falling like a seed on fertile soil, did not take long to
germinate, resulting in the creation of the Presidential Council. The new
body included government representatives and prominent citizens – Chingiz
Aitmatov, Nikolai Ryzhkov, V. Yarin, Aleksandr Yakovlev, Valentin Rasputin,
Stanislav Shatalin, V. Medvedev, and several others, including me.

The council was a good idea, but there was a slightly amateurish air about
it. The Soviet Constitution made no provision for such a body, its size and
composition being determined by the president. It had no well-defined func-
tions. It met five or seven times, considering various current issues, including
problems posed by the conversion of military industries and economic affairs.
Neither the qualifications nor the status of its members were commensurate
with the gravity of the problems at hand. In any case, it was by now futile to
offer Gorbachev advice of any sort, as he did not need it. The council's
meetings were therefore irregular and ill organized. The president found that
convening the council's meetings was a chore that soon turned into a nuisance.
This was especially true of the meeting at which he invited members to
comment on the situation in the country. For the first time, they felt needed
and able to offer their own assessments and propose their own solutions.

Gorbachev was quite taken aback by what he heard. Yarin, Rasputin, and
various others found that the people had grown tired of experiments, vacilla-
tion, and idle chatter. In most of them the word perestroika produced a
nauseous allergic reaction, as they felt a worthy cause had been spoiled and
reduced to nonsense. When I saw Gorbachev's complexion turning livid, I
knew there was trouble in the offing. Without giving the floor to all the remaining speakers, he adjourned the meeting, and was in no hurry to reconvene it.

Pacing nervously up and down his office, Gorbachev said, 'What a load of
rubbish! And these are people I trusted; I plucked them out of nowhere. And
Yarin, of all people! Though I hardly expected anything else of Valentin
Rasputin.'

The fate of the Presidential Council was sealed. In November 1990, eight months after its creation, it was disbanded. Various explanations are possible. Gorbachev may have realized its futility, or may have been unhappy with its composition; alternatively he may have been influenced by criticism from the national Supreme Soviet, whose deputies viewed it as a fount of inanity and inertia. The final decision was made so abruptly that the council's members had no advance warning of their dismissal. I knew that many of them found such high-handedness deeply offensive.

Valery Boldin, *Ten Years That Shook the World*. New York: Basic Books, 1994, pp. 254–5.

DOCUMENT 16   THE EMERGENCY COMMITTEE APPEALS TO THE SOVIET PEOPLE

The failed putsch of 19–21 August is regarded by most observers as a critical event in the fall of the Soviet Union. After taking control of the country, a State Committee for the Extraordinary Situation in the USSR was established led by Vice-President Gennady Yanayev, and based on the fiction that Gorbachev had fallen ill and was no longer able to lead the country. The address to the Soviet people highlights the official reasons why the committee decided to take control of the country.

State Committee for the State of Emergency in the USSR, 'Appeal to the Soviet People' (18 August)

Compatriots! Citizens of the Soviet Union!

In a dark and critical hour for the destiny of our country and of our peoples, we address you! A mortal danger hangs over our great homeland! The policy of reform initiated by M.S. Gorbachev, conceived as a means to ensure the dynamic development of the country and the democratization of the life of its society, has, for a number of reasons, come to a dead end. The original enthusiasm and hopes have been replaced by a lack of belief, apathy, and despair. Authority at all levels has lost the confidence of the population. Politicking has left no room in public life for concern for the fate of our country and of the citizen. Malicious mockery of all the institutions of the state is being implanted. The country in effect has become ungovernable.

Taking advantage of the freedoms that have been granted, trampling on the shoots of democracy that have only just appeared, extremist forces emerged that adopted a course of destroying the Soviet Union, seeking the collapse of the state, and aiming to seize power at all costs. They scorned the results of the nationwide referendum on the unity of the homeland. Cynical profiteering on national feelings was only a screen for the satisfaction of ambition. Neither the present misfortunes of their peoples nor the future of those peoples concerns the political adventurists. . . .

The crisis of power has had a catastrophic effect on the economy. The chaotic and uncontrolled slide toward the market has aroused an explosion of egoism – regional, departmental, group and individual. The war of laws and the encouragement of centrifugal trends has meant the destruction of the unified machinery of the national economy which has taken decades to evolve. The result has been a sharp decline in the standard of living of the great majority of Soviet people and the flourishing of speculation and the black economy. It is high time to tell people the truth. Unless we take urgent and resolute measures to stabilize the economy, we shall inevitably face, in the very nearest future, famine and a new turn of the spiral of impoverishment, from which it is but a single step to mass manifestations of spontaneous discontent, with devastating consequences. Only irresponsible people can put their hope in some sort of help from abroad. No handouts will solve our problems; our salvation is in our own hands. The time has come to measure the prestige of each person or organization by their real contribution to the recovery and development of the national economy. . . .

We intend to restore without delay, legality, law and order, to put an end to bloodshed, to declare a merciless war on the criminal world, and to root out shameful manifestations which discredit our society and humiliate Soviet citizens. . . .

We appeal to all genuine patriots, people of good will to put an end to the current time of troubles. We appeal to all citizens of the Soviet Union to recognize their duty before the motherland and extend all possible support to the State Committee on the State of Emergency in the USSR and efforts to lead the country out of the crisis.

'Obrashchenie k sovetskomu narodu,' *Sovetskaya Rossiya*, 20 August 1991, p. 1, cited in J.L. Black (ed.), *USSR Documents Annual 1991. Volume 2: Disintegration of the USSR*. Gulf Breeze, Florida: Academic International Press, 1993, pp. 176–9.

DOCUMENT 17   **THE GORBACHEV ENIGMA**

One of the most critical analysts of Mikhail Gorbachev's behaviour during the August Putsch and the last weeks of the Soviet Union analyzes the fall of the Soviet Union.

The failed coup also signaled the political demise of Mikhail Gorbachev, although it took four months for this to become fully apparent. Gorbachev, of course, had been consistently losing power to Yeltsin and to the heads of the other newly 'sovereign' republics throughout 1990 and 1991, but the failed putsch literally tore power out of his hands. Why should this have been so? First, there was the self-evident fact that the leading figures of the GKChP [Emergency Committee] had been his 'team.' In the words of writer Tat'yana

Tolstaya, Gorbachev 'chose each of these scoundrels the way one chooses melons at a market . . .' Even Gorbachev's eloquent defender Aleksandr Yakovlev had felt required to point out in an interview that much of the blame for the coup lay with Gorbachev for choosing 'a team of traitors.'

When pressed by journalists to explain why he had handpicked precisely these men to be members of his team, Gorbachev replied vaguely that 'there are stages in the development of *perestroika.*' What he meant, presumably, was that he could not outrun history; he needed a 'right-centrist' team to satisfy or keep at bay the powerful conservative forces in the USSR, in order that he could cautiously plot a 'left-centrist' course of reform. Or as one of his top aides, in an allusion to an oft-quoted dictum of American president Lyndon Johnson, pungently put it: 'Mikhail Sergeevich felt it was better to have the camels inside the tent pissing out than outside the tent pissing in. He wanted to keep them where he could see them and while they would have to take his orders. He also wanted them to put pressure on the Balts.'

This complex and risky strategy proved to be Gorbachev's undoing. He apparently thought that he could manipulate the right-centrist team he had assembled in order to placate the political right while, at the same time, using its members to 'put pressure on the Balts' and other secessionist elements, and on the 'democrats' as well. But Gorbachev's team, understandably, came to resent this manipulative game and, being authentic Soviet conservatives, they abhorred his tacks to the political 'left,' and especially . . . his decision to push for a new union treaty that would have devolved major power to the republics. . . .

There was also a discernible element of hypocrisy in Gorbachev's attitude toward the activities of his team. . . . It is not credible that Gorbachev was unaware of the 'bloody affairs' – such as the January crackdown in the Baltic – that Kryuchkov, Pugo, and other members of his national security command were involved in. The truth seems to be that Gorbachev 'did not want to know' the sordid methods by which his team was attempting to implement his policy of holding the Soviet Union together. That hypocritical stance undoubtedly filled Kryuchkov, Pugo, and Yazov with scorn for their titular leader; it also, of course, provided them with immense political clout from which to attempt to scuttle the country's progression toward democracy.

John B. Dunlop, *The Rise of Russia and the Fall of the Soviet Empire*. Princeton,
New Jersey: Princeton University Press, 1993, pp. 267–8.

DOCUMENT 18   **THE GORBACHEV ENIGMA II**

A biography of Gorbachev offers the interesting conclusion that people knew little about the real personality of Gorbachev because the Soviet leader preferred not to reveal it to the public. Instead observers saw only different images of a charismatic leader. The passage provides an interesting contrast to the previous document.

The eyes. Everyone is struck by the gleam that blazes behind his dark eyes. Presidents, Sovietologists, resident CIA psychologists, Wall Street dealmakers – all have come away from face-to-face meetings with Mikhail Gorbachev talking about some strange chemical reaction, as if with the intensity of his belief he had burned his image of a new world onto their own retinas and they will never be quite the same.

'His eyes are dark but the gleam is so hot, he conveys an intensity that is slightly abnormal,' I was told several years ago by a senior intelligence analyst who studied the Soviet leader up close at the first Washington summit. 'It's as though his temperature is a little higher than normal, and he's running a little faster than anybody else.' . . .

The eyes of Gorbachev burn with the fever of a man who sees his own world upside down, a leader who is undergoing a revolutionary transformation of vision. Where almost every world leader since the beginning of history has based his authority on military power or performance, Gorbachev dared to try to fashion a new style of leadership, ruling out the use of force, and lifting the cloud of nuclear dread under which billions of people walked around every day. Where every previous Soviet leader saw the necessity of closedness [sic], he saw the advantage of openness. Single-handedly, he transformed the image of the Soviet Union in the eyes of the world from a dangerous expansionist bear to a sympathetic if competitive partner with the courage to lead the world out of the cold war era. That is the Gorbachev we know, Gorbachev the statesman.

But about Gorbachev the man, we know almost nothing.

Oh, yes, we have seen him so often on our TV in the West, perhaps even *been seen* by him as he plunged through the streets of our own city, that we as Americans or Europeans have come to think of him as familiar, one of ours. We have given our hearts and minds over to the belief that Mikhail Gorbachev is perhaps the last real leader, and one many Americans and Europeans would prefer to our own! We are so hungry for heroes, so swept away by the peaceful revolutionary changes in Europe, that we are naturally resistant to hearing anything about this wonder man to suggest he has anything other than moral motives. As a result, Gorbachev is the first Soviet leader to be a cult figure in the West even as he became a fallen icon at home.

But did we ever really know Mikhail Gorbachev? [There] is good reason that we don't know anything about him. He wants it that way. Only if he is perceived to be somehow magically free of mortal flaws and tics and failings can a leader play God.

Gail Sheehy, *The Man Who Changed the World*.
New York: HarperCollins, 1990, pp. 3–4.

DOCUMENT 19 CONSEQUENCES OF THE BELAVEZHA
MEETING

*On 8 December, the leaders of Russia, Ukraine, and Belarus held a secret
meeting at a hunting lodge in the Brest region of Belarus to come up with
a formula to end the Soviet Union and the role of Gorbachev as Soviet
president. The result was the Commonwealth of Independent States which,
the organizers insisted, was a legal formation that ended the original 1922
agreement to found the Soviet Union – the three states all being signatories
of that agreement. The legal foundations of the agreement continue to be
debated. Neither the relative parliaments nor the leaders of other republics –
let alone Gorbachev – had been consulted beforehand.*

[Russian philosopher A.P. Butenko] is correct when he says that the Union
was broken up in order to remove a deeply disappointing president. Not a
single politician who signed the treaty creating the CIS will ever agree with
that opinion, because to agree would pass sentence upon themselves. With
one or two exceptions, these leaders did not want to see the Union break up.
But nobody had the strength to oppose the process that was under way, while
some people's anti-Gorbachev feelings overwhelmed the others, including
their attitude to the state. This is the simple truth – simple for the politicians,
but what was it like for the people?

In twentieth-century Russia there have been three leaders who were
lawyers – Kerensky, Lenin and Gorbachev. Paradoxically, these were also the
three men who placed the prospect of revolutionary reforms above the law.
Historians can produce many examples of such moves by Kerensky and
Lenin, but Gorbachev also appealed more than once for action in support of
Perestroika contrary to the law, when the laws did not fit in with the interests
of transforming the country. Moreover, while he threatened to use his powers
to defend the Constitution, he certainly did not always do what was necessary
for this defense.

It is not a question of whether the Constitution was a good one, or whether
the laws were good or bad. The truth was that they either had to be observed
or changed in good time.

There is something ominous in the unconstitutional way Gorbachev was
removed. Ominous and logical. I know how it happened, the actual procedure,
from eye-witnesses who saw almost everything. I shall say only one thing here
– it is difficult to imagine a more humiliating act at such a political level.
If I had not been a witness of similar things I would not believe it.

Vladimir K. Yegorov, *Out of a Dead End Into the Unknown:
Notes on Gorbachev's Perestroika*, translated by David Floyd.
Chicago: Edition Q, 1993, pp. 143–4.

KRYUCHKOV'S RESPONSIBILITY FOR THE FALL OF THE USSR

Among the possible causes of the collapse of the Soviet Union, the failed putsch of August 1991 is perhaps most frequently cited. Several analysts perceive the role of KGB chief Kryuchkov in this event as crucial, and thus that he above all other figures might be the person most responsible for the dissolution of the USSR. Here is one such version.

If I were to reply to the question I posed to Russian politicians regarding the person most responsible for the collapse of the Soviet Union, my answer would be Vladimir Kryuchkov.

He was the organizer of the August 1991 attempt to seize power that accelerated the disintegration and thus made it much more difficult to create a voluntary federation of at least part of the empire. No credible attempt to overthrow Gorbachev could have been mounted without the support of the KGB chief – which is one of the reasons Gorbachev failed to anticipate the movement against him. His trust in Kryuchkov's loyalty was as complete as it was misplaced.

Kryuchkov's betrayal of his president would itself justify considering him the most immediate wrecker of the Soviet Union, but his claim to the title rests on more than that act alone.

He consistently failed in his primary duty to supply Gorbachev with accurate intelligence. His reports were deliberately skewed to promote the particular policies he favored. Furthermore, he resorted to outright lies to undermine Gorbachev's trust in colleagues who did not support his views. He bears a heavy responsibility for Gorbachev's failure to recognize the strength of nationalist sentiment and the rapid growth of public hatred for the Communist Party. His shrill alarums over nonexistent foreign interference, while perhaps useful in maintaining a bloated intelligence budget, deflected attention from the real problems the Soviet Union faced, while the 'solutions' he favored were certain to exacerbate them. . . .

People do make a difference, and Vladimir Kryuchkov made a big difference. The Soviet Union might exist in some modified form today if another person had been running the KGB in 1990 and 1991.

Jack F. Matlock, Jr, *Autopsy of an Empire: The American Ambassador's Account of the Collapse of the Soviet Union*. New York: Random House, 1995, pp. 666–8.

DOCUMENT 21   **THE VIEW OF GORBACHEV'S PERSONAL ASSISTANT**

Valery Boldin was Gorbachev's personal assistant, but betrayed his leader in the days of the August coup. His memoirs indicate why he lost faith in

*Gorbachev and offer a very personal view of the collapse of the Soviet Union.
It may be described both as the view of a faithful Communist and a man who
saw the situation in very Russo-centric terms.*

The Communist Party was the most highly organized force in society, with
significant representation of the intelligentsia, workers, peasants, and the
military and technological elite. It had set in motion the restructuring of all
spheres of society known as perestroika, and was the only organized force
capable of carrying it to its logical conclusion with the least pain. Many of its
senior officials are still in the forefront of the reform movement. Yet the party
was discredited because of the mistakes of its past leaders and essentially shut
out of the creative processes under way in society. Gorbachev's own efforts
were a contributing factor. His failure to unite the party behind his leadership,
coupled with the erosion of his authority among rank-and-file Communists,
led to the destruction of that organization.

The same happened with the army. The psychological attack that began
at the first session of the Congress of People's Deputies lasted for four years.
As a result, people in military uniform were physically and morally abused
and mocked. . . . The president of the Soviet Union and commander-in-chief
of its armed forces failed in his duty to protect the army. In fact, he feared and
distrusted the army and devoted considerable efforts to weakening it and
undermining its authority. He treated the organs of the KGB the same way,
refusing even to meet with them.

It was not long before Gorbachev lost his influence among writers, journalists, and academics. The limited scope of his ideas, his passion for speech
making, television appearances, and publishing articles and books at home
and abroad, and above all his inability to act, caused the intelligentsia to
desert the ranks of his supporters. Some simply lost all interest in him, while
others became his fierce adversaries. . . .

The term 'victory in the cold war' is hardly strong enough to convey the
truth about what really happened. It was not just a victory: it was a total rout
of the disorganized units of the USSR and the moral devastation of a once
powerful adversary. But this rout was not the work of American military and
technological might, nor of its strategic genius. It resulted from the internal
capitulation of those forces opposed to the structure in place in our country.

Beyond a doubt, Gorbachev's coming to power, the notion of perestroika,
and the desire for socio-economic reforms were progressive undertakings. The
trouble was that they failed to allow for the real state of society; nor did they
have a sound theoretical or organizational basis. The idea of shifting to
market relations, for example, was not raised until 1989–90, when it was
proposed that the transition be completed in a fantastically short time. . . .

Gorbachev did not understand that, in a vast territory stretching from Bug
to the Kuriles, from Taimyr to Kushka, it was impossible to transform the

psychology of the people overnight in one huge market-oriented melting pot, while ignoring their own peculiar ways and traditions. The general secretary had obviously learned little from his efforts to leapfrog over the system formed over the previous few decades: as a result, the country began to burst at the seams from an overload of ideas and schemes, before falling apart in tiny pieces.

Valery Boldin, *Ten Years That Shook the World*, translated by Evelyn Rossiter.
New York: Basic Books, 1994, pp. 294–6.

GLOSSARY

1 + 9 Agreement   This was Gorbachev's attempt to produce a revised formulation for the Soviet Union and allow considerable autonomy to the republics. The 1 refers to the USSR and the 9 to those republics that agreed to participate in revising the Union agreement following an all-Union referendum in March 1991.

500 Days program   An economic reform program designed to transform the Soviet Union into a market economy in 500 days. Originally advanced as a platform for the Russian Federation, it was co-opted for the Soviet Union as a whole, but ultimately rejected by Mikhail Gorbachev and his Prime Minister Valentin Pavlov.

Belarusian Popular Front   A political party formed in the late Soviet period under very difficult circumstances. Unlike Popular Fronts elsewhere in the USSR, the Belarusian version was forced to hold its founding congress in Vilnius, Lithuania. Led by Zyanon Paznyak, the Front played an important role in alerting the public to Stalin's crimes, the aftermath of Chernobyl, and the plight of the Belarusian language and culture.

Brezhnev Doctrine   A policy introduced in 1968 whereby the Soviet Union (and Soviet bloc countries) would not permit a Communist regime to be overthrown from within, on the grounds that the government in question had been chosen by the 'people.' It was applied first of all in Czechoslovakia during the Communist Party of Czechoslovakia's reform movement known as the Prague Spring. The policy was abandoned during the latter part of Gorbachev's leadership.

Commonwealth of Independent States   A loose federation formed in December 1991 by the presidents of Russia and Ukraine (Boris Yeltsin and Leonid Kravchuk) along with the chairman of the Belarusian Supreme Soviet, Stanislau Shushkevich. The meeting, held at a hunting lodge in Belavezha forest (Brest region) ostensibly ended the Soviet Union by replacing it with a new body. Gorbachev regarded the legality of the agreement as dubious.

Congress of People's Deputies   Founded by the 19th Party Conference in June 1988, the Congress was the first democratically elected parliament in Soviet history and represented the highest authority in the USSR and national republics. The first congress consisted of 2,250 deputies: 1,500 from electoral districts and 750 from approved organizations. Despite its great authority, the Congress was relatively ineffective and became involved in lengthy debates rather than significant legislation.

Democratic Platform of Communist Reformers   A group founded in 1990, prior to the 28th Congress of the Communist Party of the Soviet Union with the goal of introducing a social-democratic system in Russia following the model of Western Europe. Initial support for this program embraced some 55,000 Communists of the former USSR.

Democratic Russia   The consequence of the Democratic Platform was the formation of the group Democratic Russia, though the latter focused on gaining influence in the Russian Federation rather than the USSR. It supported the formation of a market economy, a new Russian Constitution, the abolition of Article 6 in the Soviet Constitution, which gave primacy in society to the Communist Party, and general adherence to the ideals of the late dissident scientist, Andrey Sakharov.

Glasnost A term meaning 'frankness,' though often more liberally translated as 'openness,' it is associated with Gorbachev's reform program, and the stress on self-criticism and honesty in official reports, particularly in the media. Glasnost also came to be identified with the reassessment of the past and the exposure of what were termed 'blank spots' in Soviet history, particularly atrocities carried out during the Stalin period.

Gospryomka The acronym for the State Inspection of Production, established by the Gorbachev regime on 12 May 1986 to enhance quality control over production. It remained in place for two years and can be considered one of the earliest of many failed attempts to reform the Soviet economy without embarking on a radical transformation of the state-run system into one that applied full market principles.

Green World An ecological association formed in Ukraine with the purpose initially of shutting down the Chernobyl nuclear power station and bringing to an end the Soviet civilian nuclear power program in Ukraine. Its founders included its first leader, Dr Yury Shcherbak, and biologist Dmytro Hrodzynsky. Subsequently its interests widened to include industrial pollution and its impact on the natural environment of Ukraine. A political wing also formed, known as the Green Party, modeled in part on the influential political party in Germany.

Interregional Group Formed on 30 July 1989 by radical deputies in the USSR Congress of Deputies, the group included such prominent Russian politicians as Boris Yeltsin, Andrey Sakharov and Gavriil Popov, and consisted of 388 members. The declared goal was to change the Soviet Union from a totalitarian regime to a democracy. The majority of members came from the Russian Republic and formed a high-level pressure group in the Congress and the Supreme Soviet elected by it.

Izvestiya The daily newspaper of the Soviet government was initially founded on 13 March 1917 following the collapse of the Russian monarchy during the First World War. In its early months it came under the control of the Menshevik Party, the more traditional Marxist wing of the former Russian Social Democratic Workers' Party. From 9 November 1917 it was the official mouthpiece of the Soviet government. Traditionally subservient in its views to the Communist Party, it became a more liberal organ in the late 1980s and in August 1991 refused to publish the pronouncement of the leaders of the failed putsch in Moscow.

KGB The acronym of the Committee for State Security, originally founded in December 1917 as the Extraordinary Commission to Combat Sabotage and Counter-Revolution, and led by Feliks Dzerzhinsky, a Belarusian-born Pole. The organization went through several transitions: the United State Political Administration (OGPU) in 1923, the People's Commissariat of Internal Affairs (NKVD) in 1934 (divided in 1941 into the NKVD USSR and the People's Commissariat of State Security [NKGB]), the Ministry of State Security (MGB) in 1946, the Ministry of Internal Affairs (uniting Internal Affairs and State Security) in 1953, and finally the KGB on 13 March 1954. The KGB was officially subordinated to the Council of Ministers and in the Gorbachev period its leaders were V.M. Chebrikov (until 1988), V.A. Kryuchkov (1988–August 1991), and V.V. Bakatin (August–November 1991).

It was dissolved by Gorbachev on 3 December 1991. Its modern Russian equivalent is the Federal Security Service of the Russian Federation (FSB) founded by President Boris Yeltsin in April 1995.

Kolkhoz   An abbreviated form of *kollektivnoe khozyaistvo*, meaning collective farm, kolkhoz refers to the looser version of the farm established by Stalin during the collectivization period of 1929–33 (and formalized in 1935) and known as the *artel*. In theory the leading authority in the farm was a board meeting of the membership, which made decisions implemented by a council, led by a chairman and chief agronomist. In practice, Soviet collective farms were established by force, subjected to close control, and notoriously inefficient. Paid a meagre wage, the collective farmers traditionally focused on small private plots to make ends meet, and the state took priority over collective farm production through an imposed grain procurement quota.

Kommunist   The official theoretical journal of the Communist Party of the Soviet Union, *Kommunist* was regarded initially as an obstacle by Gorbachev to the imposition of his 'new thinking' because of its traditional and fairly rigid stance. Under the new leadership of Ivan T. Frolov, it became more attuned to the ideas of Glasnost and Perestroika.

Komsomol   Communist Youth League organization founded in 1918 for young people aged 14–28 as preparation for membership of the Communist Party. Komsomol members took part in a variety of activities, including industrial work, sports, health, and reading groups. The total membership by the early Gorbachev period was about 40 million, but in the late 1980s, a mass exodus occurred as young people became disillusioned with the leadership of the Communist Party. It was disbanded following the failed putsch in Moscow of August 1991.

New Democratic Movement   Formed on 1 July 1991 in opposition to the Communist Party of the Soviet Union, its founders consisted of several luminaries of the democratic movement in the late USSR, such as Aleksandr Yakovlev, Eduard Shevardnadze, Anatoly Sobchak, and Aleksandr Rutskoy. Its creation signaled that several leading politicians considered that the Communist Party had reverted back to its hard-line traditional policies.

NKVD   People's Commissariat of Internal Affairs. See *KGB* above.

Nomenklatura   A system of patronage by which senior positions in the Soviet Union were occupied, under the close control of committees of the Communist Party, it became most noticeable during the leadership of Leonid Brezhnev (1964–82). By the Gorbachev period, an elite was well established and enjoyed special privileges – such as personal chauffers, elaborate private dachas, and access to special stores containing scarce goods. The Nomenklatura provided visible evidence of the corruption of society under Communist Party leadership.

Pamyat Society   One of the results of new attention to history was the formation of the *Pamyat* Society in 1987. Though its development was a consequence of a campaign to remember Stalin's victims, *Pamyat*, under leader Dmitry Vasilev (1945–2003), developed into an extreme right wing, anti-Semitic organization that campaigned for the restoration of an autocratic monarchy in Russia, and the end to what it termed rule by Jews and Freemasons.

Perestroika   A term used to denote the 'restructuring' of Soviet society. Though used by prior Soviet leaders, it was Gorbachev who made it an official state policy, primarily for the reforming of the state economy. Often the term Perestroika is used to denote the entire series of reforms introduced during the Gorbachev years. Latterly, reference to 'Perestroika' has come to signify an era of failed reforms.

Politburo An abbreviation of Political Bureau, a small committee first established by the Bolsheviks in 1917, it became the most powerful ruling body of the Communist Party of the Soviet Union after the Civil War (replacing the Council of People's Commissars), dealing with day to day affairs. The most important position on the Politburo was that of General Secretary, a position first occupied by Stalin and then by all Soviet leaders down to Gorbachev.

Pravda Bolshevik Party newspaper founded in 1912 and the main organ of the Communist Party of the Soviet Union until 22 August 1991, when it was banned by Russian president, Boris Yeltsin. *Pravda* was regarded as the most authoritative source for the official version of events in the Soviet Union. It has since been revived and in 1990 it was the first former Soviet newspaper to appear on the Internet.

Presidential Council The Presidential Council was created in March 1990 by Gorbachev, evidently as a replacement organization for the Politburo. However, it lasted only a short period, undermined by personal conflicts among its personnel, and reportedly met only seven times before being disbanded the following November. It was replaced in turn by the Security Council, created in December 1990, which effectively became the main instrument of power in the Soviet Union the following March.

Raion A Russian term denoting a district within a province (oblast), the raion formed the lowest level of organization of party and government apparatus.

Rukh The term *Rukh* means 'movement.' This is an abbreviation of the name of a political formation, the People's Movement in support of Perestroika in Ukraine, the leading democratic organization in Ukraine at the end of the 1980s. It was formed by three leading members of the Ukrainian Writers' Union, all of whom were party members originally. The Rukh program was adopted by the democratic faction (the 'Narodna Rada' or People's Council) in the Ukrainian parliament, and largely taken up by parliamentary leader Leonid Kravchuk and his block of reformist Communists when Ukraine became independent in August 1991.

Sajudis party A democratic party founded in Lithuania on 3 June 1988, which quickly grew into Lithuania's most popular political group. At its founding congress in October 1988 it set forth the principles by which Lithuania would regain its independence, and in March 1989, the party achieved significant success during the elections to the Congress of People's Deputies. Sajudis leader, Vytautas Landsbergis, a musician, fought several political battles with Soviet leader Mikhail Gorbachev. The Sajudis, together with their Popular Front counterparts in Estonia and Latvia, spearheaded the movement of the Soviet republics for independence from the USSR.

Sovetskaya Rossiya A conservative Communist newspaper, which on several occasions during the period 1985–91 appeared to oppose the reforms of Gorbachev. The key occasion was on 13 March 1988 with the publication of a letter from a Leningrad chemistry teacher, Nina Andreeva, which criticized attacks on Stalin and some of the more radical aspects of state policy. The newspaper also backed the failed putsch of August 1991 and was included among those organs banned by President Yeltsin in late August 1991.

START Treaty   The Strategic Arms Reduction Talks took place between the United States and the Soviet Union with the goal of cutting down nuclear warheads and bombers and missile delivery systems. Earlier these talks were called Strategic Arms Limitation Talks (SALT), and US President Ronald Reagan resumed them in 1982, hoping for more radical agreements. The talks were suspended in 1983–85, but revived during the Gorbachev period and in July 1991 a new treaty was signed between the Soviet leader and US President George Bush, by which the USSR reduced its stocks of weapons by 25 per cent and the United States by 15 per cent.

Supreme Soviet   Nominally the leading organ of the Soviet state, the Supreme Soviet was elevated to an authentic power-wielding body following the election of the Congress of People's Deputies in March 1989. The Supreme Soviet was responsible for the appointment of the Chairman of the Council of Ministers and overall supervision of the Council's activities, as well as the appointment of the Defence Council. Between the meetings of the Congress, it was the chief organ of state power in 1989–91, although in practice the Communist Party still wielded great authority until August 1991.

Chernenko, Konstantin Ustinovich (1911–85). Born in the village of Novoselo, Krasnoyarsk region, Siberia, and became a member of the CPSU in 1930, embarking on a lengthy career as a clerk and close associate of Leonid I. Brezhnev (1906–82). In the 1950s joined Brezhnev in Moldavia. Became a Central Committee candidate member in 1966 and a full member in 1971, and joined the party secretariat in 1976. From 1978 he was a member of the Politburo, and became party leader upon the death of Yury Andropov in November 1984 until his death in March 1985. His period of rule is often seen as the peak of what has been termed disdainfully, 'the period of stagnation.'

Gorbachev, Mikhail Sergeyevich (1931–). Born in Privolnoye, Stavropol region into a peasant family and graduated in law from Moscow State University. Joined the CPSU in 1952 and ran the Stavropol city Komsomol organization from 1955 to 1958. In 1971 he was elected to the CC CPSU. In 1978 he served as the CC Secretary in charge of agriculture. He was promoted to a full Politburo member by Brezhnev in 1980. On the death of Chernenko he became the General Secretary of the CC CPSU and president of the USSR in 1990–91.

Grishin Viktor Vasilevich (1914–92). Born in Serpukhov (Moscow Oblast) and graduated from the Moscow College of Geodesy in 1932. A member of the CPSU since 1939, he established his party career in the Serpukhov party organization. In 1950 he moved to Moscow as the head of the Department of Machine Building. In 1952 he became a member of the Central Committee and a Supreme Soviet deputy. He was a long-time chair of the official trade unions (1956–67), a candidate member of the Politburo from 1961 to 71, and a full member from the latter year. In 1967 he took over the Moscow city party organization, a position he held until he was replaced by Boris Yeltsin in 1985. Gorbachev removed Grishin, long considered a rival for power, from the Politburo in 1986.

Ivashko, Volodymyr Antonovych (1932–). Ukrainian politician, born in Poltava. Ivashko graduated from the Kharkiv Mining Institute in 1956 and joined the CPSU in 1960. In 1978 he was appointed Secretary of the Kharkiv Oblast committee of the party. By 1986 he had been promoted to party secretariat. In 1987, Ivashko became the First Secretary of the Dnipropetrovsk party organization in Ukraine, and the second ranking Communist in that republic after V.V. Shcherbytsky. He also played the role of advisor to Soviet puppet ruler Babrak Karmal in Afghanistan from early 1980. In 1990, he was elected First Secretary of the CC CPU but resigned to take up a position in Moscow as Deputy General Secretary of the CC CPSU on 11 July 1990. His role in the failed putsch of August 1991 is debated by analysts, but he appears to have adopted a middle role between the plotters and Gorbachev.

Kryuchkov, Vladimir Aleksandrovich (1924–). Born in Tsaritsyn (Stalingrad) and worked as a prosecutor for the local administration of Stalingrad from 1946 to

1954. He was a secretary in the Soviet Embassy in Budapest from 1954–59 and thus present during the Hungarian uprising. From 1967 he worked in the apparatus of the CPSU with various posts in the KGB. He was appointed Deputy Chairman of the KGB in 1978 and rose to be Chairman in 1988, and was elevated to the CC CPSU Politburo in the following year. He is also an army general. Widely considered the initiator of the August 1991 putsch, he was arrested for treason but amnestied during Boris Yeltsin's presidency of the Russian Federation.

Ligachev, Yegor Kuzmich (1920–). Though considered the arch-enemy of Perestroika, Ligachev was a close colleague of Gorbachev for several years. Born in Novosibirsk, he graduated from the Moscow Aviation Institute (1943) and joined the party in 1944. In 1965 he became First Party Secretary of Tomsk Oblast, and was a Candidate Member of the Central Committee from 1966 to 1976. A full member in the latter year, he joined the party secretariat in 1983. In 1985, Gorbachev appointed him to the new Politburo, initially in charge of ideology, but he was transferred to the CC Agricultural Commission in 1988. Increasingly unpopular with radical reformers, he lost an election for Deputy General Secretary to Ivashko (July 1990) and was not reappointed to the Politburo at the 28th Party Congress.

Pavlov, Valentin Sergeyevich (1937–). Born in Moscow and graduated from the Moscow Financial Institute. Joined the CPSU in 1962 and worked in various capacities as an economist, including the State Planning Commission (Gosplan). From 1986 to 1991 he chaired the USSR State Committee on Prices. In 1989 he was appointed Minister of Finance. He was appointed Prime Minister when Ryzhkov became ill, and amid an intense debate on economic reform. He blamed the West for trying to destabilize the Soviet banking system and also supported the failed putsch of August 1991.

Pugo, Boris Karlovich (1937–91). Born into a Latvian Communist family in Russia. Graduated from Riga Polytechnical Institute in 1960. From 1969 to 70, he was the First Secretary of the Latvian Komsomol organization. From 1977–80 he was the Deputy Chairman of the Latvian KGB, and the Chairman from 1980 rising to the rank of Major-General. In April 1984 he was appointed the First Secretary of the Communist Party of Latvia. His elevation to the Politburo came relatively late, in September 1989, and he took up the position of Minister of Interior (chief of police) on 2 December 1991. Less than eight months later he took an active role in the August 1991 putsch and committed suicide upon its failure.

Ryzhkov, Nikolay Ivanovich (1929–). Graduated from Kramatorsk Technical School and was employed for over a decade at the Ordzhonikidze heavy machinery factory, of which he became the director in 1970–71. In 1975 he was appointed First Deputy Minister of Heavy Machinery and Transport Equipment Construction. In the period 1979–82 he was the First Deputy Chairman of the State Planning Commission (Gosplan). He joined the CC in 1981 and its Secretariat the following year. In April 1985 Gorbachev appointed him to the CC CPSU Politburo, and in September 1985 he replaced Tikhonov as Prime Minister, a position he retained until suffering a heart attack in December 1990. He finished runner-up to Boris Yeltsin in the Russian presidential election of June 1991.

Sakharov, Andrey Dmitrievich (1921–89). Born in Moscow. A doctor of physics, he became a professor and member of the staff of the Lebedev Institute of Physics of the USSR and took part in the creation of the Soviet hydrogen bomb. In the late 1950s he was an outspoken opponent of the further development of nuclear weapons. In 1970 he established the USSR Committee on Human Rights and became perhaps the USSR's best known dissident, winning the Nobel Peace Prize in 1975. In January 1980 the Soviet authorities exiled Sakharov and his wife Yelena Bonner to the town of Gorky (Nizhni-Novgorod), and remained there until Gorbachev invited him to return to Moscow. He then became an outspoken opponent of the Soviet war in Afghanistan. In 1989 he was voted a member of the Congress of People's Deputies. His state funeral in December 1989 was an occasion for a mass tribute to a man widely regarded as a heroic figure.

Shatalin, Stanislav Sergeyevich (1934–). Born in Pushkin (Tsarskoye Selo) and graduated in economics from Moscow University. An academician, and a party member since 1963, he became well known as an advocate of radical economic reform and as the author of the 500 Days program, eventually rejected by the Soviet government in 1990.

Shcherbytsky, Volodymyr Vasilevich (1918–90). Born in Verkhnedneprovsk, Dnipropetrovsk Oblast, Ukraine. In 1941 he graduated from the Dnipropetrovsk Institute of Chemical Technology. In the postwar years he rose quickly in the Ukrainian party hierarchy, initially in Dniprodzerzhinsk and then in Dnipropetrovsk. In 1961 he was elected to the CC CPSU. In 1965 he took up the position of Chairman of the Council of Ministers of the Ukrainian SSR, joining the CC CPSU Politburo in April 1971. In May 1972 he succeeded Petro Shelest as the First Party Secretary of Ukraine, ostensibly to curb national aspirations in Ukraine, retaining his position until his retirement in September 1989.

Shevardnadze, Eduard Amvrosiyevich (1928–). President of Georgia. Born in the village of Mamati, Lanchkuti region, Georgia and joined the CPSU in 1948, rising to the position of leader of the Georgian Komsomol association in 1957–61. In 1968, he became the Minister of Internal Affairs of Georgia, and four years late he was promoted to the position of First Secretary of the Communist Party of Georgia, a position he held for the next thirteen years. In 1985 he became a full member of the CC CPSU Politburo and succeeded Andrey Gromyko as the Minister of Foreign Affairs. In 1990, he was also a member of the new Presidential Council of the USSR. In this same year he resigned as Foreign Minister in protest at some recent appointments of 'hard-line' Communists by Gorbachev, though he briefly regained this position in 1991 prior to the dissolution of the Soviet Union. In November 1995 he was elected president of Georgia and re-elected in 1990. Resigned in 2003.

Yakovlev, Aleksandr (1923–). Born in Yaroslavl and educated at the Yaroslavl Pedagogical Institute as an economist. Following two years serving in the Red Army (1941–43), he joined the Communist Party in 1944, rising to the position of head of the propaganda department by 1965, a position he retained for eight years before being demoted and posted as Soviet ambassador to Canada, 1973–83. Recalled to high office by Gorbachev, he is regarded as one of the main architects of Glasnost, and remained a very significant Politburo leader in the period 1987–90, and later in 1990 in the Presidential Council.

Yanayev, Gennady Ivanovich (1937–). Born near Gorky (Nizhni Novgorod), and was a head of the Committee for Soviet Youth Groups, and involved also in cultural relations with foreign countries. In 1990 he was appointed Chairman of the Soviet Trade Unions, and became a CC Secretary and Politburo member in this same year. In December 1990, Gorbachev appointed him Vice-President. Yanayev became acting head of the USSR during the August 1991 putsch but inspired little support. Arrested for treason he was subsequently amnestied along with the other putsch leaders.

Yeltsin, Boris Nikolaevich (1931–). Born in Sverdlovsk (Yekaterinburg). Former president of the Russian Federation who retired in December 1999, Yeltsin joined the CPSU in 1961. In 1955 he graduated from the Urals Polytechnical Institute. From 1963 to 1968 he was the chief engineer and head of the House Construction combine in Sverdlovsk. His political career began in earnest after 1968 as a secretary of the Sverdlovsk Oblast committee and he was First Secretary of the same organization between 1976 and 1985. In 1981 he came a member of the CC CPSU. In 1985 Gorbachev brought the burly Siberian to Moscow, appointing him the head of the city party organization and a member of the ruling Politburo. In November 1987 he lost this position, partly owing to his systematic attack on corruption, which aroused protests among the higher echelons of the party. He then became the Deputy Chairman of the State Construction Committee. In February 1988, Yeltsin was removed from the Politburo. In March 1989 his career revived when he was elected a deputy of the Congress of People's Deputies. He was a co-founder of the reformist Inter-regional Group. In May 1990 he was voted chairman of the Russian Supreme Soviet. Yeltsin left the CC CPSU at the 28th Party Congress in July of this year. In June 1991, he was elected president of the RSFSR and played a key role both in repelling the August putsch and in the banning of the Communist Party. In December 1991, his meeting in Belarus with the president of Ukraine, Leonid Kravchuk, and leader of the Belarusian parliament, Stanislav Shushkevich, played a key role in the dissolution of the Soviet Union.

GUIDE TO FURTHER READING

The years 1985–91 elicited a vast outpouring of literature that abated as suddenly as it began, with the collapse of the USSR and the onset of a new era under Boris Yeltsin. On the other hand, many of the 'players' in the events remained on the stage, and at various times began to publish their memoirs: from Gorbachev to his associates and his political allies and opponents. The literature on the various aspects highlighted in this book tends to be, though not in every case, from the late 1980s, with a notable decline in output in the 1990s. It is necessary to be selective, since there are far too many sources to be listed here, but those included are in the author's view the most important and recognized works of the period in the English language. The place of publication is New York unless stated otherwise.

MEMOIRS AND BIOGRAPHICAL WORKS

Gorbachev's book *Memoirs* (1995) provides an attempt to justify his policies and to explain the events of his rule. Two of his staff members offer what might be termed 'antidotes' to his book: V.I. Boldin, *Ten Years that Shook the World: the Gorbachev Era as Witnessed by his Chief of Staff* (1994); and Anatoly Chernyaev, *My Six Years with Gorbachev* (University Park, PA, 2000); as to some extent does Vladimir K. Egorov's *Out of a Dead End into the Unknown: Notes on Gorbachev's Perestroika* (Chicago, 1993). Though critical, the above are by no means hostile to the Gorbachev administration. Neither is the memoir of an interpreter, Pavel Palazhenko, *My Years with Gorbachev and Shevardnadze* (1997). The same cannot be said of the memoirs of Gorbachev's chief antagonist, Boris Yeltsin, two volumes of which are pertinent to our period: *Against the Grain: an Autobiography* (1990) and *The View From the Kremlin* (1994), which like many such autobiographies are to some extent self-serving. Also very critical is Mikhail F. Nenashev, *An Ideal Betrayed: Testimonies of a Prominent and Loyal Member of the Soviet Establishment* (London, 1995). Traditional Communist views can also be gleaned from Andrei A. Gromyko, *Memoirs* (1990) and E.K. Ligachev, *Inside Gorbachev's Kremlin: The Memoirs of Yegor Ligachev* (Boulder, CO, 1996). Moving toward the more moderate reminiscences are Roy A. Medvedev, *Time of Change: An Insider's View of Russia's Transformation* (1989) and Eduard Shevardnadze, *The Future Belongs to Freedom* (London, 1991), as well as Ruslan Khasbulatov, *The Struggle for Russia: Power and Change in the Democratic Revolution* (1993). A Western perspective can be found in Jack F. Matlock, *Autopsy on an Empire: the American Ambassador's Account of the Collapse of the Soviet Union* (1995).

Biographical works on Gorbachev and his times began to appear from the very early stages of his administration. They include Christian Schmidt-Hauer,

Gorbachev: The Path to Power (London, 1986); Moshe Lewin, *The Gorbachev Phenomenon: A Historical Interpretation* (Berkeley, CA, 1988); Walter Joyce, Hillel Ticktin, and Stephen White, *Gorbachev and Gorbachevism* (London, 1989); Francoise Thom, *The Gorbachev Phenomenon: A History and Perestroika* (London, 1989); Ilya Zemtsov, *Gorbachev: The Man and the System* (New Brunswick, NJ, 1989); Barukh Hazan, *Gorbachev and his Enemies: The Struggle for Perestroika* (Boulder, CO, 1990); and Richard Sakwa, *Gorbachev and his Reforms, 1985–1990* (London, 1990). Journalistic accounts that demonstrate fascination with the Soviet leader include Dusko Doder and Louise Branson, *Heretic in the Kremlin* (1991); Robert G. Kaiser, *Why Gorbachev Happened: his Triumphs and his Failure* (New York, 1991); and Gail Sheehy, *The Man Who Changed the World: The Lives of Mikhail S. Gorbachev* (1990). Also to be included in the journalistic analyses is Michel Tatu, *Mikhail Gorbachev: The Origins of Perestroika* (Boulder, CO, 1991); while the impact of Gorbachev on Soviet history is compared to that of Lenin and Stalin in Theodore H. Von Laue, *Why Lenin? Why Stalin? Why Gorbachev? The Rise and Fall of the Soviet System* (1993), an expanded third edition of the original book.

The 1990s witnessed several biographical works that attempted to explain the fate of the Gorbachev regime, often with very close focus on the leader himself. They include two volumes by Stephen White: *Gorbachev in Power* (Cambridge, 1990) and *Gorbachev and After* (Cambridge, 1992); Archie Brown, *The Gorbachev Factor* (1996); John Miller, *Mikhail Gorbachev and the End of Soviet Power* (1993); and Gerd Ruge, *Gorbachev: A Biography* (London, 1991). The latter part of the decade has seen the appearance of several more significant works: Mark Galeotti, *Gorbachev and his Revolution* (1997); Martin McCauley, *Gorbachev* (London, 1998). Works that take a broader biographical approach or focus on other political leaders include John Morrison, *Boris Yeltsin: from Bolshevik to Democrat* (1991); Donald Murray, *A Democracy of Despots* (Montreal, 1995); George W. Breslauer's comparison of the two great rivals, *Gorbachev and Yeltsin as Leaders* (Cambridge, 2002); and Jonathan Harris, *The Public Politics of Aleksandr Nikolaevich Yakovlev, 1983–1989* (Pittsburgh, 1990).

POLITICS

The literature on politics 1985–91 can be divided into contemporary (works published during the period attempting to analyze the various changes) and reflective, i.e., those seeking to explain the demise of the Soviet Union from various perspectives. Dealing first with individually authored monographs, the onset of Glasnost saw new works by several scholars, all of which were published prior to the fall of the USSR: Wilson P. Dizard, *Gorbachev's Information Revolution: Controlling Glasnost in a New Electronic Era* (Boulder, CO, 1987); Jonathan Harris, *Ligachev on Glasnost and Perestroika* (Pittsburgh, 1989); Kristian Gerner, *Ideology and Rationality in the Soviet Model: a Legacy for Gorbachev* (London, 1989); Barukh Hazan, *Gorbachev's Gamble: the 19th All-Union Party Conference* (Boulder, CO, 1990); V. Kubalkova, *Thinking New about Soviet 'New Thinking'* (San Francisco, 1989), David Stuart Lane, *Soviet Society Under Perestroika* (Boston, 1990); Walter Laqueur, *The Long Road to Freedom: Russia and Glasnost* (Vancouver, 1989); Montecue J. Lowry, *Glasnost: Deception, Desperation, Dialectics* (1991); Thomas H. Naylor, *The Gorbachev Strategy: Opening the Closed Society* (Lexington, MA, 1988); Alec Nove, *Glasnost in Action* (London, 1989); John Sallnow, *Reform in the Soviet Union: Glasnost and the Future*

(London, 1989); Vladimir Shlapentokh, *Soviet Ideologies in the Period of Glasnost: Responding to Brezhnev's Stagnation* (1988); and George Soros, *Opening the Soviet System* (London, 1990).

Other works of this period included analyses of domestic and foreign policy: Susan L. Clark, *Gorbachev's Agenda: Changes in Soviet Domestic and Foreign Policy* (Boulder, CO, 1989) (but see also Foreign Policy below); history, Robert W. Davies, *Soviet History in the Gorbachev Revolution* (Bloomington, Indiana, 1989); the succession question, Richard Owen, *Comrade Chairman: Soviet Succession and the Rise of Gorbachev* (1987); corruption, Leslie Holmes, *The End of Communist Power: Anti-Corruption Campaigns and the Legitimization Crisis* (1993); and a plethora of works on the political reform process at its various stages: F. Barnard, *Pluralism, Socialism, and Political Legitimacy: Reflections on Opening Up Communism* (1991); Astrid von Borcke, *Gorbachev's Perestroika: Can the Soviet System be Reformed?* (Cologne, 1987); Giulietti Chiesa, *Transition to Democracy in the USSR: Ending the Monopoly of Power and New Political Forces* (Washington, DC, 1990); Leo Cooper, *Soviet Reforms and Beyond* (Basingstoke, 1991); Martin Crouch, *Revolution and Evolution: Gorbachev and Soviet Politics* (1989); Padma Desai, *Perestroika in Perspective: the Design and Dilemmas of Soviet Reform* (Princeton, NJ, 1989); Ben Eklof, *Soviet Briefing: Gorbachev and the Reform Period* (Boulder, CO, 1989); Marshall I. Goldman, *What Went Wrong with Perestroika?* (1991); Darrell Hammer, *The Politics of Oligarchy* (Boulder, CO, 1990); Richard D. Little, *Governing the Soviet Union* (1989); and Vera Tolz, *The USSR's Emerging Multiparty System* (1990).

The period provided an interesting one for journalists, several of whom published books during or following their stint in the Soviet Union. Most notable in this regard are David Remnick, *Lenin's Tomb: The Last Days of the Soviet Empire* (1993); Hedrick Smith, *The New Russians* (London, 1990); Steve Crawshaw, *Goodbye to the USSR* (London, 1992); Patrick Cockburn, *Getting Russia Wrong: the End of Kremlinology* (London, 1989); Mark Frankland, *The Sixth Continent: Russia and the Making of Mikhail Gorbachev* (London, 1987); Michael Dobbs, *Down with Big Brother: The Fall of the Soviet Empire* (1997); Jonathan Steele, *Eternal Russia: Yeltsin, Gorbachev, and the Mirage of Democracy* (Cambridge, MA, 1994); Martin Walker, *The Waking Giant: Gorbachev's Russia* (1988); and Fred Weir, *The Soviet Revolution: Shaking the World Again. A Canadian Journalist's Eyewitness Account* (Toronto, 1990). One who became briefly a victim of the Soviet authorities and suffered incarceration was Nicholas Daniloff, *Two Lives, One Russia* (Boston, 1988). The failed putsch of August 1991 receives mention and sometimes detailed accounts in several works, but fewer monographs devoted specifically to those few days. An exception is James Billington, *Russia Transformed. The Breakthrough to Hope: Moscow, August 1991* (1992). The transformation of the extensive military weapons system is covered by Julian Cooper, *The Soviet Defence Industry: Conversion and Economic Reform* (1991).

Several authors focus on what is termed the 'Gorbachev revolution,' a phrase that seems somewhat captured in time from the perspective of the early 21st century, but which include fairly recent works, such as Gordon M. Hahn, *Russia's Revolution From Above 1985–2000: Transition and Revolution in the Fall of the Communist Regime* (New Brunswick, NJ, 2002); Jerry F. Hough, *Democratization and Revolution in the USSR, 1985–1991* (Washington, DC, 1997); David M. Kotz, *Revolution From Above: the Demise of the Soviet System* (London, 1997); and Michael E. Urban, *More*

Power to the Soviets: the Democratic Revolution in the USSR (Aldershot, 1990). Rapid changes are discussed in Ronald J. Hill and Jan Ake Dellebrant, *Gorbachev and Perestroika: Towards a New Socialism?* (Aldershot, 1989); Vladislav Krasnov, *Russia Beyond Communism: A Chronicle of National Rebirth* (Boulder, CO, 1991); and Geoffrey A. Hosking, *The Awakening of the Soviet Union* (Cambridge, MA, 1990). Other scholars have naturally offered their reflections on how the world's first Communist power collapsed so suddenly and unexpectedly in December 1991: Robert V. Daniels, *The End of the Communist Revolution* (London, 1993); Brendan Kiernan, *The End of Soviet Politics: Elections, Legislatures, and the Demise of the Communist Party* (Boulder, CO, 1993); William E. Watson, *The Collapse of Communism in the Soviet Union* (Westport, CT, 1998); Philip Roeder, *Red Sunset: The Failure of Soviet Politics* (Princeton, NJ, 1993); and Stephen White, *Communism and its Collapse* (London, 2001).

Perhaps no other period of Soviet history has elicited so many edited collections. Today they are of varying usefulness and we will cite here only a selection. Early but valuable works are Seweryn Bialer (ed.), *Politics, Society, and Nationality in Gorbachev's Russia* (Boulder, CO, 1988); Archie Brown (ed.), *Political Leadership in the Soviet Union* (Bloomington, Indiana, 1990); Alexander Dallin and Condoleeza Rice (eds), *The Gorbachev Era* (Stanford, CA, 1986); and Martin McCauley (ed.), *The Soviet Union under Gorbachev* (Basingstoke, 1987). There are important examinations of the changes in the Soviet media and other outlets under Glasnost: Alexander Dallin and Gail W. Lapidus (eds), *The Soviet System in Crisis: A Reader of Western and Soviet Views* (Boulder, CO, 1991); Vitalii Korotych and Cathy Porter (eds), *The New Soviet Journalism: the Best of the Soviet Weekly 'Ogonyok'* (Boston, 1990); Andrei Melville and Gail W. Lapidus (eds), *The Glasnost Papers: Voices on Reform from Moscow* (Boulder, CO, 1990); James Riordan and Susan Bridges (eds), *Dear Comrade Editor: Readers' Letters to the Soviet Press Under Perestroika* (Bloomington, Indiana, 1992); Ron McKay (ed.), *Letters to Gorbachev: Life in Russia through the Postbag of 'Argumenty i Fakty'* (London, 1991); and Isaac J. Tarasulo (ed.), *Perils of Perestroika: Viewpoints from the Soviet Press, 1989–1991* (Wilmington, DE, 1992).

On political parties in the late Soviet period, see M.A. Babkina and A.M. Babkina (eds), *New Political Parties and Movements in the Soviet Union* (1992); Geoffrey A. Hosking, Jonathan Aves, and Peter J.S. Duncan (eds), *The Road to Post-Communism: Independent Political Movements in the Soviet Union, 1985–1991* (London, 1992); and Stephen White, Alex Pravda, and Zvi Gitelman (eds), *Developments in Soviet and Post-Soviet Politics* (Durham, NC, 2002). Several comparative studies exist in the format of edited collections. On China, see, for example, Mel Gurtov (ed.), *The Transformation of Socialism: Perestroika and Reform in the Soviet Union and China* (Boulder, CO, 1990). On Eastern Europe, see Nancy Bermeo (ed.), *Liberalization and Democratization: Change in the Soviet Union and Eastern Europe* (Baltimore, MD, 1992); and Charles Bukowski and J. Richard Walsh (eds), *Glasnost, Perestroika, and the Socialist Community* (1990). Of the general analyses of the collapse of the USSR, one or two works have retained their pertinence and are worthy of study: Ed A. Hewett and Victor H. Winston (eds), *Milestones in Glasnost and Perestroyka* (Washington, DC, 1991); David Lane (ed.), *Elites and Political Power in the USSR* (Aldershot, 1988); and Theodore Taranovski (ed.), *Reform in Modern Russian History: Progress or Cycle* (Cambridge, 1995). Many other works, while worthy of examination, have become obsolete over time. One that does link the Soviet era to the current one is

Archie Brown and Lilia Fedorovna Shevtsova (eds), *Gorbachev, Yeltin, and Putin: Political Leadership in Russia's Transition* (Washington, DC, 2001).

THE NATIONAL QUESTION

In recent years, more and more analysts are recognizing the significance of the nationalities question in the demise of the USSR. It is useful to begin with theoretical works pertaining to the former Soviet empire. These include Ben Fowkes, *The Disintegration of the Soviet Union: A Study in the Rise and Triumph of Nationalism* (1997); Alexander J. Motyl, *Sovietology, Rationality, Nationality: Coming to Grips with Nationalism in the USSR* (1990); and Ronald G. Suny, *The Revenge of the Past: Nationalism, Revolution, and the Collapse of the Soviet Union* (Stanford, CA, 1993). A good introduction to the changes brought about by Gorbachev's reforms is Charles Furtado and Andrea Chandler, *Perestroika in the Soviet Republics* (Boulder, CO, 1992). General works published during the Gorbachev period include Leon Aron, *Gorbachev's Mounting Nationalities Crisis* (Washington, DC, 1989); Lubomyr Hajda (ed.), *The Nationalities Factor in Soviet Politics and Society* (Boulder, CO, 1990); Stephan Kux, *Soviet Federalism: A Comparative Perspective* (Boulder, CO, 1990); Alastair McAuley (ed.), *Soviet Federalism, Nationalism, and Economic Decentralization* (Leicester, 1991); Bohdan Nahaylo and Victor Swoboda, *Soviet Disunion: A History of the Nationalities Problem in the USSR* (1990); Uri Ra'anan, *The Soviet Empire: The Challenge of National and Democratic Movements* (Lexington, MA, 1990); and Graham Smith (ed.), *The Nationalities Question in the Soviet Union* (London, 1990).

Two post-Soviet additions to the general literature are Marco Buttino, *In a Collapsing Empire: Underdevelopment, Ethnic Conflicts and Nationalisms in the Soviet Union* (Milan, 1992) and Gail Lapidus and Victor Zaslavsky (eds), *From Union to Commonwealth: Nationalism and Separatism in the Soviet Republics* (Cambridge, 1993). Of the literature on the Russian republic, the works have been both valuable and often controversial. The following are good starting points: Stephen Carter, *Russian Nationalism: Yesterday, Today, and Tomorrow* (1990); John B. Dunlop, *The Rise of Russia and the Fall of the Soviet Empire* (Princeton, NJ, 1993); Darrell Hammer, *Russian Nationalism and Soviet Politics* (Boulder, CO, 1988); and Miron Rezun (ed.), *Nationalism and the Breakup of an Empire: Russia and its Periphery* (Westport, CT, 1992).

The initial impetus for changes in the federal structure of the USSR came from the Baltic States. A general introduction to the events is Kristian Gerner and Stefan Hedlund (eds), *Baltic States and the End of the Soviet Empire* (London, 1993); and Anatol Lieven, *The Baltic Revolution: Estonia, Latvia, Lithuania and the Path to Independence* (New Haven, CT, 1993). See also Rasma Karklins, *Ethnopolitics and the Transition to Democracy: The Collapse of the USSR and Latvia* (Washington, DC, 1994) and George J. Neimanis, *The Collapse of the Soviet Empire: A View from Riga* (Westport, CT, 1997). Belarus is covered by Jan Zaprudnik, *Belarus: at a Crossroads in History* (Boulder, CO, 1993); and David R. Marples, *Belarus: from Soviet Rule to Nuclear Catastrophe* (1996). There is quite a significant body of literature on Ukraine in 1985–91. One can begin with Taras Kuzio and Andrew Wilson, *Ukraine: Perestroika to Independence* (1994), which was subsequently brought out in a new edition authored by Kuzio alone (2000), and which forms a natural sequel to David R. Marples, *Ukraine under Perestroika: Ecology, Economics, and the Workers' Revolt* (1991).

The question of dissent in Ukraine is strictly speaking not relevant to this study, but it does provide an important background into the sources of discontent in this significant republic. Thus worthy of note is J. Bilocerkowycz, *Soviet Ukrainian Dissent* (Boulder, CO, 1987). A general conference to investigate the changes taking place in Ukraine and held at York University in Toronto resulted in the publication Romana Bahry (ed.), *Echoes of Glasnost in Soviet Ukraine* (North York, Ontario, 1989). A collection of interviews with Ukrainian luminaries of these years is Roman Solchanyk, *Ukraine: The Road to Independence* (1994), while the same author discusses the coming of independence in Ukraine in the first two chapters of Roman Solchanyk, *Ukraine and Russia: The Post-Soviet Transition* (London, 2001). In terms of detail, the most complete account of the transition of Ukraine from a Soviet republic to an independent state is Bohdan Nahaylo, *The Ukrainian Resurgence* (Toronto, 1999). Works on Central Asia and the Caucasus are somewhat scarcer. Westview Press initiated a series on the Soviet republics, which overlapped the collapse of the USSR, meaning that while some volumes are of relevance, others appeared too early to be pertinent to this topic. Three books that cover the period of attainment of independence in detail are: Vytas Stanley Vardys, *Lithuania: the Rebel Nation* (Boulder, CO, 1997); Rein Taagepera, *Estonia: Return to Independence* (Boulder, CO, 1993); and Gregory Gleason, *The Central Asian States: Discovering Independence* (Boulder, CO, 1997).

Generally, the Baltic States have received adequate treatment and attention. On Lithuania, see Alfred Erich Senn, *Lithuania Awakening – 1988* (Berkeley, CA, 1990); and on Latvia, Juris Dreifelds, *Latvia in Transition* (Cambridge, 1996). On the Baltic States as a whole, there are several relevant collections, including Jan Arveds Trapans (ed.), *Toward Independence: The Baltic Popular Movements* (Boulder, CO, 1991); Kristian Gerner and Stefan Hedlund, *The Baltic States and the End of the Soviet Empire* (1993); and a book whose range is much broader than its title suggests, Ole Norgaard, with Dan Hindsgaul, Lars Johannsen, and Helle Willumsen, *The Baltic States after Independence* (Cheltenham, 1996).

THE ECONOMY

Initially, it appeared that the Gorbachev administration might take some ambitious steps toward economic reform and scholars formulated their monographs accordingly. By the early 1990s, the focus was rather on 'crisis' or 'collapse.' Of the general works in the early years of perestroika, one should note two books by Abel G. Aganbegian, *The Economic Challenge of Perestroika* (Bloomington, Indiana, 1988) and *Inside Perestroika: The Future of the Soviet Economy* (London, 1989), as well as Misha Belkindas, *Privatization of the Soviet Economy under Gorbachev* (Durham, NC, 1989). Another early study was Jerry F. Hough, *Opening up the Soviet Economy* (Washington, DC, 1988). Several works can be categorized as general introductions to the dilemmas of economic reform: David A. Dyker, *Restructuring the Soviet Economy* (1992); Janos Komai, *The Road to a Free Economy* (1992); Heidi Kroll, *Reform and Monopoly in the Soviet Economy* (Providence, RI, 1990); Susan J. Linz and William Moskoff (eds), *Reorganization and Reform in the Soviet Economy* (1988); and Vladimir V. Popov, *Soviet Economic Reforms: Lost Opportunities and Remaining Hopes* (Toronto, 1991).

Concerning books on specific topics within economic reform, currency reform is treated in Josef C. Brada and Michael P. Claudon, *Reforming the Ruble: Monetary Aspects of Perestroika* (1990). Soviet technological backwardness is covered in Marshall I. Goldman, *Gorbachev's Challenge: Economic Reform in the Age of High Technology* (1987). The classic work on Soviet energy policy remains Thane Gustafson, *Crisis amid Plenty: the Politics of Soviet Energy under Brezhnev and Gorbachev* (Princeton, NJ, 1991). The high-level discussions concerning the transition to a market economy are the focus of Anthony Jones (ed.), *The Great Market Debate in Soviet Economics: An Anthology* (1991). One of the few works on the cooperative movement is Anthony Jones, *Ko-ops: The Rebirth of Entrepreneuship in the Soviet Union* (Bloomington, Indiana, 1991). A later overview of the economic changes with concentration on Russia is Anders Aslund, *How Russia Became a Market Economy* (Washington, DC, 1995).

Turning to agriculture, while the output was not voluminous, there are several books worthy of consultation, and written during the Gorbachev period. They include Josef C. Brada and Karl-Eugen Waedekin (eds), *Soviet Agriculture in Transition: Organizational Response to Falling Performance* (Boulder, CO, 1988); Boris Z. Milner and Dmitry S. Lvov (eds), *Soviet Agriculture and Trade under Perestroika* (London, 1990); William Moskof (ed.), *Perestroika in the Countryside: Agricultural Reform in the Gorbachev Era* (1990); and John Yin, *Infrastructure of the* [sic] *Soviet Agriculture* (Sudbury, Ontario, 1991). Finally, the collapse of the Soviet Union elicited a number of works that analyzed the role of the economic crisis or collapse and its impact on the regime. Most notable are Robert W. Campbell, *The Failure of Soviet Economic Planning: System, Performance, Reform* (Bloomington, Indiana, 1992); Philip Hanson, *From Stagnation to Catastroika: Commentaries on the Soviet Economy, 1983–1991* (1992); Paul C. Roberts, *Meltdown: Inside the Soviet Economy* (Washington, DC, 1990); Peter Rutland, *The Politics of Economic Stagnation in the Soviet Union: The Role of Local Party Organs in Economic Management* (Cambridge, 1993); and Hillel Ticktin, *Origins of the Crisis in the USSR: Essays on the Political Economy of a Disintegrating System* (1992).

CHERNOBYL AND ENVIRONMENTAL ISSUES

Works on Chernobyl can be divided into several categories, and I am omitting here what may be termed 'technical books' concerning the nature of the nuclear accident and confining myself to those that relate to the ultimate fate of the Soviet Union. These can be divided into Soviet and non-Soviet, and in the former case they derive from eyewitnesses to the accident and/or its aftermath. One of the chief figures involved in the medical aspects is L.A. Il'in, *Chernobyl: Myth and Reality* (Moscow, 1995). From the perspective of a medical doctor turned environmental activist, and in contrast to the opinions of the above, there is Yurii Shcherbak, *Chernobyl: A Documentary Story* (1988). A fine book by former Soviet geneticist now resident in the UK is Zhores A. Medvedev, *The Legacy of Chernobyl* (Oxford, 1990). His namesake but no relation, a former engineer, wrote two books that bitterly attacked the way the Soviet civilian nuclear reactors were operated: Grigorii Medvedev, *The Truth about Chernobyl* (1991); and Grigorii Medvedev, *No Breathing Room: the Aftermath of Chernobyl* (1993). Another indictment of the Soviet authorities can be found in Alla Yaroshinskaya, *Chernobyl: the Forbidden Truth* (Lincoln, NE, 1995), written by a former delegate of the USSR Supreme Soviet from Ukraine.

Western books on Chernobyl and/or the Soviet nuclear industry are quite numerous. The first doctor on the scene from the West wrote an account shortly afterward: Robert Peter Gale, *Final Warning: the Legacy of Chernobyl* (1988). Other early books include Viktor Haynes and J. Marko Bojcun, *The Chernobyl Disaster* (1988); David R. Marples, *Chernobyl and Nuclear Power in the USSR* (London, 1987); Richard F. Mould, *Chernobyl – The Real Story* (1988); and Chris Park, *Chernobyl: The Long Shadow* (1989). A dramatic account is Piers Paul Read, *Ablaze: the Story of the Heroes and Victims of Chernobyl* (1993). On the social consequences, see David R. Marples, *The Social Consequences of the Chernobyl Disaster* (1988) and for the impact on democracy, see Peter Gould, *Fire in the Rain: the Democratic Consequences of Chernobyl* (Cambridge, 1990). A more recent work that explores the nuclear industry in the former USSR is Paul R. Josephson, *Red Atom: Russia's Nuclear Program from Stalin to Today* (1999). On environmental issues in general, see Philip Pryde, *Environmental Management in the Soviet Union* (Cambridge, 1991); D.J. Peterson, *Troubled Lands: The Legacy of Soviet Environmental Destruction* (Boulder, CO, 1993); and the harrowing outline of environmental destruction in Murray Feshbach and Alfred Friendly Jr, *Ecocide in the USSR* (1993).

SOCIAL ISSUES

Soviet workers and the problems that emerged for them are analyzed in several works. They range from the question of unemployment, J. Porket, *Work, Employment, and Unemployment in the Soviet Union* (1989); labor issues, Donald Filtzer, *Soviet Workers and the Collapse of Perestroika: The Soviet Labour Process and Gorbachev's Reforms, 1985–1991* (Cambridge, 1994); and David Mandel, *Perestroika and the Soviet People: Rebirth of the Labour Movement* (Montreal, 1991); poverty, William Moskoff, *Hard Times – Impoverishment and Protest in the Perestroika Years: The Soviet Union 1985–1991* (1993); and political issues: Walter Connor, *The Accidental Proletariat: Workers, Politics, and Crisis in Gorbachev's Russia* (Princeton, NJ, 1991). Social issues *per se* are dealt with in Anthony Jones, Walter Connor, and David Powell (eds), *Soviet Social Problems* (Boulder, CO, 1994); Michael Rywkin, *Soviet Society Today* (1989); and Judith Sedaitis and Jim Butterfield (eds), *Perestroika From Below: Social Movements in the Soviet Union* (Boulder, CO, 1991). A valuable comparative approach is Elizabeth Teague, *Solidarity and the Soviet Worker: the Impact of Polish Events of 1980 on Soviet Internal Politics* (London, 1988).

Social issues can be divided into a number of subjects. On alcohol, see, for example, Boris Segal, *The Drunken Society. Alcohol Abuse and Alcoholism in the Soviet Union: A Comparative Study* (1990). Soviet culture in the Gorbachev period is covered by Nancy Ries, *Russian Talk: Culture and Conversation During Perestroika* (Ithaca, NY, 1997); and Marsha Siefert (ed.), *Mass Culture and Perestroika in the Soviet Union* (Oxford, 1991). These can be supplemented by the final chapter (dealing with Perestroika) of Richard Stites, *Russian Popular Culture: Entertainment and Society since 1900* (Cambridge, 1992). On organized crime, see Arkady Vaksberg, *The Soviet Mafia* (1991); and Stephen Handelman, *Comrade Criminal: Russia's New Mafiya* (New Haven, CT, 1997), which also deals with this subject in the post-independence period. Several works have addressed the topic of Soviet women in the period 1985–91, including Mary Buckley (ed.), *Perestroika and Soviet Women* (Cambridge, 1992); and Chanie Rosenberg, *Women and Perestroika* (London, 1989). The important subject of television was addressed in the early Gorbachev period in Ellen Propper Mickiewicz, *Split Signals: Television and Politics in the Soviet Union* (London, 1988).

FOREIGN RELATIONS AND DISARMAMENT

The end of the Cold War coincided with the collapse of the USSR and in many works is identified closely with it. At the same time, numerous important USA–USSR summit and arms control meetings occurred in 1985–91; the period can be termed one of the most fruitful in the lengthy process of weapons reduction that falls under the general headings of SALT (Strategic Arms Limitation Treaty) and then START (Strategic Arms Reduction Treaty), embracing the presidencies of Reagan, Bush, and Clinton on the American side, and Gorbachev and Yeltsin on the Russian. Most of the works listed below fall into one of the two categories. Thus one can deal first with other topics. The link between the USSR and the changes in Eastern Europe is explored in Karen Dawisha, *Eastern Europe, Gorbachev, and Reform: The Great Challenge* (Cambridge, 1990). National security issues receive perusal in Coit D. Blacker, *Hostage to Revolution: Gorbachev and Soviet Security Policy* (1993); and Michael McGwire, *Perestroika and National Security Policy* (Washington, DC, 1991); and ideology in foreign policy in Sylvia Woodby, *Gorbachev and the Decline of Ideology in Soviet Foreign Policy* (Boulder, CO, 1989).

Two general surveys provide an overall picture of Soviet foreign policy: Robert Miller, *Soviet Foreign Policy Today: Gorbachev and the New Political Thinking* (1991); and Richard Staar, *Foreign Policies of the Soviet Union* (Stanford, CA, 1991). The war in Afghanistan, which Gorbachev inherited from the Brezhnev administration is examined from two angles: its impact on the collapse of the Soviet Union is the focus of Anthony Arnold, *The Fateful Pebble: Afghanistan's Role in the Fall of the Soviet Empire* (Novato, CA, 1993); and the Soviet withdrawal of troops is the subject of Sarah Elizabeth Mendelson, *Changing Course: Ideas, Politics and the Soviet Withdrawal from Afghanistan* (Princeton, NJ, 1998). A related work is William C. Green, ed. *Gorbachev and his Generals: The Reform of Soviet Military Doctrine* (Boulder, CO, 1990). Very specific geographical concentration is provided in Robert Owen Freedman, *Soviet Policy Toward Israel under Gorbachev* (1991); Roy U.T. Kim, *Japanese-Soviet Relations under Gorbachev* (Pittsburgh, 1988); and David Shumaker, *Gorbachev and the German Question: Soviet-West German Relations, 1985–1990* (Westport, CT, 1995).

Works on the Cold War clearly date very quickly. Those written prior to 1992 have to be treated with some caution, though they may merit study for detail rather than interpretation. The statement applies, for example, to Michael Cox, *Beyond the Cold War: Superpowers at the Crossroads* (Lanham, MD, 1990); Gregory Flynn and Richard E. Greene (eds), *The West and the Soviet Union: Politics and Policy* (1990); Jerry F. Hough, *Russia and the West: Gorbachev and the Politics of Reform* (New York, 1988); and Robbin Laird and Susan L. Clark (eds), *The USSR and the Western Alliance* (Boston, 1990); and Don Oberdorfer, *The Turn: From the Cold War to a New Era: The United States and the Soviet Union, 1983–1990* (1991). A general survey that covers the 1980s decade is Mike Bowker and Robin Brown (eds), *From Cold War to Collapse: Theory and World Politics in the 1980s* (Cambridge, 1992). A work that looks at the changing and improving relations between the United States and the Soviet Union is Marshall Brement, *Reaching out to Moscow: from Confrontation to*

Cooperation (1991). Two other books deal with similar topics: Robert Jervis and Seweryn Bialer (eds), *Soviet-American Relations after the Cold War* (Durham, NC, 1991); and Allen Lynch, *The Soviet Breakup and US Foreign Policy* (1992). The view of a former US senator represents a rather one-sided paean to Gorbachev, comparing him with Abraham Lincoln and Franklin D. Roosevelt: Gary Hart, *Russia Shakes the World: the Second Russian Revolution and its Impact on the West* (1991).

Concerning arms control, good starting points are Paul Bennett, *The Soviet Union and Arms Control: Negotiating Strategy and Tactics* (1989); Daniel Calingaert, *Soviet Nuclear Policy under Gorbachev: a Policy of Disarmament* (1991); and Patrick Glynn, *Closing Pandora's Box: Arms Races, Arms Control, and the History of the Cold War* (1991). The relationship between Gorbachev's domestic policy and US arms build-up is treated in William W. Kaufmann, *Glasnost, Perestroika, and US Defense Spending* (Washington, DC, 1990); while Soviet aspects are examined in Alan B. Sherr, *The Other Side of Arms Control: Soviet Objectives in the Gorbachev Era* (Boston, 1988). The summit meetings between the presidents elicited a lot of publicity and receive analysis in Joseph G. Whelan, *The Moscow Summit, 1988: Reagan and Gorbachev in Negotiation* (Boulder, CO, 1990), as well as Joseph G. Whelan, *Soviet Diplomacy and Negotiating Behavior – 1988–90: Gorbachev-Reagan-Bush Meetings at the Summit* (Washington, DC, 1991). Lastly, the background to Gorbachev's thinking on foreign policy forms the basis of Allen Lynch, *Gorbachev's International Outlook: Intellectual Origins and Political Consequences* (1989).

REFERENCES

Breslauer, George W. (2002) *Gorbachev and Yeltsin as Leaders*. Cambridge: Cambridge University Press.

Bush, Keith (1991) Pavlov's Anticrisis Program. *Report on the USSR*, Vol. 3, No. 20, 17 May: 1–6.

Chernyaev, Anatoly (2000) *My Six Years with Gorbachev*. University Park, Pennsylvania: The Pennsylvania State University Press.

Dunlop, John B. (1993) *The Rise of Russia and the Fall of the Soviet Empire*. Princeton, New Jersey: Princeton University Press.

Foye, Stephen (1991) Gorbachev Denies Responsibility for Crackdown. *Report on the USSR*, Vol. 3, No. 4, 25 January: 1–3.

Gorbachev, Mikhail (1995) *Memoirs*. New York: Doubleday.

Hanson, Philip (1990) The Shatalin Plan and the Future of the Soviet Presidency. Unpublished paper, 2 October, Krasnyi Arkhiv, Central European University, Budapest.

Khasbulatov, Ruslan. (1993) *The Struggle for Russia*, edited by Richard Sakwa. London: Routledge.

Matlock, Jack F. Jr (1995) *Autopsy of an Empire: the American Ambassador's Account of the Collapse of the Soviet Union*. New York: Random House.

McNeill, Terry (1988) Gorbachev's First Three Years in Power: Not So New Political Thinking in Foreign Policy. *Radio Liberty Research Bulletin*, RL75/88, 2 March: 1–4.

Palazchenko, Pavel (1997) *My Years with Gorbachev and Shevardnadze: the Memoir of a Soviet Interpreter*. University Park, Pennsylvania: The Pennsylvania State University Press.

Rutland, Peter (1990) Abalkin's Strategy for Soviet Economic Reform. *Report on the USSR*, Vol. 2, No. 21, 25 May: 3–6.

Tatu, Michel (1986) The Central Committee Elected at the Twenty-seventh Congress. *RFE/RL Research Bulletin*, 10 March.

Tedstrom, John (1991) Gorbachev the Economist. *Report on the USSR*, Vol. 3, No. 35, 30 August: 11–12.

Voices of Glasnost: Letters from the Soviet People to Ogonyok *Magazine, 1987–1990*, Selected and edited by Christopher Cerf and Marina Albee with Lev Gushchin; consulting editor, Lynn Visson; translator, Hans Fenstermacher; with an introduction by Vitaly Korotich. London: Kyle Cathie Limited, 1990.

White, Stephen (1990) *Gorbachev in Power*. Cambridge: Cambridge University Press.

Yeltsin, Boris (1994) *The View from the Kremlin*. London: HarperCollins.

INDEX

STUART BRITAIN

Social Change and Continuity: England 1550–1750 (Second edition)
Barry Coward   0 582 29442 8

James I (Second edition)
S.J. Houston   0 582 20911 0

The English Civil War 1640–1649
Martyn Bennett   0 582 35392 0

Charles I, 1625–1640
Brian Quintrell   0 582 00354 7

The English Republic 1649–1660 (Second edition)
Toby Barnard   0 582 08003 7

Radical Puritans in England 1550–1660
R.J. Acheson   0 582 35515 X

The Restoration and the England of Charles II (Second edition)
John Miller   0 582 29223 9

The Glorious Revolution (Second edition)
John Miller   0 582 29222 0

EARLY MODERN EUROPE

The Renaissance (Second edition)
Alison Brown   0 582 30781 3

The Emperor Charles V
Martyn Rady   0 582 35475 7

French Renaissance Monarchy: Francis I and Henry II (Second edition)
Robert Knecht   0 582 28707 3

The Protestant Reformation in Europe
Andrew Johnston   0 582 07020 1

The French Wars of Religion 1559–1598 (Second edition)
Robert Knecht   0 582 28533 X

Philip II
Geoffrey Woodward   0 582 07232 8

The Thirty Years' War
Peter Limm   0 582 35373 4

Louis XIV
Peter Campbell   0 582 01770 X

Spain in the Seventeenth Century
Graham Darby   0 582 07234 4

Peter the Great
William Marshall   0 582 00355 5

EUROPE 1789–1918

Britain and the French Revolution
Clive Emsley   0 582 36961 4

Revolution and Terror in France 1789–1795 (Second edition)
D.G. Wright   0 582 00379 2

Napoleon and Europe
D.G. Wright   0 582 35457 9

The Abolition of Serfdom in Russia 1762–1907
David Moon   0 582 29486 X

Nineteenth-Century Russia: Opposition to Autocracy
Derek Offord   0 582 35767 5

The Constitutional Monarchy in France 1814–48
Pamela Pilbeam   0 582 31210 8

The 1848 Revolutions (Second edition)
Peter Jones   0 582 06106 7

The Italian Risorgimento
M. Clark   0 582 00353 9

Bismarck & Germany 1862–1890 (Second edition)
D.G. Williamson   0 582 29321 9

Imperial Germany 1890–1918
Ian Porter, Ian Armour and Roger Lockyer   0 582 03496 5

The Dissolution of the Austro-Hungarian Empire 1867–1918 (Second edition)
John W. Mason   0 582 29466 5

Second Empire and Commune: France 1848–1871 (Second edition)
William H.C. Smith   0 582 28705 7

France 1870–1914 (Second edition)
Robert Gildea   0 582 29221 2

The Scramble for Africa (Second edition)
M.E. Chamberlain   0 582 36881 2

Late Imperial Russia 1890–1917
John F. Hutchinson   0 582 32721 0

The First World War
Stuart Robson   0 582 31556 5

Austria, Prussia and Germany 1806–1871
John Breuilly   0 582 43739 3

Napoleon: Conquest, Reform and Reorganisation
Clive Emsley   0 582 43795 4

The French Revolution 1787–1804
Peter Jones   0 582 77289 3

The Origins of the First World War (Third edition)
Gordon Martel   0 582 43804 7

The Birth of Industrial Britain
Kenneth Morgan   0 582 30270 6

EUROPE SINCE 1918

The Russian Revolution (Second edition)
Anthony Wood   0 582 35559 1

Lenin's Revolution: Russia 1917–1921
David Marples   0 582 31917 X

Stalin and Stalinism (Third edition)
Martin McCauley   0 582 50587 9

The Weimar Republic (Second edition)
John Hiden   0 582 28706 5

The Inter-War Crisis 1919–1939
Richard Overy   0 582 35379 3

Fascism and the Right in Europe 1919–1945
Martin Blinkhorn   0 582 07021 X

Spain's Civil War (Second edition)
Harry Browne   0 582 28988 2

The Third Reich (Third edition)
D.G. Williamson   0 582 20914 5

The Origins of the Second World War (Second edition)
R.J. Overy   0 582 29085 6

The Second World War in Europe
Paul MacKenzie   0 582 32692 3

The French at War 1934–1944
Nicholas Atkin   0 582 36899 5

Anti-Semitism before the Holocaust
Albert S. Lindemann   0 582 36964 9

The Holocaust: The Third Reich and the Jews
David Engel   0 582 32720 2

Germany from Defeat to Partition 1945–1963
D.G. Williamson   0 582 29218 2

Britain and Europe since 1945
Alex May   0 582 30778 3

Eastern Europe 1945–1969: From Stalinism to Stagnation
Ben Fowkes   0 582 32693 1

Eastern Europe since 1970
Bülent Gökay   0 582 32858 6

The Khrushchev Era 1953–1964
Martin McCauley   0 582 27776 0

Hitler and the Rise of the Nazi Party
Frank McDonough   0 582 50606 9

The Soviet Union Under Brezhnev
William Tompson   0 582 32719 9

NINETEENTH-CENTURY BRITAIN

Britain before the Reform Acts: Politics and Society 1815–1832
Eric J. Evans   0 582 00265 6

Parliamentary Reform in Britain c. 1770–1918
Eric J. Evans   0 582 29467 3

Democracy and Reform 1815–1885
D.G. Wright   0 582 31400 3

Poverty and Poor Law Reform in Nineteenth-Century Britain
1834–1914: From Chadwick to Booth
David Englander   0 582 31554 9

The Birth of Industrial Britain: Economic Change 1750–1850
Kenneth Morgan   0 582 29833 4

Chartism (Third edition)
Edward Royle   0 582 29080 5

Peel and the Conservative Party 1830–1850
Paul Adelman   0 582 35557 5

Gladstone, Disraeli and later Victorian Politics (Third edition)
Paul Adelman   0 582 29322 7

Britain and Ireland: From Home Rule to Independence
Jeremy Smith   0 582 30193 9

TWENTIETH-CENTURY BRITAIN

The Rise of the Labour Party 1880–1945 (Third edition)
Paul Adelman   0 582 29210 7

The Conservative Party and British Politics 1902–1951
Stuart Ball   0 582 08002 9

The Decline of the Liberal Party 1910–1931 (Second edition)
Paul Adelman   0 582 27733 7

The British Women's Suffrage Campaign 1866–1928
Harold L. Smith   0 582 29811 3

War & Society in Britain 1899–1948
Rex Pope

0 582 03531 7

The British Economy since 1914: A Study in Decline?
Rex Pope

0 582 30194 7

Unemployment in Britain between the Wars
Stephen Constantine

0 582 35232 0

The Attlee Governments 1945–1951
Kevin Jefferys

0 582 06105 9

The Conservative Governments 1951–1964
Andrew Boxer

0 582 20913 7

Britain under Thatcher
Anthony Seldon and Daniel Collings

0 582 31714 2

Britain and Empire 1880–1945
Dane Kennedy

0 582 41493 8

INTERNATIONAL HISTORY

The Eastern Question 1774–1923 (Second edition)
A.L. Macfie

0 582 29195 X

India 1885–1947: The Unmaking of an Empire
Ian Copland

0 582 38173 8

The United States and the First World War
Jennifer D. Keene

0 582 35620 2

Women and the First World War
Susan R. Grayzel

0 582 41876 3

Anti-Semitism before the Holocaust
Albert S. Lindemann

0 582 36964 9

The Origins of the Cold War 1941–1949 (Third edition)
Martin McCauley

0 582 77284 2

Russia, America and the Cold War 1949–1991 (Second edition)
Martin McCauley

0 582 78482 4

The Arab–Israeli Conflict
Kirsten E. Schulze

0 582 31646 4

The United Nations since 1945: Peacekeeping and the Cold War
Norrie MacQueen

0 582 35673 3

Decolonisation: The British Experience since 1945
Nicholas J. White

0 582 29087 2

The Collapse of the Soviet Union
David R. Marples

0 582 50599 2

WORLD HISTORY

China in Transformation 1900–1949
Colin Mackerras   0 582 31209 4

Japan Faces the World 1925–1952
Mary L. Hanneman   0 582 36898 7

Japan in Transformation 1952–2000
Jeff Kingston   0 582 41875 5

China since 1949
Linda Benson   0 582 35722 5

South Africa: The Rise and Fall of Apartheid
Nancy L. Clark and William H. Worger   0 582 41437 7

US HISTORY

American Abolitionists
Stanley Harrold   0 582 35738 1

The American Civil War 1861–1865
Reid Mitchell   0 582 31973 0

America in the Progressive Era 1890–1914
Lewis L. Gould   0 582 35671 7

The United States and the First World War
Jennifer D. Keene   0 582 35620 2

The Truman Years 1945–1953
Mark S. Byrnes   0 582 32904 3

The Korean War
Steven Hugh Lee   0 582 31988 9

The Origins of the Vietnam War
Fredrik Logevall   0 582 31918 8

The Vietnam War
Mitchell Hall   0 582 32859 4

American Expansionism 1783–1860
Mark S. Joy   0 582 36965 7

The United States and Europe in the Twentieth Century
David Ryan   0 582 30864 X

The Civil Rights Movement
Bruce J. Dierenfield   0 582 35737 3